Tradition in the
Twenty-First Century

Tradition in the Twenty-First Century

Locating the Role of the Past in the Present

Edited by Trevor J. Blank and
Robert Glenn Howard

Utah State University Press
Logan

© 2013 by University Press of Colorado

Published by Utah State University Press
An imprint of University Press of Colorado
5589 Arapahoe Avenue, Suite 206C
Boulder, Colorado 80303

 The University Press of Colorado is a proud member of
the Association of American University Presses.

The University Press of Colorado is a cooperative publishing enterprise supported, in part, by Adams State University, Colorado State University, Fort Lewis College, Metropolitan State University of Denver, Regis University, University of Colorado, University of Northern Colorado, Utah State University, and Western State Colorado University.

Cover design by Dan Miller
Cover illustration © Mark Aplet / Shutterstock
Chapter 1, "Thinking through Tradition," was originally published in Oring, *Just Folklore*, Cantilever Press. © 2012 Elliott Oring

ISBN: 978-0-87421-900-5 (e-book)
ISBN: 978-0-87421-899-2 (paper)

Library of Congress Cataloging-in-Publication Data

Tradition in the twenty-first century : locating the role of the past in the present / edited by Trevor J. Blank and Robert Glenn Howard.
     pages cm
  Includes index.
  ISBN 978-0-87421-899-2 (pbk.) — ISBN 978-0-87421-900-5 (e-book)
  1. Folklore. 2. Tradition (Philosophy) 3. Oral tradition. 4. Communication in folklore. 5. Semiotics and folk literature. I. Blank, Trevor J.
  GR71.T73 2013
  398.2—dc23
                                    2013009390

To

Bill Ivey

Contents

Acknowledgments

What first began as a stimulating conversation about tradition in contemporary folkloristics morphed into an exciting conference panel on the subject; ultimately, our extended conversation developed into this book, and its publication has been over four years in the making. As editors, we are indebted to many people for their help in making this volume a reality.

First and foremost, we would like to thank the wonderful staff at Utah State University Press and the University Press of Colorado, especially Michael Spooner, Dan Miller, and Laura Furney. John Alley was instrumental in developing the book from a lively panel into an expansive collaborative work. We are grateful to the American Folklore Society for providing an initial forum for exploring this book's subject matter. As always, we would like to thank our families' ongoing support at home because that is the private well from which our public expressions draw.

Our colleagues reliably provided robust feedback and unwavering moral support, as well as inspiration, through their ideas both in writing and face-to-face. In particular, we would like to thank Donald Allport Bird, Anthony Bak Buccitelli, Charley Camp, Bill Ellis, Tim Evans, Lisa Gabbert, Barbara Kirshenblatt-Gimblett, Spencer Lincoln Green, Robert Georges, Michael Owen Jones, Tim Lloyd, John McDowell, Jay Mechling, Montana Miller, Dorothy Noyes, Andrew Peck, Leonard Primiano, David Puglia, Kate Schramm, Moira Smith, Steve Stanzak, Jeff Tolbert, Elizabeth Tucker, and Daniel Wojcik. Additionally, we are thrilled and honored to have worked with such an esteemed group of contributors, all of whom put a great deal of time and effort into seeing this project through from start to finish.

Finally, we would like to especially recognize Bill Ivey. Without his powerful speech at the American Folklore Society conference in 2007 to spur us on, you would not be reading these words today. In his generation or any other, few have done more to forward the field of folklore studies than he. It is our pleasure to dedicate this book to him.

Trevor J. Blank
Robert Glenn Howard

Tradition in the
Twenty-First Century

Introduction

Living Traditions in a Modern World

In his 2007 presidential address to the American Folklore Society (AFS), later published in the *Journal of American Folklore*, Bill Ivey boldly asserted that "antimodernism is a central motivating engine that runs through all of folklore" (Ivey 2011, 11). Painting a vivid picture of the archetypical homes where folklore researchers live, he described how they keep their "black-and-white TV set tucked far into the corner" while opting to "sing or dance" in their living rooms. Counting those in the audience that day among his dancers, Ivey proclaimed that we who research folklore are "temperamentally disposed against the forces of modernity" (11). His compelling speech jarred the soon-to-be-coeditors of this book to attention—and out of a significant rut in the shared ideological road that folklorists travel.

Is it really true that folklore and the researchers who study it are "disposed against the forces of modernity" by temperament? With tradition both thoroughly embedded in modern life and at the center of folklore studies, can a student of folklore actually be inherently antimodern? We decided to put together a panel for the 2009 American Folklore Society Annual Meeting in Boise, Idaho, that would explore "tradition" as it manifests among us today. Joined by folklorists Simon J. Bronner, Merrill Kaplan, Elliott Oring, and Tok Thompson, we set out to demonstrate that tradition is indeed alive and well in the twenty-first century. In doing so, the panel helped to facilitate a vibrant discourse that generated ongoing discussions, debates, and disagreements. We explored the very nature of tradition as a concept, as well its role within folkloristics, and that discussion continued well after the session concluded. Ultimately, these ongoing debates about tradition have yielded the diverse body of essays that comprise this volume.

To set the stage for the broad ground traveled in this collection, our introduction aims to more fully explore the position that folklore scholarship

DOI: 10.7330/9780874218992.c00

might be antimodern and consider what such a possibility suggests about tradition as a central concept within the field of folklore studies. We begin by briefly exploring the meanings of the word *folklore* in relationship to tradition. Next, we address the concept of "modernity" in an effort to locate why some folklorists may feel that it is at odds with folklore studies and how tradition is central to that tension. In that discussion, it becomes clear that insofar as we are modern, we are also the bearers and users of tradition. Bringing tradition with us conserves our links to the past, even as those links are enacted in the present. Thus, throughout the course of this introduction, we also argue that voicing an antimodern temperament serves to undermine the contributions that folklore studies can offer to current thinking about the contemporary human experience.

Folklore studies' valuation of tradition has a lot to offer current research on today's globalized, media driven, and technologically infused world. To better realize that contribution, however, tradition should be imagined as one aspect of what is modern—and we will discuss at least one conception of tradition in which it is. From that perspective, even as tradition gestures to the past, it also carries us forward to our communal future. We describe how tradition can be seen to emerge when, in moments of individual action, we breathe our humanity into the perceived links that allow us to imagine a shared future. Finally, we conclude by offering the reader a synoptic teaser that describes the breadth, depth, and incredibly wide variety of scholarship we have been honored to gather together in pursuit of the diverse manifestations of tradition in the twenty-first century.

FOLKLORE AND TRADITION

Pioneering American folklorist Stith Thompson wrote that the "common idea present in all folklore is that of tradition, something handed down from one person to another and preserved either by memory or practice rather than written record" (quoted in Leach and Fried 1984, 403). The generation before Thompson imagined "folklore" as a kind of evolutionary artifact—an object of sorts—that moved from the past into the present, where it could then be "collected" and preserved as historical evidence of humanity's shared cultural past. For them, folklore consisted of literally "old" objects, which most commonly took the form of ideas: stories, beliefs, and practices (Georges and Jones 1995, 59). As Thompson and his contemporaries shifted their focus from preserving these historical relics toward documenting their transmission, the idea of "type" came to the fore as a way to document and analyze the similarities in different folkloric artifacts. From this perspective, genres and types are transmitted as individuals innovate on them in specific behaviors to create new but perceptibly traditional objects (Georges and Jones 1995, 93). This conception remains dominant in the field, as evidenced when the editors of the 2011 anthology *The Individual and Tradition: Folkloristic Perspectives* define "tradition" as a process "not unlike recycling" characterized by the use of "accessible raw materials, the handed-down knowledge and ways of knowing, with which an individual may go to work" (Cashman, Mould, and Shukla 2011, 3).

In Ivey's 2007 speech, a similar conception of tradition enables him to exclaim, "Antimodernism gives us [folklorists] our critical stance, revivalism a path to action and reform" (Ivey 2011, 11). For Ivey, the "recyclables" of tradition allow people to "go to work" on social transformation. This linkage of the "old" cultural resources and contemporary activism was a powerful force among the folklorists of his generation. Ivey attended his first AFS meeting in 1969, and his emergence as a scholar coincided with a time in US history marked by a powerful struggle between institutional limitations and a counterculture bursting with the youthful energy of romanticism. In that fray, many looked backward to imagine a great premodern past in which humans were more connected to each other and their environments. The innovative activists and scholars of the 1960s and 1970s helped to make this "revivalist" attitude part of the struggle for civil rights, and those struggles helped define a whole generation.

This generation of folklorists created new sorts of folklore studies that emphasized the contextualized performance of folklore as enacted in individual innovations on empirically verifiably shared traditions. With this new perspective, folklore could be recognized not so much as specific traditional artifacts, or even types. Instead, folklore could be found in the elements of specific performances that exhibited human connections. Most often these connections related to a communal past, a tradition. In one extreme case, that of Dan Ben-Amos, tradition itself was even rejected as a heuristic for what counts as folklore (Ben-Amos 1971).

Alan Dundes was one of the first and most influential of this generation to take on their redefinition of folklore. In 1965 he famously imagined the "folk" as "[a]ny group of people whatsoever who share at least one common factor. It does not matter what the linking factor is—it could be a common occupation, language or religion—but what is important is that a group

formed for whatever reason will have some traditions which it calls its own"
(Dundes 1965, 2).

Following up with his laundry list of what appear to be folkloric genres,
Dundes offered a courageous first step toward redefining folklore for a
new generation of performance scholars by acknowledging that American
academics (just as much as the peasants of nineteenth-century Europe) have
traditions. A few years later, Dan Ben-Amos presented his more radical stance.

For Ben-Amos, folklore is a communication process, and his definition
remains one of the most quoted today, despite its explicit rejection of
tradition: "As an artistic process, folklore may be found in any communicative
medium; musical, visual, kinetic, or dramatic . . . In sum, folklore is artistic
communication in small groups" (Ben-Amos 1971, 13). While Ben-
Amos opened folklore to "any communicative medium," he effectively
downplayed mass-mediated contexts by limiting folkloric communication
to "small groups" that he defines as "face-to-face" (12). For Ben-Amos,
the concept of tradition cannot be a heuristic because "the cultural use
of tradition as sanction is not necessarily dependent upon historical fact"
(13). Which is to say that in some cases, scholars might deem something
traditional when its practitioners do not or vice-versa. Most important
for Ben-Amos is the "small-group" context. While that context refuses to
romanticize the antiquity of a given folkloric process, it does romanticize
the context itself in ways that also suggest an antimodern stance. The small
group sitting face-to-face engaging in a folkloric "communicative process"
could easily be the near neighbors (if not close kin) of Ivey's singing and
dancing folklorists, with their blank televisions bearing cold witness from
dark corners.

Since Ben-Amos's attempt to capture his generation's new brand of
folklore studies by rejecting both mediated communication and tradition,
scholars have not been fully satisfied with those exclusions. As a result, they
have explored more open ways to characterize what constitutes folklore.
Some, like Linda Dégh, have argued that folklore is found in mass media
and thus should be studied by folklore scholars (Dégh 1994). Dorothy Noyes
has powerfully reimagined tradition as performative action in which the
performers imagine themselves responsible for passing along their combined
"metaknowledge" in both lore and practice as "a job that must be done"
(Noyes 2009, 248). Others have expanded the idea to include human creative
expression more generally, such as Henry Glassie's definition of tradition as
"volitional, temporal action," which he invokes in richly poetic descriptions

of diverse examples (Glassie 2003, 192). Possibly on the opposite side of the spectrum from Glassie, Robert A. Georges and Michael Owen Jones provide a jarringly scientific-sounding "folkloristic" definition of folklore that mutes the romanticized tones more characteristic of their contemporaries:

> The word *folklore* denotes expressive forms, processes, and behaviors (1) that we customarily learn, teach, and utilize or display during face-to-face interactions, and (2) that we judge to be traditional (a) because they are based on known precedents or models, and (b) because they serve as evidence of continuities and consistencies through time and space in human knowledge, thought, belief, and feeling. (Georges and Jones 1995, 2)

Georges and Jones's definition manages to systematically capture the basic ides of their generation while moderating its tendencies in two important ways. First, they add the word "customarily" to the phrase "face-to-face." By adding this phrase, folklore can take forms associated with a face-to-face exchange but might (in any given case) actually be exchanged by phone, television, or mobile computing device. Second, they emphasize that folklore emerges in those forms that "we judge to be traditional" instead of those that the scholar empirically demonstrates *are* traditional.

Unlike Ben-Amos, Georges and Jones retain the "traditional" element of folklore without making it an absolute heuristic. Folkloric expression may "serve as evidence of continuities and consistencies." However, the source of those claims to evidence are not necessarily scientific because folklore emerges in what "we judge to be traditional." Here the sentence suggests that this "we" is the same "we" that customarily learns, teaches, and utilizes the folklore in the line before. In that sense, the users seem to be the experts who judge their expression "traditional" and (if they do) it is folkloric. This formulation of "tradition" is very much akin to when Ben-Amos rejected judgments of what is traditional because "tradition" is often merely a "rhetorical device" used by folk practitioners (Ben-Amos 1971, 14). In Georges and Jones's definition of folklore, the authors walk a fine line between a continuation of the past and an opening to the new forms folklore increasingly takes in the twenty-first century. In particular, reclaiming "tradition," as less an empirical scholarly claim and more a "rhetorical device" that is perceived by individuals engaging in folkloric communication, opens folklore studies to the important work that needs to be done in the new global, mediated, and technology driven contexts of the modern world.

If the academic study of folklore is, as Simon J. Bronner asserts, "as close as you will come to a 'science of tradition,'" then folklorists must strike a subtle bargain between the perception of the traditional as that which is handed-down from the past and the technologies that are changing the means and scope of those "handing down" processes (Bronner 1998, 12). Both inside and outside of folkloristics, "tradition" has been conceptualized as a complex and contradictory term. On the one hand, that which is traditional is that which a community conserves. In this sense, the authority of the past is a force that resists change; it conserves ideas about the individual, gender roles, family, nationhood, duty, and so forth. In doing so, this authority stands against progressive attempts at change. On the other hand, tradition offers the everyday individual a resource with which to act alongside, but apart from, the reified power of impersonal institutions. In this sense, it offers a potential alternate authority to that held by those in power—and, in this alterity, traditions are not stuck in any rut (perceived or real) created by their resistance to modernity. In the next section, we examine how a range of historical conceptions of modernity have led some to set it in opposition to tradition.

TRADITION AND MODERNITY

Like many complex ideas, "modernity" has a long and intricate history. It has evolved a subtle range of meanings that vary between historical moments as well as academic discourses. The word itself comes from the Latin *modernus,* meaning "of the present time." First used in Latin to distinguish the Christian era from the previous domination of the pagan cultures of Western Europe, it came particularly into vogue in the seventeenth-century debates about the value of the great achievements of Classical culture in comparison to "modern" feats of the contemporary time.

For today's historically oriented scholars, "modernity" refers to a period ranging from 1500 to 1989 BCE (Berman 1988; Osborne 1992). This usage gives rise to a more generally understood conception of "modernity" that casts the term in a negative light. Early sociologist Max Weber described modernity as a process of "rationalization" that began with a new way of thinking during the Enlightenment and resulted in new means of material production and divisions of labor that differentiated the "modern" from the "traditional" periods in a society (Larraín 2001). Previously, Karl Marx and Friedrich Engels had imagined a similar process of rationalization but in more strongly negative terms; they connected rationality to the rise of capitalism and the distancing of the individual from the production of goods in their community. In both cases, modernism is pitted against tradition.

Another strain of thought often termed "modernism" actually aligned itself with tradition as a justification for European cultural hegemony, and this deeply problematic association renders this tradition-friendly brand of modernism unacceptable today—or so we should hope. Tradition in this hegemonic sense is probably best known from T. S. Eliot's famous 1921 essay "Tradition and the Individual Talent." Eliot decries the Romantic Period's elevation of individual genius in art to suggest that the true poet is the rare person who can assimilate the great art of Europe's past so fully that she or he can refashion that tradition to suit her or his own age. His description of the process states, "The existing monuments form an ideal order among themselves, which is modified by the introduction of the new (the really new) work of art among them" (Eliot 1921, 4). While his hegemonic claims sometimes go unnoticed in this essay, Eliot's later elaborations on his theory of tradition render them crystal clear.

In his book on the topic, Eliot (1934) articulated how the "ideal order" of tradition must be kept pure from "foreign" influence. He described how the social conditions "likely to develop tradition" must be fostered where "a spirit of excessive tolerance is to be deprecated": "The population should be homogeneous; where two or more cultures exist in the same place they are likely either to be fiercely self-conscious or both to become adulterate. What is still more important is unity of religious background; and reasons of race and religion combine to make any large number of free-thinking Jews undesirable" (Eliot 1934, 20). Even while glorifying tradition, Eliot's open advocacy for cultural purity grates against any contemporary folklorist's valuation of everyday, hybrid, and alternative cultural forms.

Following the revelations in World War II about the dangers inherent in excessive desires for purity, critical theorists like Herbert Marcuse, Max Horkheimer, and Theodor Adorno became popular for emphasizing a powerful negative view of modernity's process of rationalization. They expanded on Weber and Marx to argue that modernity's new forms of production created damaging processes of "alienation" for everyday individuals (Adorno and Horkheimer 2007; Marcuse 1964). Meanwhile, I. A. Richards spurred the so-called New Critics. Richards's expansion of Eliot's earlier conceptions into a pedagogical practice he termed "practical criticism" was introduced to US educational institutions through the 1945 recommendations of Harvard's influential Committee on the Objectives of a General Education in a Free Society. An easily adopted educational method, these recommendations helped instantiate Eurocentric ideals as push back against a perceived increase in cultural fragmentation after the war (Conant 1955 [1945]). As a result, a "tradition" of "great literature" was taught through sets of canonical high art texts offered without historical or cultural context and often including few or no folkloric examples of everyday expression. Supporters felt that mere contact with this "great Tradition" would connect students to a common European-American system of values (Graff 1989, 167–79).

Today, in the globalized and transnational world of the twenty-first century, critical theorists have largely rejected the high art canons of the past as students of literature increasingly turn to explore the cultural and aesthetic dimensions of more diverse objects like comic books, televised fiction, movies, vernacular discourse, and non-European artistic expressions. In this environment, the imagined cultural purity in Eliot's vision can no longer masquerade as an accurate or just alliance between modernity and tradition. At the same time, as many postcolonial theorists have pointed out, even the well-intentioned deployment of the modern/traditional dichotomy associated with more liberal thinkers can function as a means by which colonial power transmits itself into our postcolonial age because it can reify essentialized conceptions of ethnic difference and elide the diversity inherent in the human condition.

Despite this long history of foibles emerging out of the distinctions made between tradition and modernity, a negative sense of "modernity" that pits it against tradition, still seems to ring true for some folklorists. Simon Bronner has described these thinkers as imagining modernity as a period that begins for societies with the ending of "traditional" ways of life (Bronner 1998, 43). Here modernity includes an increased sense of individualism brought on by the modern technologies of mass production, communication, and travel. Individuals prone to follow Weber along these lines might see modernity's liberating technologies as having reduced violence and human suffering while carrying a potential for alienation that we must guard against; other thinkers, more closely following Adorno and Horkheimer, might emphasize alienation by lamenting a loss of connection between humans and their communities associated with the modern world and its technologies.

Both positions engage the reified notion of modernity and set it in opposition to tradition. However, folklore researchers who have spent a generation romanticizing "face-to-face" human communication seem to side more with Adorno and Horkheimer in their distrust of modernity (though not necessarily agreeing with their infamously negative assessment of the folk themselves). In so doing, these folklore scholars pit their perception of "tradition" against modern technologies and the changes those technologies have brought to communication contexts. In our view, maintaining this dichotomy is unprofitable.

Scholars in sociology first documented the basic flaw in the traditional versus modernity distinction long ago (Gusfield 1967). The problem is that whichever concept is privileged—whether rationality has improved traditional society or alienated us from our true selves—both claims assume that there is a linear progression that societies follow from one overarching set of characteristics to the historically next set of overarching characteristics. That simplified view of history is rightly considered problematic for two reasons. First, it suppresses the very real diversity in the experiences of different societies and different individuals living in those societies. Modernity is different in rural Afghanistan than it is in Chicago, just as modern Chicago is different for Barack Obama than it is for a schoolteacher on the city's southwest side. Second, this linear view of history suggests that characteristics from one period (tradition in the face of "modern" technologies, for example) will be discarded in the next historical period. In the twenty-first century, it is more realistic to imagine an unending, dynamic, and changing flux of lived experience where social categories like tradition are emergent in, around, and as the "modern" stuff of everyday contemporary life.

While change is certainly the only constant, that does not mean that traditions have disappeared. Even if we radically limit our claims to only contemporary US researchers interested in folklore, this social group has not yet moved from a wholly "premodern" or "traditional" society to a wholly "modern" or "post-traditional" one. Instead, our traditional performances continue, even as they render us different from the past. In the imagined living room where contemporary folklorists dance and sing in front of a lifeless television screen, both the television and the dancing are participating in their own modernity.

But what happens when the songs being sung are learned from YouTube? Or what if the dancers pause their celebration to settle a debate about the specific geographic and historical origins of their movements by consulting

Wikipedia? Are these folkloric performances no longer traditional because they engage with both the technological and global aspects of modernity? In our view, the processes of tradition remain, even as their modes of expression and transmission change.

To us, it seems safe to say that tradition remains at least because humans (modern or otherwise) need it. We need it to enact our connection with each other. Such connection gains credence as it reaches back to the past and offers hope as it looks forward to imagine a shared future. Today, increasing numbers of connections use modern technology to transcend geographic, ethnic, and class differences and imagine a better future: a future in which these differences unify humans instead of divide them. From this perspective, modernity is more in league with tradition than a force against it. Facilitated by technologies as old as language itself or as new as networks of mobile computing devices, tradition enacts a present in which the past increasingly connects us all to our shared future. With this reconciled view of modernity and tradition, our next section forwards the preliminary argument that refusing to reconcile modernity and tradition in folklore studies could reduce the important contribution our field should be making to the vast and rapidly growing research on modern instances, forms, and modes of traditional expression.

MODERN TRADITIONS

In this modern age, scholars of folklore studies have rich and diverse folkloric material to document and analyze. As network communication technologies increasingly penetrate the daily lives of people from all locations, ethnicities, and social classes, the implications are far-reaching. Acting as conduits and purveyors of tradition or traditional knowledge, social networking mediums, amateur and professional websites, personal and genre-specific blogs, and other ubiquitous forms of digital participatory engagement are now penetrating folk culture in all its forms, thereby influencing and mediating future modifications to the conceptualization of tradition. As the essays in this volume attest, tradition persists in these most modern of communication contexts; folklore studies originated the study of lived tradition, and tradition will remain in folklore studies' purview as long as its advocates, practitioners, and scholars do not abandon it.

Anthropologist Franz Boas influentially posited that folklore "mirrors" societal and cultural values, and thus folklorists should be able to interpret the meaningful expressive behaviors found in symbolic interactions as they occur (see Boas 1925; Smith 1959). In a time when scholars of North American folklore sought to distinguish themselves from their European counterparts, Boas's contention was most significant in that it cogently presented folklore as being *alive*.

Instead of studying the origins or dead survivals of European folklore, North American scholars sought to analyze the reflexive qualities and contexts of the expressive behaviors and oral traditions found in contemporary society. As a result, the North American approach shifted from the European model's concern with "the past" to an interest in both the "the past and the present," going beyond the study of cultural "survivals" to also include the context of functioning elements in the interpretation of folklore materials (Dundes 1966, 242; see also Bronner 2002). This approach breathed life into the field founded on the premise that its subject matter was "fast-vanishing," dying, and fading away into oblivion. The North American approach flourished because folklore was not vanishing but adapting and changing to the vast and often violent changes caused by the influx of Europeans into North America.

Just as Boas and his contemporaries helped to invite new perspectives on folklore, the greatest periods of subsequent growth and prosperity for folkloristics have also occurred amid fundamental shifts in the field's approaches to methodologies, subject matter, and theoretical orientations— all of which opened new avenues for inquiry (Bascom 1954; Ben-Amos 1971; Botkin 1993 [1944]; Dorson 1952, 1976; Dundes 1965; Paredes and Bauman 1972).[1] Boas's contemporaries were reluctant to acknowledge the existence of a wholly "American" brand of folklore, but the compelling allure of oral traditions and the belief that face-to-face communications could be interpreted as reflexive vernacular expressions ultimately gained traction (Abrahams 2006 [1964]; Lord 1960), especially as folklorists developed methodologies for conducting ethnographic fieldwork (Goldstein 1974) and began to underscore the value of both material and verbal folk cultures (Glassie 1968). Similarly, Richard Dorson (1970) broke new ground by contemplating the "folk in the city," and Alan Dundes and Carl R. Pagter (1978, 1987, 1991, 1996) argued for an interpretation of folklore

---

1   This list is, of course, subjective and truncated. See Bronner (2002) for a more thorough historiography of the ideas and contexts that facilitated the creation of a distinctive American approach to folklore studies by the twentieth century and Bronner (1998) for the role of tradition more specifically.

that included nonverbal forms of expression. Ultimately, these thinkers participated in the emergence of the performance- and context-based redefinition of folklore that led Dan Ben-Amos to reject tradition itself as central to the field.

Of course, tradition did not disappear—and still has not. This may well be because, much as Boas imagined long ago, tradition is not a transmittable entity or a surviving form that is no longer being produced. While forms emerge, change, and fade, tradition is the living enactment of a community's perception about its own links to the past. It can be seen to emerge in specific performed events when individuals or groups enact forms they perceive to be deeply connected to their past. Imagining that connection to the past, individuals also imagine those with whom they are connected: the community or communities with whom their share their traditions. As they locate themselves in relation to those who have come before, they also locate themselves as bearers of those traditions into the future. They are imagining a future in which they have played their part in the community to come. They live tradition because, as Boas noted, traditions are alive.

If some folklorists imagine themselves resisting what is "modern," new, or infused with technology, they are alienating themselves from the new domains where many contemporary and future traditions live. The pitting of tradition against modernity encourages some folklorists to resist introducing new ideas of community, vernacular expression, and ethnographic methods. As a result, scholars of folklore are not fully engaged in considering significant emergent factors influencing folkloric expression today. Despite this resistance, our changing world demands that we reexamine the assumptions that we have inherited from our training. We must strive for a truly encompassing, multifaceted collection and interpretation of contemporary folklore that more accurately documents folk, mass, and popular culture. In doing so, we do not mean to suggest that the tried-and-true approaches of folkloristics are erroneous or irrelevant. Rather, we hope to present clear evidence of another dimension of folkloric expression and transmission so that it may be recognized—as it clearly is to us—as the emerging apparatus of contemporary folklore.

TRADITION IN THE TWENTY-FIRST CENTURY

In the long history of folklore studies, researchers have struggled to locate the sources of tradition and account for the boundaries of the traditional.

In the twenty-first century, new means of communication, travel, and globalized cultural and economic dependence have complicated our task. In this environment, is a folkloristic definition of "tradition" still possible? And, if so, how should it be defined? What would be its purposes and what are its definitive traits? Is "tradition" an empirically verifiable quality or is it better imagined as a "social imaginary?" Is it an empirically factual concept or is it also one that suggests a critical role for the folklorist? Renegotiating these questions today is important not only because of the dawn of the digital era but because folklorists now recognize how they can reinscribe power relations by judging a document or artifact worthy of preservation based on its perception as "traditional." *Tradition in the Twenty-First Century* does not aim to finally answer these questions. It aims to inspire and encourage folklorists to engage this centrally important discussion in ways that challenge us to innovate, even as we conserve the rich discipline we share. Our aim in publishing this volume is to present new, salient viewpoints on the dynamics of tradition in modern society. Along the way, we hope that the contents of this volume will have at least some small influence on the ways that folklorists conceptualize tradition as they define the scope and identity of the folklore discipline always anew.

In our capacity as editors, we have purposely encouraged our contributors to utilize new or underexplored analytical approaches while penning their chapters; to be confident and unapologetic in supporting their contentions; and/or to test out ideas that have not yet been fully fleshed out in contemporary folkloristic discourse. More pointedly, we have asked contributors to reflect upon these factors while also considering the current state of folkloristic inquiry: Is tradition still the driving concept in folklore studies? If so, do we need to adjust our conception of it based on the host of new means of communication we all use? And how should we go about accomplishing this? Each essay addresses these and related questions in its own way: shedding the new light of the twenty-first century onto the perennial and important concept of tradition.

Tradition in the Twenty-First Century begins with Elliot Oring's provocative essay, "Thinking through Tradition." Oring opens with a bold assessment of the definitional core behind the term "tradition" and explains how folklorists have historically used (and misused) it. Noting the role of "tradition" in the history of folkloristics, he asks if a "science of tradition" such as that imagined repeatedly throughout our discipline's existence (including in this very volume) can be based on a concept that is so "scattered, inchoate, and soft." Oring compels folklorists to harden their conception and consider "tradition" a form of "cultural reproduction." From this perspective, the term is neutral: an empirical assessment that refuses to "privilege the oral and face-to-face" or "serve as a critique of modern life."

Clearly distinct from Oring's scientific perspective on tradition, a "critical folklore studies" approach seeks to overtly advocate certain political perspectives while critiquing and challenging others in an effort to promote social justice. In chapter 2, "Critical Folklore Studies and the Revaluation of Tradition," author Stephen Olbrys Gencarella articulates a robust version of this perspective. Gencarella begins by arguing that any study of folklore that examines tradition must *also* examine the exclusions that attend the tradition. Invoking the scholarship of philosophers Friedrich Nietzsche, Giorgio Agamben, and Kenneth Burke, Gencarella asserts that any set of traditions can only be understood in reference to the values and morality in whose constitution it participates. Since all discursive constitutions are also necessarily exclusions, he argues that the values both included and excluded by a tradition must be viewed with critical attention. With this attention, folklore studies can turn to engage in critical praxis that goes beyond the scientific descriptions and aesthetic celebrations of the discipline's past.

Chapter 3, Robert Glenn Howard's "Vernacular Authority: Critically Engaging 'Tradition,'" offers a potential "middle way" between the scientific and critical perspectives articulated in the first two chapters. Howard begins with the supposition that "tradition" has at least two aspects: empirical verifiability and vernacular assertion. Because these two aspects are not yoked together, folklorists can use the concept of "vernacular authority" to imagine what is deemed traditional in any specific communication event. From this "discursive" perspective, he suggests, an expression that appeals to tradition indicates an individual choice (consciously or not) to invoke (successfully or not) a shared conception of an authority that contrasts with those of institutions. Using this conception of performed vernacular authority, Howard posits that folklore researchers can bring their expertise and valuation of everyday artistry to the scholars currently adapting media criticism to study the many hybrid forms emerging in the twenty-first century.

Building off these foundations, Casey R. Schmitt further explores the intersection of tradition and vernacular authority in chapter 4, "Asserting Tradition: Rhetoric of Tradition and the Defense of Chief Illiniwek." Schmitt's essay explores how individuals within a community may invoke tradition in an effort to assert vernacular authority and assign values to a community's conceptualization of traditionality and authenticity. Through the use of rhetoric that espouses communally sanctioned values or practices, he argues, an individual communicator may invoke tradition in order to equate or amalgamate certain ideas with the rhetorical power enjoyed by tradition, which serves as a symbol of unassailable vernacular authority.

Chapter 5, "Curation and Tradition on Web 2.0," features the work of Merrill Kaplan, who takes Handler and Linnekin's (1984) famous argument that tradition is interpretative—having no essential essence apart from its application in the interpretive act—and applies it to the vernacular practice of "curation." Kaplan contends that the unmistakably analogous practices of vernacular curation are now persistently manifesting online; more importantly, though, is the fact that this virtualized curatorial adaptation may actually represent the greatest boom in the documentation and preservation of folkloric materials in world history. However, she notes, the mere acknowledgment of this possibility blurs the boundaries between the privileged discourse of professional folklorists and that of the "folk" themselves.

Returning to etymological contexts and their influence on present and future discourse, Tok Thompson examines tradition as a "living word" in chapter 6, "Trajectories of Tradition: Following Tradition into a New Epoch of Human Culture." He asserts that the term is constantly being adapted in use and is thus productively changing human action. As a "self-conscious performance," tradition is dynamically performed as an ongoing part of both individual and group identity. Tracing this function back in time, Thompson offers a definition of tradition that is not only applicable in the technologically infused cultures of today, but it can also address both the pasts and possible futures of "tradition."

In chapter 7, "And the Greatest of These is Tradition: The Folklorist's Toolbox in the Twenty-First Century," Lynne S. McNeill revisits Diane Goldstein's (1993) observation of the distinguishing characteristics of folklore scholarship—namely, the field's emphasis on genre, transmission, and especially tradition. Through the microcosm of several popular Internet memes, McNeill demonstrates how technologically mediated vernacular expression continues to support the contention that tradition does not exclude official or institutional cultures but rather blurs the boundaries of the "official" and "vernacular."

Finally, in chapter 8, "The 'Handiness' of Tradition," Simon J. Bronner explores and summarizes many of this volume's overarching considerations by revisiting the conceptual origins of the term *tradition*. After noting the ways in which these origins still manage to inform the use of "tradition" in the present day, Bronner locates the term's center of gravity around "handiness" and proceeds to explore how individuals' "sense of tradition" seem to function as cognitive reference points for decoding and thus assigning symbolic meaning to the activities or situations that comprise their daily lives. In closing, he argues that a folkloristic definition of tradition for rhetorical and analytic purposes is not only possible but relevant for deepening our understanding of the complexities that distinguish contemporary folk culture.

In reviewing the synopsis of the chapters, the diverse body of contributions to this volume represents a wide range of scholarly opinions and interpretations on how folklorists should conceptualize and document "tradition" in the twenty-first century. Predictably, some contributors do not agree with their colleagues' observations or approaches; at times, they may even draw different conclusions from the same materials, contexts, and terms. Some authors downplay the importance of communication technologies while others see them as the most important locus of vernacular expression in contemporary society. Despite the sometimes contradictory or divergent contentions advocated by the contributors to this volume, at least one unifying belief remains among them: a modern understanding of tradition cannot be fully realized without a thoughtful consideration of the past's role in shaping the present. Even so, we wish to predominantly emphasize how tradition adapts, survives, thrives, and continues to mutate (or when applicable, remains stable) in today's modern world, with specific attention paid to how traditions now resist or expedite dissemination and adoption by individuals and communities.

So while all of the contributors to this volume may not always agree with one another, they collectively represent a complex, intimate portrayal of tradition in the twenty-first century. Read together, the chapters in this volume offer a comprehensive overview of the folkloristic and popular conceptualizations of tradition from past to present and offer a thoughtful assessment and projection of how "tradition" will fare in years to come. We should note that our goal in producing this book is not to contend that there is a "right way" to study or interpret tradition today; nor do we wish to propagate a simplified impression of how tradition is currently transmitted or conceptualized by tradition bearers and receivers. Instead, we aim to present the viewpoints of scholars who critically engage one of the field's core areas of scholarly inquiry (Bronner 1998; Glassie 1995; Goldstein 1993; Handler and Linnekin 1984; Jones 2000). Collectively, we hope that contributors' insights convey a more holistic report on the state of tradition today—both in and outside the context of folkloristics—while also challenging readers to broaden their own perspectives on the malleability of tradition and the contexts that perpetually influence its persistence. Above all, we hope that this volume will further promote the development of folklore theory, especially as it pertains to the theoretical underpinnings that inform our scholarly interpretations of tradition.

This remains an important theoretical pursuit because if the "traditional" can be both a conservative authority and a resource to resist institutions—perhaps the most powerful conservator of shared values—then the conceptualization of tradition stands at the interface between the individual innovator and the communities in which she or he seeks to act. Without codification, tradition is free for the taking, and this freedom is as rich and powerful in today's globalized and technology-driven modern world as it has been in years past. Unquestionably, the digital age continues to facilitate a hybridization of folk and mass culture into a shared, collaborative, and simulative space online in which emic notions of tradition are in a constant state of flux. Longstanding conceptualizations of tradition within folklore studies often emphasize the power of face-to-face interactions as a prerequisite determinant for identifying genuine folkloric interaction. But with the widespread adoption of computer-mediated communications for the purpose of vernacular expression, the "folk" who utilize these technologies for knowledge sharing, symbolic interaction, and civic engagement have deployed them in extraordinarily multifaceted ways (Blank 2009a, 2012; Fine and Ellis 2010; Howard 2011; Jenkins 2008; Prensky 2001; Turkle 1995, 2005; Wasik 2009).[2]

Folklorist William Westerman may have said it best when he wrote, "All knowledge is folk knowledge" (Westerman 2009, 123). As folklorists, we should take care to remind ourselves that folk knowledge can be found in more venues than in those where we first recognized it. The Internet,

---

2   For applied case studies and additional evidence of digital folk culture development and emergent notions of tradition in the digital age, see Aldred (2010); Blank (2009b); Bronner (2009); Ellis (2003); Foote (2007); Frank (2004, 2011); Gray (2009); Howard (2008a, 2008b); and Moore, Gathman, and Ducheneau (2009). For research that explores relevant historical contexts, as well as early Internet cultures, in more detail, see Dorst (1990); Jennings (1990); Kirshenblatt-Gimblett (1995, 1996); Rheingold (2000); and Tapscott (1999, 2008).

modern technology, or even the changing dynamics of folkloristics may seem to alienate our long-held conceptualizations of the field, and some scholars argue that we are wasting our energies revisiting of tradition as a core concept of contemporary folklore studies. Ironically, many of these same critics work in academia and likely find themselves engaging the Internet and other such conduits of tradition on a daily basis, for a multitude of reasons. It does not take much effort to observe a folkloric process on an Internet message board, in the comments section of any major online news story or popular blog, or even in your own e-mail inbox. The twenty-first century is inundated with the influence of technology, and our purview of folklore and tradition should accommodate this reality. As editors, it is our hope that this volume will help to accomplish this goal.

REFERENCES

Abrahams, Roger D. 2006 [1964]. *Deep Down in the Jungle: Black American Folklore from the Streets of Philadelphia*. Piscataway, NJ: Aldine Transaction.

Adorno, Theodor, and Max Horkheimer. 2007 [1947]. *Dialectic of Enlightenment (Cultural Memory in the Present)*, ed. Gunzelin Schmid Noerr and trans. Edmund Jephcott. Palo Alto, CA: Stanford University Press.

Aldred, B. Grantham. 2010. "Identity in 10,000 Pixels: LiveJournal Userpics and Fractured Selves in Web 2.0." *New Directions in Folklore* 8 (1/2): 6–35.

Bascom, William. 1954. "Four Functions of Folklore." *Journal of American Folklore* 67 (266): 333–49. http://dx.doi.org/10.2307/536411.

Ben-Amos, Dan. 1971. "Toward a Definition of Folklore in Context." *Journal of American Folklore* 84 (331): 3–15. http://dx.doi.org/10.2307/539729.

Berman, Marshall. 1988. *All That Is Solid Melts into Air: The Experience of Modernity*. New York: Penguin.

Blank, Trevor J. 2009a. *Folklore and the Internet: Vernacular Expression in a Digital World*. Logan: Utah State University Press.

Blank, Trevor J. 2009b. "Moonwalking in the Digital Graveyard: Diversions in Oral and Electronic Humor Regarding the Death of Michael Jackson." *Midwestern Folklore* 35 (2): 71–96.

Blank, Trevor J. 2012. *Folk Culture in the Digital Age: The Emergent Dynamics of Human Interaction*. Logan: Utah State University Press.

Boas, Franz. 1925. "Stylistic Aspects of Primitive Literature." *Journal of American Folklore* 38 (149): 329–39. http://dx.doi.org/10.2307/535235.

Botkin, Benjamin A. 1993 [1944]. *A Treasury of American Folklore*. New York: Random House Value.

Bronner, Simon J. 1998. *Following Tradition: Folklore in the Discourse of American Culture*. Logan: Utah State University Press.

Bronner, Simon J. 2002. *Folk Nation: Folklore in the Creation of American Tradition*. Wilmington, DE: SR Books.

Bronner, Simon J. 2009. "Digitizing and Virtualizing Folklore." In *Folklore and the Internet: Vernacular Expression in a Digital World*, ed. Trevor J. Blank, 21–66. Logan: Utah State University Press.

Cashman, Ray, Tom Mould, and Pravina Shukla. 2011. *The Individual and Tradition: Folkloristic Perspectives*. Bloomington: Indiana University Press.

Conant, James Bryant, ed. 1955 [1945]. *General Education in a Free Society: Report of the Harvard Committee*. Cambridge, MA: Harvard University Press.

Dégh, Linda. 1994. *American Folklore and the Mass Media*. Bloomington: Indiana University Press.

Dorson, Richard M. 1952. *Bloodstoppers and Bearwalkers: Folk Traditions of the Upper Peninsula*. Cambridge, MA: Harvard University Press.

Dorson, Richard M. 1970. "Is There a Folk in the City?" *Journal of American Folklore* 83 (328): 185–216. http://dx.doi.org/10.2307/539108.

Dorson, Richard M. 1976. *Folklore and Fakelore: Essays toward a Discipline of Folk Studies*. Cambridge, MA: Harvard University Press.

Dorst, John. 1990. "Tags and Burners, Cycles and Networks: Folklore in the Telectronic Age." *Journal of Folklore Research* 27 (3): 179–90.

Dundes, Alan. 1965. *The Study of Folklore*. Englewood Hills, NJ: Prentice Hall College Division.

Dundes, Alan. 1966. "The American Concept of Folklore." *Journal of the Folklore Institute* 3 (3): 226–49. http://dx.doi.org/10.2307/3813799.

Dundes, Alan, and Carl R. Pagter. 1978 [1975]. *Work Hard and You Shall Be Rewarded: Urban Folklore from the Paperwork Empire*. Bloomington: Indiana University Press.

Dundes, Alan, and Carl R. Pagter. 1987. *When You're up to Your Ass in Alligators: More Urban Folklore from the Paperwork Empire*. Detroit: Wayne State University Press.

Dundes, Alan, and Carl R. Pagter. 1991. *Never Try to Teach a Pig to Sing: Still More Urban Folklore from the Paperwork Empire*. Detroit: Wayne State University Press.

Dundes, Alan, and Carl R. Pagter. 1996. *Sometimes the Dragon Wins: Yet More Urban Folklore from the Paperwork Empire*. Syracuse, NY: Syracuse University Press.

Ellis, Bill. 2003. "Making a Big Apple Crumble: The Role of Humor in Constructing a Global Response to Disaster." In *Of Corpse: Death and Humor in Folklore and Popular Culture*, ed. Peter Narváez, 35–82. Logan: Utah State University Press. Earlier version published in *New Directions in Folklore*, June 6, 2002, https://scholarworks.iu.edu/dspace/handle/2022/6911.

Eliot, T. S. 1921. "Traditional and the Individual Talent." In *The Sacred Wood: Essays on Poetry and Criticism*, 1–18. New York: Alfred A. Knopf.

Eliot, T.S. 1934. *After Strange Gods: A Primer of Modern Heresy*. London: Faber and Faber.

Fine, Gary Alan, and Bill Ellis. 2010. *The Global Grapevine: Why Rumors of Terrorism, Immigration, and Trade Matter*. London: Oxford University Press.

Foote, Monica. 2007. "Userpicks: Cyber Folk Art in the 21st Century." *Folklore Forum* 37 (1): 27–38.

Frank, Russell. 2004. "When the Going Gets Tough, the Tough Go Photoshopping: September 11 and the Newslore of Vengeance and Victimization." *New Media & Society* 6 (5): 633–58. http://dx.doi.org/10.1177/146144804047084.

Frank, Russell. 2011. *Newslore: Contemporary Folklore on the Internet*. Jackson: University Press of Mississippi.

Georges, Robert A., and Michael Owen Jones. 1995. *Folkloristics: An Introduction*. Bloomington: Indiana University Press.

Glassie, Henry. 1968. *Pattern in the Material Folk Culture of the Eastern United States*. Philadelphia: University of Pennsylvania Press.

Glassie, Henry. 1995. "Tradition." *Journal of American Folklore* 108 (430): 395–412. http://dx.doi.org/10.2307/541653.

Glassie, Henry. 2003. "Tradition." In *Eight Words for the Study of Expressive Culture*, ed. Burt Feintuch, 176–97. Urbana: University of Illinois Press.

Goldstein, Diane E. 1993. "Not Just a 'Glorified Anthropologist': Medical Problem Solving Through Verbal and Material Art." *Folklore in Use* 1 (1): 15–24.

Goldstein, Kenneth S. 1974. *A Guide for Field Workers in Folklore*. Detroit, MI: Gale Research.

Graff, Gerald. 1989. *Professing Literature: An Institutional History*. Chicago, IL: University of Chicago Press.

Gray, Mary. 2009. *Out in the Country: Youth, Media, and Queer Visibility in Rural America*. New York: New York University Press.

Gusfield, Joseph R. Jan 1967. "Tradition and Modernity: Misplaced Polarities in the Study of Social Change." *American Journal of Sociology* 72 (4): 351–62. http://dx.doi.org/10.1086/224334. Medline:6071952

Handler, Richard, and Jocelyn Linnekin. 1984. "Tradition, Genuine or Spurious." *Journal of American Folklore* 97 (385): 273–90. http://dx.doi.org/10.2307/540610.

Howard, Robert Glenn. 2008a. "Electronic Hybridity: The Persistent Processes of the Vernacular Web." *Journal of American Folklore* 121 (480): 192–218. http://dx.doi.org/10.1353/jaf.0.0012.

Howard, Robert Glenn. 2008b. "The Vernacular Web of Participatory Media." *Critical Studies in Media Communication* 25 (5): 490–513. http://dx.doi.org/10.1080/15295030802468065.

Howard, Robert Glenn. 2011. *Digital Jesus: The Making of a New Christian Fundamentalist Community on the Internet*. New York: New York University Press.

Ivey, Bill. 2011. "Values and Value in Folklore (AFS Presidential Plenary Address, 2007)." *Journal of American Folklore* 124 (491): 6–18. http://dx.doi.org/10.5406/jamerfolk.124.491.0006.

Jenkins, Henry. 2008. *Convergence Culture: Where Old and New Media Collide*. New York University Press.

Jennings, Karla. 1990. *The Devouring Fungus*. New York: W. W. Norton.

Jones, Michael Owen. 2000. "'Tradition' in Identity Discourses and an Individual's Symbolic Construction of Self." *Western Folklore* 59 (2): 115–40. http://dx.doi.org/10.2307/1500156.

Kirshenblatt-Gimblett, Barbara. 1995. "From the Paperwork Empire to the Paperless Office: Testing the Limits of the 'Science of Tradition.'" In *Folklore Interpreted: Essays in Honor of Alan Dundes*, ed. Regina Bendix and Rosemary Levy Zumwalt, 69–92. New York: Garland.

Kirshenblatt-Gimblett, Barbara. 1996. "The Electronic Vernacular." In *Connected: Engagements with Media*, ed. George E. Marcus, 21–66. Chicago, IL: University of Chicago Press.

Larraín, Jorge. 2001. *Identity and Modernity in Latin America*. Cambridge, UK: Polity Press.

Leach, Maria, and Jerome Fried. 1984. *Funk & Wagnalls Standard Dictionary of Folklore, Mythology, and Legend*. New York: Harper and Row.

Lord, Albert. 1960. *The Singer of Tales*. Cambridge, MA: Harvard University Press.

Marcuse, Herbert. 1964. *One-Dimensional Man*. Boston, MA: Beacon Press.

Moore, Robert J., E. Cabell Hankinson Gathman, and Nicolas Ducheneau. 2009. "From 3D Space to Third Place: The Social Life of Small Virtual Spaces." *Human Organization* 68 (2): 230–40.

Noyes, Dorothy. 2009. "Tradition: Three Traditions." *Journal of Folklore Research* 46 (3): 233–68. http://dx.doi.org/10.2979/JFR.2009.46.3.233.

Osborne, Peter. 1992. "Modernity Is a Qualitative, Not a Chronological, Category: Notes on the Dialectics of Differential Historical Time." In *Postmodernism and the Re-reading of Modernity*, ed. Francis Barker, Peter Hulme, and Margaret Iversen, 23–45. Manchester, UK: Manchester University Press.

Paredes, Américo, and Richard Bauman, eds. 1972. *Toward New Perspectives in Folklore.* Austin: University of Texas Press.

Prensky, Marc. 2001. "Digital Natives, Digital Immigrants." *Horizon* 9 (5): 1–6. http://dx.doi.org/10.1108/10748120110424816.

Rheingold, Howard. 2000. *The Virtual Community: Homesteading on the Electronic Frontier.* Cambridge, MA: MIT Press.

Smith, Marian W. 1959. "The Importance of Folklore Studies to Anthropology." *Folklore* 70 (1): 300–12. http://dx.doi.org/10.1080/0015587X.1959.9717162.

Tapscott, Don. 1999. *Growing Up Digital: The Rise of the Net Generation.* Columbus, OH: McGraw-Hill.

Tapscott, Dan. 2008. *Grown up Digital: How the Net Generation is Changing Your World.* Columbus, OH: McGraw-Hill.

Turkle, Sherri. 1995. *Life on the Screen: Identity in the Age of the Internet.* New York: Simon & Schuster.

Turkle, Sherri. 2005. *The Second Self: Computers and the Human Spirit.* Cambridge, MA: MIT Press.

Wasik, Bill. 2009. *And Then There's This: How Stories Live and Die in Viral Culture.* New York: Viking Press.

Westerman, William. 2009. "Epistemology, the Sociology of Knowledge, and the Wikipedia Userbox Controversy." In *Folklore and the Internet: Vernacular Expression in a Digital World,* ed. Trevor J. Blank, 123–58. Logan: Utah State University Press.

1

Thinking through Tradition

Elliott Oring

THE WORD *TRADITION* IS ITSELF TRADITIONAL IN FOLKLORE studies. John Aubrey used it in his *Miscellanies* in 1696. In 1777 John Brand identified tradition—indeed, oral tradition—as central in the preservation of the rites and opinions of the common people (Dorson 1968a, 1:8). W. J. Thoms referred to "local traditions" in his 1846 letter to the *Athenaeum* where he proposed his neologism "folklore" (Dorson 1968a, 1:53), and E. Sydney Hartland, in the last years of that century, characterized folklore as the "science of tradition" (Dorson 1968a, 2:231). Tradition has remained central to most definitions of folklore ever since (Brunvand 1998, 3). Indeed, it is considered one of a few "keywords" in folklore studies (in addition to the terms *art, text, group, performance, genre, context,* and *identity* [Feintuch 2003]). But what is the status of tradition in folklore studies? What role does it play and what achievements can the field attribute to its deployment?

In his essay "The Seven Strands of Tradition," Dan Ben-Amos (1984) identified a variety of ways that folklorists have used *tradition*: as lore, canon, process, mass, culture, langue, and performance. *Lore* refers to past knowledge of a society that has inadvertently survived but is in danger of dying out (104). *Canon* refers to that body of literary and artistic culture that has gained acceptance in a particular social group (106). *Process* refers to the dynamics of cultural transmission over time (117). *Mass* refers to what is transmitted by tradition; it is not the result of superorganic process but rather is changed by those who transmit it (118). *Culture* suggests that tradition is synonymous with the anthropological conception of thought and behavior in social life (120–21). *Langue* refers to the concepts, categories, and rules that engender culture. As in Ferdinand de Saussure's linguistics, it refers to

DOI: 10.7330/9780874218992.c01

the abstract system that underlies and generates speech and behavior (121). *Performance* refers to enactment, and although enactment is always in the present, tradition always exists in the minds and memories of people as a potential (122–23).

These differences in the uses of the term *tradition* are not always crystal clear, but Ben-Amos was trying to sort out the usages of the term by folklorists from different periods and publications. His was an attempt to construct a descriptive history of the term. He found that folklorists did not use *tradition* consistently, nor did they examine their usages critically. Curiously, Ben-Amos concludes that none of the uses of the term *tradition* are more adequate or proper than any other. Tradition, he states, is a metaphor that guides folklorists in dealing with "an inchoate world of experiences and ideas" (Ben-Amos 1984, 124). Simon J. Bronner, writing a decade and a half later, was perhaps less forgiving. He characterizes the use of *tradition* in folklore as reflecting "multiple meanings" and betraying a "conceptual softness" (Bronner 1998, 10).

Can a "science of tradition" be based on a concept that is so scattered, inchoate, and soft? Ben-Amos's seeming unconcern with the ways folklorists deployed the term *tradition* probably stemmed from the fact that he had no personal investment in the concept. He had eliminated tradition from his definition of folklore more than a decade before. For him, folklore was "artistic communication in small groups" (Ben-Amos 1972, 14). Tradition played no part. Ben-Amos nevertheless claimed that folklorists think *with* the term *tradition* even if they did not think much *about* it. Do folklorists think with tradition? Is tradition an analytical concept that helps folklorists to perceive, explore, and explain the world? These are some of the questions addressed below.

TRADITION AS PROCESS AND PRODUCT

The word *tradition* comes from the Latin roots *trans* + *dare*—literally, "to give across"—that is, to hand over, deliver, or transfer.[1] Thus, *tradition* involves the notion of transferring or transmitting and has been applied

---

1   The meanings of *surrender* or *betrayal* that exist both in Latin and English (*Oxford English Dictionary*, 1989, 2nd. ed., s.v. "tradition") should be noted as well. In English, the related term *traduce* not only means "to transfer" but also to "speak falsely," "misrepresent," "betray," and "bring into disgrace" (*Oxford English Dictionary*, 2nd ed., s.v. "traduce").

to the *act* of handing over or handing down as well as to those *objects* that are handed over or handed down. Consequently, *tradition* refers to both processes and products.

Although folklorists have consistently noted the duality of the term, they have focused almost exclusively on the products of tradition (see Ben-Amos 1984, 116–19; Final Discussion 1983, 241; Gailey 1989, 144; Sims and Stephens 2005, 65; Vansina 1985, 3).[2] They have been drawn to the field by quilts, proverbs, remedies, legends, songs, and tales. The study of folklore has always been rooted in the study of particular traditions; and the study of those traditions only sometimes turned toward the question of the means by which they were passed on.[3] Folklore did not begin with a study of process and then turn to the outcomes of that process. The process was used to label objects of interest and set them apart. The process itself, however, has always remained somewhat opaque.[4]

Dan Ben-Amos's survey of the uses of *tradition* noted that the term was employed to denote both process and product, but that distinction was obscured as he listed all seven uses indiscriminately. Process is listed with six other uses that refer to products of tradition—namely, lore, canon, mass, culture, langue, and performance (Ben-Amos 1984, 102–25). These products are the ideas, knowledge, objects, behaviors, or rules that are transferred and transmitted through time. Had Ben-Amos arranged the categories taxonomically, however, with the first distinction drawn between *process* and *product*, the fact that the other six categories were—or dealt with—product would have stood out more clearly. Then the deficiency of attention to tradition as process would have been underscored, as *process* would have included no further categories.

The collapse of process and product into a simple list obscures the fact that process is not just another entry. It does not constitute a mere one-seventh

---

2   The products are what Hermann Bausinger called objectified cultural "goods" (Bausinger 1969, 28).

3   In a folklore encyclopedia entry on "Tradition," the term *traditions* is referred to by the second sentence. The entry goes on to note that *tradition* is an adjective modifying specific genres (Allison 1997, 2:800).

4   It is important to note that John Brand, who first used the term *oral tradition*, did not think it constituted a special type of process or demanded particular kinds of social relations for its operation. Rather, the public written record had been censored to remove references to the rites and ceremonies of earlier times. Oral tradition was important because it was not so censored (Brand in Dorson 1968a, 1:6–12). Here is one source of the notion of folklore as "unofficial culture" (Dorson 1968b, 37) and the culture of resistance (Rodriguez 1998).

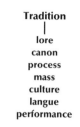

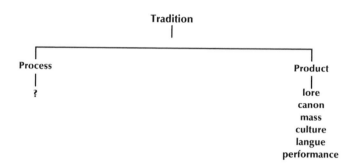

of the meanings of tradition. It represents a fundamentally different conceptualization of what constitutes tradition. Process is more fundamental than product. Traditions are traditions only by virtue of some process that makes them so. Process creates product. Without the process, traditions would be indistinguishable from all other cultural ideas and practices.

What, then, is this process? The process of tradition, I contend, is the process of *cultural reproduction*. Cultural reproduction refers to the means by which culture is reproduced in transmission and repetition.[5] It depends on the assimilation of cultural ideas and the reenactment of cultural practices. Reproduction may be accomplished in an act of transmission from one person to another. Or it may be accomplished when individuals produce something they have reproduced before, such as singing a song they have sung in the past (Bartlett 1932, 63, 118). My use of *cultural reproduction* refers to a much broader sphere of activity than that addressed by Pierre Bourdieu in his study of French educational institutions. The term should not be restricted to school learning or the learning of "high" or "official" culture. A study of cultural reproduction need not focus on the ways that it preserves

---

5 Cultural reproduction need not be regarded from the perspective of "cultural capital" or "symbolic violence" (Bourdieu 1973; Bourdieu and Passeron 1977).

social stratifications (Bourdieu 1973; Bourdieu and Passeron 1977). Indeed, folklorists should be more interested in how social organizations enable cultural reproduction than the reverse. In reality, cultural reproduction is achieved through a number of different processes. *Cultural reproduction* is merely an umbrella term for these processes—the processes of tradition.

It is even possible to identify some of these processes within Ben-Amos's essay. When he discusses the sense of tradition as canon, for example, he talks about creativity and how folklorists view creativity as necessary to the maintenance of tradition. Creativity—or better, *re-creation*—would then be one of the processes of tradition. Canons are products, but *canonization* is a process, so it might be included as well. Beyond Ben-Amos's essay, other processes spring immediately to mind: *education, memorization, rehearsal, comparison,* and *traditionalization.*[6]

TRADITION AND CREATIVITY

Everything changes. What comes from the past mutates and is modified, transformed, or disappears. There are two possible approaches to the past and change: take the past as given and describe and explain change; or take change as given and describe and explain that which perseveres. The attention of contemporary folklorists is unequally distributed with respect to these approaches. For the most part, folklorists take the past as given and address themselves to variation (Ben-Amos 1984, 114). Each instantiation of a tradition is regarded as a performance with its own peculiar variables. Rather than being something handed down, it is highlighted as something new and unique.[7] It has even been claimed that "tradition is change" (Final Discussion 1983, 236; Toelken 1996, 7).

---

6   *Comparison* refers to checking what one has learned against other sources. *Performance* involves taking aesthetic responsibility for an action. To the extent that a performance depends upon the reproduction of something from the past, a performer might be censured for what is regarded as excessive or inappropriate deviation. Performance might prove less a matter of individual creativity and more a process of learning and faithful reproduction. *Traditionalization* refers to the human propensity to turn experiences and texts into traditions by linking them to the past (Bauman 2004, 146–49; Hymes 1975, 353–54) or creating the desire, need, and conditions for their future reproduction.

7   Since all culture is subject to constant change, it has been argued, there can only be what is new. *Tradition*, consequently, becomes an interpretive term applied to ideas and practices that are new that take on symbolic value as old. Conversely, as everything is necessarily derived from the past, everything is to some extent old, but it takes on symbolic value under the terms *new* or *modern* (M. E. Smith in Handler and Linnekin

Of late, the attention of folklorists has been directed to one type of change: change that is deliberate, crafted, and aesthetic. The terms for this type of change are *innovation, improvisation,* and *creativity*.[8] Folklorists hold that it is creativity that keeps tradition alive by making an inheritance from the past relevant in the present (Ben-Amos 1984, 113; Glassie 1995, 395).[9] However, there are several problems with this proposition.

There is a presumption that the changes that occur to past ideas, expressions, and behaviors are *necessary* ones. For example, "Folklore lives through a generally selective process that ensures . . . that traditions will maintain their viability, or change so they can, or die off" (Toelken 1996, 43). "Only those forms are retained that hold a functional value for the given community" (Jakobson and Bogatyrev 1980 [1929], 6). "Creative storytellers are the ones who modernize and renew the folktale tradition to make it attractive for current consumption" (Dégh 1995, 44). "The creative impulse speaks to the fact that tradition is not and has never been something static, the most stable aspect of any tradition being its ability to change in response to changing needs" (Neulander 1998, 226). These claims, however, are merely assertions. Change and adaptation have not been assessed independently but are defined in terms of one another. The change of past forms is required for survival in the present; survival in the present demands change in forms from the past.[10] However, without some empirical

---

1984, 273). While one can view "new" and "old" as interpretive categories, it seems extreme to regard "new" and "old" strictly as designations. Such an approach depends on the utter disconnection of all ideas and practices from one another so that they exist only in the present and are old or new by arbitrary attribution. There are, however, thoughts and behaviors that are relatively new, and thoughts and behaviors that are very close reproductions of earlier models. In the early twenty-first century, quantum computing seems very new even if electronic digital computing may now seem somewhat old.

8 What kind of changes count as creative is unclear. Does "creativity" indicate a qualitative evaluation of a particular change, and if so, who makes the determination? Definitions are rare, and when they are occasionally offered—(e.g., "a heuristic process, of an expressive character, put into service of direct aims and results in the development of personality" [Voigt 1983, 181])—they do not clear anything up.

9 Ben-Amos pointed to the inherent contradiction in this formulation. Changing the past, paradoxically, is what keeps the past alive (Ben-Amos 1984, 114–15).

10 This claim is, in fact, belied by actual experience. Bertrand Harris Bronson points out that there is objective evidence to suggest that many changes—creative or otherwise—meet with no community support. They simply remain in the province of the individual singer and produce curious clashes when that community performs together (Bronson 1969, 148–49).

determination of what constitutes necessary and incidental change, what has been proposed is tautology: the changes that have occurred to an expression from the past enable its survival; expressions from the past that have not survived did not change appropriately to suit current conditions. In other words, that which survives, survives; that which has not, has not.[11]

Creativity is a term for a process that is applied to a product. Because creativity is a process, it is conflated with the process of tradition itself. But the process of tradition, whatever its particular characteristics, must conceptually relate to a process of cultural reproduction, not innovation. Things from the past can be altered. Things from the past are altered. Things from the past are "creatively" or otherwise revised. But to call this the process of tradition is to largely ignore continuity and stability. Continuity and stability depend on what people preserve—for good or ill, consciously or unconsciously—of the thought and behavior of the past. To study tradition, folkloristics must come to understand the means by which cultural reproduction is accomplished—to grasp the forces that direct the present through the conduit of past practice.

The notion of creativity as employed by folklorists is not the process *of* tradition but a process *acting upon* particular traditions (Bronson 1969, 144–45). For example, would the creative refashioning of a ballad or folktale constitute the operation of tradition or an operation performed on a traditional expression? The use of a single term to at once refer to both a process and a product is probably the source of many problems with the term *tradition*. Some statements that might be true about tradition as product (e.g., "traditions change") are ambiguous, meaningless, or false when applied to tradition as process (e.g., "tradition is change" [Final Discussion 1983, 236; Toelken 1996, 7]). Some statements that might be true about tradition as process (e.g., "tradition never dies") are ambiguous, meaningless, or false when applied to a product (e.g., "traditions never die").

Contemporary folklorists have been trapped by tradition. Like Ben-Amos (1972), they have moved away from the concept. Unlike Ben-Amos, they did not consciously or precipitously abandon it. Almost alchemically, they transformed it. The continuity of the past was regarded as a given. The focus was on change, particularly creative change, which became the touchstone of tradition: "Tradition . . . is an innovative adaptation of the old" (Glassie 1995, 395); "The artist's own unique talents of inventiveness

---

11   See Bronson's (1954) critique of "selection."

within the tradition . . . are expected to operate strongly" (Toelken 1996, 37); "The pattern of creative activity within the forms of one's own society is valid not only in such folk arts as pottery or storytelling, but equally in the most extreme forms of self-expression in modern European painting" (Crowley 1966, 136); "The linking of creativity and tradition . . . succeeds the Romantic notion of art as the domain of exceptional and cultivated minds" (Bronner 1992, 2). Tradition was thus made to exhibit the quality that defines art in our culture—it was dynamic, innovative, original, and creative. In other words, *"creativity" was the means by which folklorists recuperated tradition as art.*[12] Tradition, consequently, has been something of a "survival" in contemporary folkloristics. It has lost much of its original meaning and has made its way into "a new state of society different from that in which . . . [it] had . . . [its] original home" (Tylor 1871, 1:16). Yet the older sense of the term haunts the discipline like an unlaid ghost, and it indexes, ironically, the influence of tradition in the operation of contemporary folklore scholarship.

TRADITION: ETIC AND EMIC

Where an etic and superorganic notion of tradition dominated folklore scholarship in the past—under theories of evolution, diffusion, function, and structure—an emic sense of tradition is privileged today. Richard Handler and Jocelyn Linnekin dismiss the idea that *tradition* might refer to a core of culture traits inherited from the past and regard it solely as a symbolic construction—an interpretation of the past enacted in the present (Handler and Linnekin 1984, 273). The traditional is what people claim their traditions to be. Whether those claims can be substantiated by empirical evidence is another matter entirely.[13] Barry M. McDonald, writing in response to Henry Glassie's (1995) essay on tradition, is more forgiving. He feels that practitioners and folklorists need to negotiate "some mutually intelligible core meanings for the concept" (McDonald 1997, 52). The

---

12   Glassie, for example, attempts to find tradition in Ben-Amos's otherwise traditionless definition of folklore (Glassie 1995, 400–1).

13   Max Radin (1935, 15:62–63) felt that "tradition" should be distinguished from "custom" because traditions were judged as valuable by their bearers. They were symbolic. Walter Hävernick (1968) proposed a distinction between "tradition" and "continuity" with the former relating to the symbolic elements of social groups and the latter to the elements of an unconscious, unsymbolic past.

meaning of the term, he feels, should not be determined by the folklorist's critical viewpoint alone.

Both propositions seem problematic. Handler and Linnekin base their claim for an interpretive concept of tradition on their independent investigations of particular cases in Quebec and Hawaii. However, the cases only evidence that tradition can be constructed and deployed for symbolic purposes—for purposes of cultural identity. Identity formation and maintenance are important uses made of the past and the perceived past—or what might be called "the rhetorical past."[14] They hardly seem to exhaust the possible roles that past ideas, objects, and practices might play in contemporary affairs, nor do they engage at all with tradition as process.[15]

What would happen to the field of folklore were it restricted only to those practices deemed traditional by their practitioners? Many people tell jokes, cure illnesses, dance, sing, and make quilts simply to engage in those activities. Tradition may have nothing to do with the reasons for the performance. That the joke is a funny one, the remedy an effective one, the song a moving one, the dance a sensual one, and the quilt a warm one is often more than sufficient justification for the endeavor. People may know that the joke, the remedy, the song, the dance, and the quilt pattern have been around for a while, but it may have little to do with why they joke, heal, sing, dance, and stitch. In fact, it is often the folklorist who raises questions about the past and introduces traditionality into folk consciousness and discourse. In any event, much of what folklorists consider to be folklore would evaporate overnight were *folklore* defined simply as tradition and *tradition* defined in terms of people's claims about what constituted the practices of their ancestors.

And what might be achieved by McDonald's notion of a negotiated concept of tradition? It is quite possible—indeed likely—that scholars and the people they study will have different, sometimes radically different, notions of the past. The scholar certainly needs to be aware of these differences. It may be that etic and emic concepts illuminate one another or talk past one another, but what exactly is to be negotiated? How would the outcome of such a negotiation be decided? Why should etic and emic concepts of anything agree? What would be gained from such agreements and, more

---

14   Social identities may also coalesce around things that are not traditional—or regarded as traditional—at all (e.g., sports teams).

15   In fact, the construction of tradition in Handler and Linniken's formulation would be a process, but they are more interested in the functions of the products constructed.

importantly perhaps, what would be lost? It is precisely in the disparities between the assessments of scholars and practitioners that some of the most fruitful questions about human thought and behavior are engendered.[16]

Traditions can be unconscious. Ideas, knowledge, and behaviors can be received and acted upon without the recipient's awareness of their nature, origin, or consequences. Some hold the idea of unconscious tradition as "theoretically 'deficient' and potentially offensive to its practitioners" (McDonald 1997, 58). Wherein lies the deficiency and offense? Is all knowledge consciously acquired and accessible to consciousness? If so, why is it that native speakers usually cannot describe the rules that govern their language production? They clearly follow rules but often have a hazy grasp, if any grasp at all, of what those rules are. People—ourselves included—often do not know exactly what they are doing, how they do it, or how they acquired the means do it.

The unconscious aspects of cultural practice—the principles that seem to be operating outside the awareness of cultural actors—are the most fascinating part of a cultural system. This proposition is not cultural paternalism. It is not some imposition upon subaltern peoples. Cultural analysis is most trenchant when it identifies a pattern of thought or behavior governing our *own* culture of which we are unaware.[17] Victorian folklorists regularly pointed to behaviors in their own society that seemed devoid of sense and showed that these derived from the beliefs and practices of earlier times. Diffusionists have shown that ideas and behaviors that were central to a cultural system often—usually—came from the outside (Wissler 1926). Evolutionary and diffusionist perspectives have long been abandoned, but they demonstrated that numerous forms of behavior are rooted—unbeknownst to their practitioners—in forms from other times and places (Linton 1937). A strong case has been made, in fact, that real tradition consist of tacit rather than explicit knowledge (McKeon 2004).

16 Imagine a case in which an individual's sense of his childhood is filled with pleasant and loving memories. Is it not possible that this individual suffered greatly in childhood and that his personality might have crystallized around those negative childhood experiences? Might not the fond memories—the symbolic past—be a mask and serve as compensation for a real past? The memories of childhood are a symbolic construction, but to accept them as the only notion of that individual's past would be to abdicate the ability to understand that particular construction of childhood or understand anything that might have been conditioned by actual childhood experience.

17 A simple example: in American culture, food picked up with a utensil is to be placed entirely in the mouth; food picked up with the hands can be taken away from the mouth and brought back to the plate. Which foods qualify as hand foods and utensil foods is a separate problem. What is theoretically deficient or offensive in this observation?

Folklorists need to be attentive to the uses of the word, or any words that serve to denote the relation between past and present. They need to record what people select from the panoply of past belief and practice as "traditional"; describe how claims of traditionality are negotiated; and understand the effects of such attributions in specific situations and in society more generally. Understanding tradition emically is to understand something significant about the conduct of human affairs both large and small. How people imagine their pasts contributes directly to the maintenance and modification of past beliefs and practices. However, there may be other forces beyond an individual's or group's ken that influence thought and behavior. Folklorists cannot ignore the emic notion of tradition, but the view that tradition is a symbolic construction only allows for the exploration of the ways we make use of the past; it does not allow for an understanding of the ways that the past makes use of us.[18]

TRADITION AND MODERNITY

Tradition has not only been applied to products and processes. The term has also been used to designate periods of time. *Tradition* has been used to label what is conceived to be the predecessor and opposite of modernity. *Modernity* (from the Latin *modo* meaning "lately") is a term that postulates a radical break with the past. It designates that period in which technology, social and economic organization, aesthetic expression, values, and lifestyles were utterly transformed from what they had been. Modernity is marked by industrialization, capitalism, nationalism, individualism, rationalized and secularized social institutions, and parliamentary democracy. It is defined against tradition: the "premodern," "old," "old-fashioned," "antique," "conservative," "classic," "primitive," "feudal," "folk," and "traditional." In

---

18   Twenty-five years ago, I attended a psychoanalytic seminar. The speaker was a psycho-analyst working with adolescent delinquents with whom the analyst claimed some success. In discussing one case, the analyst indicated that his patient believed that his father was trying to kill him. I asked whether his father was indeed trying to kill him, as that would seem to make a difference in his evaluation and treatment. If his father was, in fact, trying to kill him, it might explain important aspects of the patient's problem. At the very least, his belief about his father would not be a symptom but a fact. The psychoanalyst could not seem to grasp the distinction. In his view, everything that one imagined about oneself and one's world was open to analysis and psychologi-cal amelioration. This seemed a dangerous theory—especially if the patient were killed when he got home.

this framework, *tradition* cannot be defined except from within modernity. Consequently, *modernity* and *tradition* are not simply descriptive terms but comparative and evaluative ones (Anttonen 2005, 13–14, 28). Whether tradition takes a positive or negative value in this formulation depends on whether one takes a positive or negative view of contemporary society and culture. Modernity may be seen as something to be escaped—in which case tradition may be celebrated and venerated; or modernity may be seen as something to be embraced—in which case tradition is a shackle from which society needs to be freed.[19]

The discourse on "tradition versus modernity" has profoundly shaped the field of folklore from its inception. Folklore was born, after all, in the concern for how the past might serve to improve and invigorate an anemic present (Wilson 1989, 27). Even for folklorists today, tradition often figures as the opposite of and as an alternative to modernity. Folklorists often identify, describe, and attempt to preserve traditions because they feel that bygone ways of life are valuable, beautiful, and ultimately more humane. The work of folklorists has in large part been an effort to engender respect and sympathy for past or marginalized ways of life (Abrahams 1992, 25; Feintuch 1988, 1–16; Gailey 1989, 159; Hofer 1984, 133). Thus, the studies, publications, and exhibits of traditions become homilies whose purpose is the aesthetic and moral edification of the citizens of modern society. Scholars who adhere to this approach to folklore cannot ignore how their reactions to modernity shape their scholarly perspectives or how their scholarly perspectives participate in the response to and critique of modernity.[20]

Tradition and modernity are just one of many polar categorizations of society and culture: folk/urban, mechanical/organic, religious/secular, oral/literate, status-based/contractual, communal/societal, highbrow/lowbrow, local/global. They often prove evaluative concepts as well. As such, they probably obscure as much as, if not more than, they clarify. Few would contest that urban life in a first world country in the twenty-first century is qualitatively different from life on a European feudal manor in the ninth. There are fundamental differences in their technologies, social organizations, and worldviews. However, a folkloristic definition of

---

19   This is not an all-or-nothing proposition. One can take a negative view of some aspects of modernity while being totally committed to others. It is difficult—perhaps impossible—to find someone who is opposed to all aspects of the modern world.

20   The centrality of folklore scholarship in the construction of national, ethnic, and other social identities is a particular case in point (Anttonen 2005, 124–77).

tradition is not something that can only be accomplished in relation to modernity, nor need the definition necessarily engage the value of either past or present.[21] Defined as *cultural reproduction*, tradition can be value neutral. One can investigate how cultural continuities are created and disturbed independent of whether the continuities or transformations are for better or for worse. There is no society, regardless of how "modern," in which tradition—as a process of cultural reproduction—plays no great part.[22] Similarly, there is no society, no matter how "traditional," in which the automatic and exact reproduction of past ways of life and thought determines uniformity of belief and practice. In every society, there is innovation and deviation.[23]

FOLKLORE AND TRADITION

Since everything is necessarily derived to some extent from the past—so that everything is, to some extent, traditional—what part of tradition constitutes folklore? Is folklore some special sort of tradition? Henry Glassie (1995) maintains that it is. He regards tradition as a matter of people keeping

---

21   The use of *tradition* to denote something handed down—usually orally—from the past is found in English in 1380 (*OED*). The Hebrew word *masoret* means "tradition" and goes back at least to the 6th century CE It is a close analogue of *tradition*, since it is based on the root *masar*—to "give over" or "transmit." Interestingly, *masor* means "informer" or "traitor"—one who betrays someone over to the authorities and thus is analogous to the word *traduce*, to which *tradition* is related (Jastrow 1950). *Masorah*—a word found even in ordinary English dictionaries—relates to the information employed to insure the faithful reproduction of the biblical text as well as to the text itself. There is no hint of an opposition between modernity and tradition in these uses—only the sense of a faithful reproduction of the past.

22   It is more than ironic that the great replicative technologies—printing, machine manufacture, photography, analog recording, broadcasting, digitization—are technologies of modernity. The close reproduction of cultural knowledge and practice is made possible by these contemporary technologies. The technologies of the past—oral transmission, customary example, and writing—seem a more uncertain basis for cultural reproduction in the long term. Yet modernity is thought of as opposed to convention—as a world of innovation rather than of mindless reproduction.

23   DaBore, the subject of Philip L. Newman's anthropological fieldwork in New Guinea, disbelieved in lightning balls, although all the men of his society fervently set to dig them up after lightning strikes and used them in garden magic. This was the only part of the belief system of the Gururumba of New Guinea in which DaBore did not believe. He built a spirit house in his garden and assigned misfortunes to witches, ghosts, and sorcerers like everyone else. His view of lightning balls was completely idiosyncratic (Newman 1965, 104–105).

"faith with the past" and "with themselves." Tradition is a responsibility that individuals voluntarily assume (Glassie 1995, 402; see also Noyes 2009, 248). Those who do what others make them do are mere "slaves." Oppression is the opposite of tradition (Glassie 1995, 396).[24] Barry McDonald, who disagrees with Glassie on a number of points about tradition, also regards tradition as rooted in choice and a "personal relationship" (McDonald 1997, 57–58). Both seem to privilege tradition as a kind of cultural reproduction rooted in particular relationships and responsibilities.

Undoubtedly, such relationships and responsibilities inform the maintenance of certain traditions. But is there justification in limiting the application of *tradition* to this sphere alone? One can think of situations—religious beliefs and practices immediately come to mind—in which the maintenance of the past can be a matter of imposition and oppression. Belief is scrutinized, behavior is supervised, threats are made, and punishments and rewards meted out in the maintenance of conformity. Should such situations be exempted from the category of tradition a priori? Would it not be better to include all instances of cultural reproduction within *tradition*, and then distinguish them by type, organization, and motivation?[25]

Glassie's and McDonald's conceptions are consonant with the notion that traditions represent the good and the beautiful that survive in the modern world and that goodness and beauty can only be forged through free and humane practice. Folklorists have focused almost exclusively on traditions that reflect positive value—traditions that evidence creativity, resilience, cooperation, commitment, and community. Studies of racist, classist, and even sexist traditions are, for the most part, absent in the folklore literature.[26] This evaluative approach to tradition significantly narrows the scope of inquiry and severely limits the possibility that folkloristics can participate in a general science of tradition.

---

24 Bengt Holbek put forth a similar view (Final Discussion 1983, 240). Bourdieu feels, however, that cultural reproduction depends on "symbolic violence" (Bourdieu and Passeron 1977, 4–68).

25 In fact, folklore needs to concern itself with *tradition*, *custom*, *habit*, and even *fad*. These terms raise similar questions and involve some of the same processes.

26 An exception to this rule might be found in the work of Alan Dundes. Because Dundes adopted a psychoanalytic perspective on folklore, he sought out the unseemly side of folklore and explored its racism, classism, and sexism (Dundes 1984, 1997a, 1997b). Although a major figure in the discipline, his psychoanalytic interpretations had little influence and were sometimes ridiculed. Other exceptions are Montell (1986) and Bronner (2008).

If a limitation is to be imposed on *tradition* for the folklorist, it should be that the term avoids the invocation of evaluative and moral criteria. Let folklore be those parts of tradition that deal with the oral or handmade, that are transmitted face-to-face and are, to a great extent, aesthetic in nature.[27] This limitation in scope presumes nothing about the goodness or morality of the products of tradition or the goodness or morality of the process of their reproduction. It is true that the concern of folklore studies with oral, face-to-face communication came about because these were the touchstones of those communities eradicated or marginalized by industrial and market forces. The loss was felt to be a moral one. But if folklore as a field was founded in concerns over the costs of modernity, the field need not remain rooted in that accounting. Folklore can define itself without privileging the oral and face-to-face morally and without presuming that its study must serve as a critique of modern life.

In limiting themselves to aesthetic reproduction achieved through oral and face-to-face channels, folklorists could not claim to be scientists of tradition at large, nor claim to be the only scientists of tradition. There are many areas of cultural reproduction in which folklorists have no interest or expertise and about which they have had little to say. Most prominent are those broad areas of language and social organization to which folklorists—at least American folklorists—have paid little or no attention. While folklorists have been interested in linguistic products such as tales, riddles, and proverbs, they have not concerned themselves with language systems as a whole—the means by which lexicons, morphologies, grammars, and pragmatic rules are acquired and maintained. Nor have they worried about the reproduction of institutional and bureaucratic organizations and practices. While these areas may fall outside the folklorist's purview, at some level they still need to be noted in order to grasp the larger questions of cultural continuity to which the study of folklore can contribute. In exploring such questions, all kinds of traditions need to be examined: oral and literary, contemporary and ancient, conscious and unconscious, individual and institutional, artistic and ordinary. The folkloristic focus on the oral, the face-to-face, and the aesthetic is likely to contribute to an understanding of tradition only within this larger frame. Consequently, folklorists will have to become informed

---

27   To label something "aesthetic" does not presume it is of "good" quality, only that it is structurally distinct and conspicuous with respect to its background—a proverb in relation to ordinary speech, for example. On the question of whether folklore should be limited to "*oral* tradition" see Smith (1975).

about these other areas of reproduction even if they do not stand at the center of their researches.

TRADITION AS A CONTEMPORARY SUBJECT

The raison d'être of folklore studies was that traditions were dying and should be observed and recorded before they vanished entirely. Once gone, these traditions would be beyond documentation and understanding. Some scholars have scoffed at folklore's claim that tradition was dying because folklorists had been using the same justification for more than three centuries (Bauman and Briggs 2003, 306). Of course, no one ever claimed that tradition was dying—if what is meant by tradition is the process of cultural reproduction—but only that particular traditions die out, which is demonstrably true. In addition, societies that perpetuated traditions almost exclusively through oral and face-to-face transmission were disappearing or rapidly changing—also demonstrably true. The relatively isolated societies rooted in face-to-face, oral communication and hand- rather than machine-work were, in fact, vanishing in Europe and America, where the discipline of folklore developed.

It is claimed that folkloristics' myopic concern with dying and marginalized practices can only serve to marginalize it as a discipline. Barbara Kirshenblatt-Gimblett felt that folklore must struggle "to find a truly contemporary subject, one that is not just *in* the present, but truly *of* the present" (Kirshenblatt-Gimblett 1995, 70). But is the value of a field to be based on the contemporaneity of its subject matter? Are archaeology or paleontology somehow deficient as disciplines because they engage the ancient or prehistoric? Are classical and medieval history inadequate because they deal with periods and peoples long past? The answers to these questions should be obvious. Nevertheless, there is no barrier to folklore engaging a fully contemporary subject. *The contemporary can only be defined in terms of what it replaces, marginalizes, or renders superfluous.* A focus on the persistence and disappearance of past practices is, therefore, an utterly contemporary matter. The field of folklore would prove of inestimable value to the study of society in being able to describe and explain how and why the persistence and replacement of cultural ideas and practices occur. Furthermore, the attention to cultural maintenance and replacement does not demand a commitment to either the practices that are maintained or those that are being replaced. The old and the new need not be conceptualized positively or negatively. They need not be moral categories. The need is to understand why the new replaces the old, when it does, and how and why certain past practices continue even when everything else seems to be changing around them.[28]

THE FORCE OF TRADITION

The claim that tradition could not be understood as a core of inherited traits but as a symbolic construction (Handler and Linnekin 1984, 273–90) was related to larger moves in the humanities and social sciences in the 1970s and 1980s: moves away from notions of essence, description, cause, universality, and science to notions of resemblance, interpretation, motive, contingency, and the literary. One particularly influential book in encouraging a change in the view of tradition was *The Invention of Tradition*, edited by Eric Hobsbawm and Terence Ranger. Its series of essays demonstrated how much of what had been presented as an inheritance from the ancient past was, in fact, no more than the invention of comparatively recent times. Even when the content of a tradition was not entirely factitious, the claim for its continuity was, since much tradition was a deliberate revival and reformulation rather than a continuous handing down. Thus, the traditions that people cherished and around which they rallied—those traditions whose perusal might be said to be the very reason for folklore studies— were often invented to provoke those sentiments and provide a point about which people could come together. The traditions with which folklorists were concerned turned out to be the result of deliberate crafting—often for transparent political purposes (Hobsbawm and Ranger 1984, 9).[29]

Nevertheless, the concepts of tradition as inheritance and invention are interrelated. The power of invented traditions—which is considerable—is rooted in the belief that what is inherited from the past matters. Traditions that have been invented, revived, or reformulated can only have force if

---

28 The study of why the new replaces the old is commonly known as the study of "social change." The persistence of the old—even when under pressure by new practices— might be termed the study of "social unchange" (see Noyes 2009, 239).

29 "I contend that Tradition is always being created anew, and that traditions of modern origin are as much within our province as ancient ones," wrote E. Sidney Hartland more than a century ago (Burne, Alvarez, and Hartland 1885, 120). G. Malcolm Laws, Jr. indexed American ballads that were recent New World creations (Laws 1964). It is the political manipulation of tradition that struck folklorists in the late twentieth century, not the idea that new traditions were being created.

what is handed down from "previous generations" is thought to have bearing in directing, supporting, and validating current thought and action. An invented tradition is consequently engendered by the same forces as a genuine one.

The relation of invented traditions to genuine traditions is somewhat analogous to the relation between truth and lie. Lies are employed to achieve specific ends. They have functional value. But lies can only function effectively if they are represented and accepted as truth. Lies are utterly dependent on the power of truth. Invented traditions, though they may be crafted for particular purposes, depend on the same warrant that genuine traditions possess.

Consequently, some very basic questions about tradition—whether inherited or invented—remain the same: How does the past acquire and assert its authority? How is the past sustained in the present? How is following precedent made to seem necessary or desirable?[30] When does the past trump contemporary experience, and under what circumstances, and in what ways does contemporary experience substitute new rationales for past ideas and behaviors? Why and how do new rationales succeed and why and how do old rationales fail? In what areas of thought and behavior in contemporary society is the inherited past still appealed to, and in what areas does it continue to operate? (These may not be the same.) Conversely, in what areas does the past lose its power as a model for present thought and action, and why?

DIRECTIONS IN THE STUDY OF TRADITION

Tradition needs to be approached on a number of levels—social, psychological, and aesthetic—although these are not entirely separate. The approach can be both etic and emic. Approaching reproduction on the social level would involve ascertaining the fields of choice available in a social group. It would also require a close examination of the kinds of pressures—personal, social, religious, political, legal, aesthetic—that engender conformity and the preservation of precedent (Thompson 1953, 592). Furthermore, the extent to which ideas and behaviors are embedded in or attached to other forms and practices that constrain the possibility of their variation needs

---

30 This has been termed the "normativeness" of tradition (Shils 1981, 200). Bauman has approached certain aspects of this question in his discussion of "authorization"—the process of making discourses authoritative (Bauman 2004, 150–58).

to be examined.[31] Attention to the conditions and circumstances in which individuals and groups invoke *tradition* is likewise needed.

The psychological level would involve, for example, some investigation of the processes of memory. Folklorists have pretty much avoided a confrontation with the question of memory and of learning more generally. Folklorists have to make themselves familiar with some of this literature as it helps to understand the process of tradition which begins as a process of learning.[32] The aesthetic and the psychological are closely intertwined, and psychologists, folklorists, anthropologists, and oral historians have made contributions to such research (Anderson 1951, 1956; Bartlett 1920; Oring 1978; Rubin 1995; Vansina 1985). The theory of oral formulaic composition did turn folklorists and literature scholars to the question of how traditions are remembered and reproduced (Foley 1988; Lord 1960). Much of this work focused on the study of poetic narratives, but it seems there is a lot more to do.[33] The codes and symmetries in the particular forms of folklore that serve as aids to memory and guides to reproduction need to be identified (Rubin 1995).[34] Folklorists need to understand what parts of an expression or practice are relatively fixed and what parts are free—and under what conditions (Bronson 1954, 6; 1969, 151; Glassie 1995, 406; Smith 1986, 6). The critical responses of audiences need to be observed and described in order to see whether and how they affect subsequent performance. Folklorists have talked about this, but they have not done very much in the way of reporting it, let alone analyzing it (Bauman 1977, 11; Glassie 1995, 407; Toelken 1996, 39).

Because it has often been thought of as some accumulated mass of belief and custom—some lifeless, superorganic entity—tradition has not often

---

31   Constraints may be internal or external. An internal constraint relates to performance—the way that meter, rhyme, or music might constrain certain lexical choices in a song, for example. External constraints would condition the performance as a whole, as when certain ritual occasions demand performances of a certain kind. How certain institutional practices are a function of other practices involve something like functional analysis, but not the type familiar from past folklore theory (see Cancian 1960).

32   There is a whole subfield in linguistics on language acquisition, but there is precious little in folklore on tradition acquisition.

33   A notable exception is Glassie's (1975) work on the recreation of folk housing.

34   A code is something that "preserves a message and aids its communication" (du Sautoy 2008, 282). Mozart's ability to memorize Gregorio Allegri's *Miserere*—a piece which the pope had prohibited being copied or played outside the Vatican—owed much to the musical symmetries in that work (du Sautoy 2008, 253–54).

been thought of in ethnographic terms. The presumption has been that one can do an ethnographic study of particular traditions but not of tradition itself. As cultural reproduction, however, an ethnographic approach to tradition is possible. Henry Glassie describes tradition as a keeping of faith—a faith, among others, with deceased teachers (Glassie 1995, 402). But where are the close descriptions of the relationships through which traditions are learned and maintained? Glassie is undoubtedly right that student artisans in Turkish ateliers do not receive much in the way of formal instruction but "breathe the air of experience" (408). But what does this involve? The folklore literature is remarkably thin on the descriptions of interactions of teachers and students or students with their fellow students.[35] When "influences" are written about, they are often inferred from texts and performances rather than from observations of formal and informal situations of instruction.[36] Likewise, there is little or no ethnographic data on performance review, self-assessment, and rehearsal.[37] These are areas to which folklorists might give considerably more attention. The observation and analysis of these micro processes might prove unique and important contributions to the study of tradition.[38]

THE PROBLEM OF TRADITION

Despite claims for the centrality of tradition in folklore, tradition has not served as an analytical concept—that is, it has not helped folklorists think about the materials that they study, nor has it provided an orientation for

---

35 This is a textured view of what is called "the social organization of tradition" (Bauman 2001, 15821).

36 "If the preferred terminology of 'stability' and 'change' is to have any validity in the future, it must be understood in the concrete particularization of the relationship between singers. It is simply not enough to pursue the sterile exercise of comparing songs solely with each other or with their supposed predecessors" (Russell 1987, 336).

37 A recent article on "coaxing" and the *corrido* has some relation to rehearsal, but it is viewed from the perspective of performance, and not from what it can add to an understanding of how performers conceive the song that needs to be reproduced (McDowell 2010).

38 Henry Glassie has probably attended more to the ways folk artists learn their skills than most, but not in close detail (Glassie 1989, 92–110). Understandably, it is difficult to reprise the learning processes of individual artists who are encountered by the folklorist in their mature years. But it suggests that folklorists might attend as much to novices learning their crafts as well as to "stars." See Glassie's description of carpet-weaving sisters in Ahmetler, Turkey (Glassie 1993, 669–77).

their investigations. Folklorists do not study tradition but tradition*s*. They are interested in tales, quilts, ballads, and proverbs to be found, primarily, in certain—largely marginal—social groups. The focus is on the objects themselves rather than what the study of such objects and practices contribute to an understanding of a process of "handing over" or "handing down."[39] The traditions that folklorists focus upon are regarded as *expressions*. Even traditionality itself has most often been regarded in expressive terms (Oring 1994, 243)—that is, as a sign and symbol of individual and community (e.g., Anttonen 2005; Gailey 1988; Johnson 1998, 658–59; Jones 2000; Radin 1935; Sims and Stephens 2005, 66–67). Folklorists, therefore, have been interested in discovering the meanings and functions of the traditions that they collect. Only rarely have they broached the questions identified above that might be regarded as central in a study of tradition as process: How are beliefs and practices taught and learned; what is the source of the authority of tradition and how does its force make itself felt; how do past practices continue to operate in the present and how and why do new practices come to destroy or marginalize the old? Folklore fieldwork can speak to these questions in important ways but, for the most part, it does not. It is not surprising, therefore, that folklorists have written no major treatises on tradition, and those that have been written are by scholars in other fields (Boyer 1990; Hobsbawm and Ranger 1984; Shils 1981; but see Bronner 1998). These works make little use of folklore research—much to the consternation of folklorists (Bendix 2002, 110).

Contrary to what Dan Ben-Amos (1984) suggests in his essay, folklorists do occasionally think *about* tradition, but rarely do they think *with* it.[40] *Tradition* is a word they frequently *use* but largely to mark territory. Something called a "tradition" or "traditional" is deemed to fall within the

---

39 Paul Smith is an exception. He has thought about tradition as a learning process and developed models of what might affect the stability of any particular tradition in its transmission (Smith 1974, 1975, 1978, 1986). Smith's essays were published in a somewhat obscure journal. Nevertheless, the extent to which they have been ignored—even by those writing on the concept of tradition—evidences the lack of interest of folklorists in process. Ian Russell has also developed a model of folksong transmission that identifies both continuity and change. Nevertheless, he addresses change more than continuity (Russell 1987, 331).

40 For example, see Baker (2000); Bronner (2000a, 2000b); Finnegan (1991); Gailey (1989); Glassie (1995); Gomme (1910); Handler and Linnekin (1984); Honko (1983); Jacobs (1893); Jones (2000); Klein (2000); McDonald (1997); Opie (1963); and Smith (1974, 1975, 1978, 1986).

folkloristic purview.[41] It becomes something which folklorists feel justified observing and discussing.[42] However, only when folklorists start attending to *tradition* as a process of cultural reproduction will the term acquire a measure of conceptual depth.[43] This is not to suggest that folklorists stop studying the particular traditions with which they are enamored and about which they have some interesting things to say. Nor does it suggest that folklorists should ignore change or creativity. Tradition, however, has been regarded somewhat like inertia: an object in motion tends to stay in motion; an object at rest tends to stay at rest. This may prove adequate for classical physics, but it does not seem adequate for the study of folklore. Folklorists need to grasp the means by which thought and practice are reproduced over time. Tradition needs to be regarded as a problem and not simply a given. In fact, *the major problem of tradition in folklore studies is that it has not sufficiently been regarded as a problem.* Only when the term *tradition* directs folklorists to frame substantive questions can it gain any conceptual value for the discipline.

The pursuit of tradition in the twenty-first century will not prove fruitful if it remains the enterprise it was in the nineteenth and twentieth. If *tradition* only serves to label new objects and claim new territories—primarily on the World Wide Web—it is hard to imagine how the field will advance. There

---

41 Thirty papers at an American Folklore Society conference contained "tradition," "traditions," or "traditional" in their titles (American Folklore Society 2005). These words were embedded in such phrases as "oral tradition," "shy tradition," "tradition of religious songs," "folk traditions," "traditional beliefs," "traditional foodways," and "traditional and popular culture." Judging from the abstracts of these papers, the terms were mainly employed to refer to knowledge and practices connected to the past that are maintained or reintroduced into contemporary life and literature. The term, however, seems to have little or no analytic, or even descriptive, value. This is not to suggest that the papers presented at the conference did not have something worthwhile to say. They just don't seem to have said it with *tradition*.

42 The effort to corral Internet communication within the folkloristic domain is but another example of the use of *tradition* to claim territory (American Folklore Society 2009, 56; Blank 2009). If tradition can be said to exist on the World Wide Web, then the web becomes an object for folkloristic scrutiny. In this way it can be claimed that folkloristics does not only attend to the flotsam and jetsam of a fading past but is, in fact, a scrupulously contemporary discipline. As it has been argued above, however, folkloristics would be a contemporary discipline with a contemporary subject without having to attach itself to any contemporary technology or medium.

43 It may be that cultural reproduction is close to Hermann Bausinger's suggestion that folklore, as the study of tradition, might be conceived as "diffusion research," which would possess a dynamic, processual character (Bausinger 1986 [1969], 34).

will, of course, be studies of art, legend, ritual, and humor on the web. Undoubtedly there will be a range of new forms to observe, record, and ponder as well. But to what larger questions will these forms speak? To note that some legend on the web is an updated version of an old and widespread one, and even to comment tellingly on its communicative import, will not engage matters of tradition. Until tradition is confronted for what it is—a process of reproduction—folklore studies will remain unchanged despite its focus on an ever-changing world of mediated communication. *Tradition* is a word that is more closely bound to folklore than to any other field; it is a word that has the potential to focus research on a particular set of problems and give the field a distinctive role to play in the social and human sciences. It is time that *tradition* conveyed a sense of intellectual purpose and became a concept with which and through which folklorists can truly think.

REFERENCES

Abrahams, Roger D. 1992. "The Public, the Folklorist, and the Public Folklorist." In *Public Folklore*, ed. Robert Baron and Nicolas Spitzer, 17–27. Washington, DC: Smithsonian Institution Press.

Allison, Randal S. 1997. *Folklore: An Encyclopedia of Beliefs, Customs, Tales, Music, and Art.* 2 vols. Ed. Thomas A. Green, 799–802. Santa Barbara, CA: ABC-CLIO.

American Folklore Society. 2005. *Program and Abstracts: Folklore, Equal Access, and Social Justice.* Columbus, OH: American Folklore Society.

American Folklore Society. 2009. *Program and Abstracts: Examining the Ethics of Place.* Columbus, OH: American Folklore Society.

Anderson, Walter. 1951. *Ein Volkskundliches Experiment.* FF Communications No. 141. Helsinki: Suomalainen Tiedeakatemia Fennica.

Anderson, Walter. 1956. *Eine Neue Arbeit zur Experimentellen Volkskunde.* FF Communications No. 168. Helsinki: Suomalainen Tiedeakatemia Fennica.

Anttonen, Pertti J. 2005. *Tradition through Modernity: Postmodernism and the Nation-State in Folklore Scholarship.* Helsinki: Finnish Literature Society.

Baker, Ronald L. 2000. "Tradition and the Individual Talent in Folklore and Literature." *Western Folklore* 59 (2): 105–14. http://dx.doi.org/10.2307/1500155.

Bartlett, F. C. 1920. "The Functions of Images." *British Journal of Psychology* 11: 320–37.

Bartlett, Frederic C. 1932. *Remembering: A Study in Experimental Social Psychology.* Cambridge, UK: Cambridge University Press.

Bauman, Richard. 1977. *Verbal Art as Performance.* Prospect Heights, IL: Waveland.

Bauman, Richard. 2001. "The Anthropology of Tradition." In *International Encyclopedia of the Social and Behavioral Sciences,* 26 vols., ed. Neil J. Smelser and Paul P. Bates, 15819–15824. Amsterdam: Elsevier. http://dx.doi.org/10.1016/B0-08-043076-7/00970-0

Bauman, Richard. 2004. *A World of Others' Words: Cross-Cultural Perspectives on Intertextuality.* Malden, MA: Blackwell.

Bauman, Richard, and Charles L. Briggs. 2003. *Voices of Modernity: Language Ideologies and the Politics of Inequality.* Cambridge, UK: Cambridge University Press. http://dx.doi.org/10.1017/CBO9780511486647

Bausinger, Hermann. 1986 [1969]. "A Critique of Tradition: Observations on the Situation of Volkskunde." In *German Volkskunde: A Decade of Theoretical Confrontation, Debate, and Reorientation (1967–1977)*, ed. and trans. James R. Dow and Hannjost Lixfeld, 26–40. Bloomington: Indiana University Press.

Ben-Amos, Dan. 1972. "Toward a Definition of Folklore in Context." In *Toward New Perspectives in Folklore*, ed. Americo Paredes and Richard Bauman, 3–15. Austin: University of Texas Press.

Ben-Amos, Dan. 1984. "The Seven Strands of Tradition: Varieties and Its Meaning in American Folklore Studies." *Journal of Folklore Research* 21 (2/3): 97–131.

Bendix, Regina. 2002. "The Uses of Disciplinary History." *Radical History Review* 84: 110–14. http://dx.doi.org/10.1215/01636545-2002-84-110.

Blank, Trevor J., ed. 2009. *Folklore and the Internet: Vernacular Expression in a Digital World*. Logan: Utah State University Press.

Bourdieu, Pierre. 1973. "Cultural Reproduction and Social Reproduction." In *Knowledge, Education and Cultural Change*, ed. Richard Brown, 71–112. London: Tavistock.

Bourdieu, Pierre, and Jean-Claude Passeron. 1977. *Reproduction in Education, Society, and Culture*. Sage Studies in Social and Educational Change, vol. 5. London: Sage Publications.

Boyer, Pascal. 1990. *Tradition as Truth and Communication*. Cambridge, UK: Cambridge University Press. http://dx.doi.org/10.1017/CBO9780511521058

Bronner, Simon J. 1992. "Introduction." In *Tradition and Creativity in Folklore: New Directions*, ed. Simon J. Bronner, 1–38. Logan: Utah State University Press.

Bronner, Simon J. 1998. *Following Tradition: Folklore in the Discourse of American Culture*. Logan: Utah State University Press.

Bronner, Simon J. 2000a. "The Meanings of Tradition: An Introduction." *Western Folklore* 59 (2): 87–104. http://dx.doi.org/10.2307/1500154.

Bronner, Simon J. 2000b. "The American Concept of Tradition: Folklore in the Discourse of Traditional Values." *Western Folklore* 59 (2): 143–70. http://dx.doi.org/10.2307/1500157.

Bronner, Simon J. 2008. *Killing Tradition: Inside Hunting and Animal Rights Controversies*. Lexington: University Press of Kentucky.

Bronson, Bertrand Harris. 1954. "The Morphology of the Ballad-Tunes (Variation, Selection, and Continuity)." *Journal of American Folklore* 67 (263): 1–13. http://dx.doi.org/10.2307/536803.

Bronson, Bertrand Harris. 1969. *The Ballad as Song*. Berkeley: University of California Press.

Brunvand, Jan Harold. 1998. *The Study of American Folklore: An Introduction*. New York: W. W. Norton.

Burne, Charlotte S., Antonio Machado y Alvarez, and E. Sidney Hartland. 1885. "The Science of Folklore." *Folk-Lore Journal* 3 (2): 97–120.

Cancian, Francesca. 1960. "The Functional Analysis of Change." *American Sociological Review* 25 (6): 818–27. http://dx.doi.org/10.2307/2089979.

Crowley, Daniel. 1966. *I Could Talk Old-Story Good: Creativity in Bahamian Folklore*. Berkeley: University of California Press.

Dégh, Linda. 1995. *Narratives in Society: A Performer-Centered Study of Narration*. Helsinki: Suomalainen Tiedeakatemia.

Dorson, Richard M., ed. 1968a. *Peasant Customs and Savage Myths: Selections from the British Folklorists*. 2 vols. Chicago: University of Chicago Press.

Dorson, Richard M., ed. 1968b. "What Is Folklore?" *Folklore Forum* 1 (4): 37.

Dundes, Alan. 1984. *Life Is Like a Chicken Coop Ladder: A Study of German National Character through Folklore*. New York: Columbia University Press.

Dundes, Alan. 1997a. *Two Tales of Crow and Sparrow: A Freudian Folkloristic Essay on Caste and Untouchability*. Lanham, MD: Rowman & Littlefield.

Dundes, Alan. 1997b. *From Game to War and Other Psychoanalytic Essays on Folklore*. Lexington: University Press of Kentucky.

Du Sautoy, Marcus. 2008. *Symmetry: A Journey into the Patterns of Nature*. New York: Harper.

Feintuch, Burt. 1988. "Introduction." In *The Conservation of Culture: Folklorists and the Public Sector*, ed. Burt Feintuch, 1–16. Lexington: University Press of Kentucky.

Feintuch, Burt. 2003. *Eight Words for the Study of Expressive Culture*. Urbana: University of Illinois Press.

Discussion, Final. 1983. "On the Analytical Value of the Concept of Tradition." In *Trends in Nordic Tradition Research*, ed. Lauri Honko and Pekka Laaksonen, 233–49. Helsinki: Suomalaisen Kirjallisuuden Seura.

Finnegan, Ruth. 1991. "Tradition, But What Tradition and for Whom?" *Oral Tradition* 6 (1): 104–24.

Foley, John Miles. 1988. *The Theory of Oral Composition: History and Methodology*. Bloomington: Indiana University Press.

Gailey, Alan. 1988. "Tradition and Identity." In *The Uses of Tradition: Essays Presented to G. B. Thompson*, ed. Alan Gailey, 61–67. Ulster: Ulster Folk and Transport Museum.

Gailey, Alan. 1989. "The Nature of Tradition." *Folklore* 100 (2): 143–61. http://dx.doi.org/10.1080/0015587X.1989.9715762.

Glassie, Henry. 1975. *Folk Housing in Middle Virginia: A Structural Analysis of Historic Artifacts*. Knoxville: University of Tennessee Press.

Glassie, Henry. 1989. *The Spirit of Folk Art: The Girard Collection at the Museum of International Folk Art*. New York: Harry N. Abrams.

Glassie, Henry. 1993. *Turkish Traditional Art Today*. Bloomington: Indiana University Press.

Glassie, Henry. 1995. "Tradition." *Journal of American Folklore* 108 (430): 395–412. http://dx.doi.org/10.2307/541653.

Gomme, G. Laurence. 1910. "Heredity and Tradition." *Folklore* 21 (3): 385–86.

Handler, Richard, and Jocelyn Linnekin. 1984. "Tradition, Genuine or Spurious." *Journal of American Folklore* 97 (385): 273–90. http://dx.doi.org/10.2307/540610.

Hävernick, Walter. 1968. "Tradition und Kontinuation." *Zeitschrift für Volkskunde* 64: 22–24.

Hobsbawm, Eric, and Terence Ranger. 1984. *The Invention of Tradition*. Cambridge: Cambridge University Press.

Hofer, Tamás. 1984. "The Perception of *Tradition* in European Ethnology." *Journal of Folklore Research* 21 (3/4): 133–47.

Honko, Lauri. 1983. "Research Traditions in Tradition Research." In *Trends in Nordic Tradition Research*, ed. Lauri Honko and Pekka Laaksonen, 13–22. Helsinki: Suomalaisen Kirjallisuuden Seura.

Hymes, Dell. 1975. "Folklore's Nature and the Sun's Myth." *Journal of American Folklore* 88 (350): 345–69. http://dx.doi.org/10.2307/538651.

Jacobs, Joseph. 1893. "The Folk." *Folklore* 4, no. 2: 233–38.

Jakobson, Roman, and Petyr Bogatyrev. 1980 [1929]. "Folklore as a Special Form of Creation," trans. John M. O'Hara. *Folklore Forum* 13 (1): 3–21.

Jastrow, Marcus. 1950. *A Dictionary of the Targum, the Talmud Bavli and Yerushalmi, and the Midrashic Literature*. 2 vols. New York: Pardes.

Johnson, John William. 1998. "Tradition." In *Encyclopedia of Folklore and Literature*, ed. Mary Ellen Brown and Bruce A. Rosenberg, 658–60. Santa Barbara, CA: ABC-CLIO.

Jones, Michael Owen. 2000. "Tradition in Identity Discourses and an Individual's Symbolic Construction of Self." *Western Folklore* 59 (2): 115–40. http://dx.doi.org/10.2307/1500156.

Kirshenblatt-Gimblett, Barbara. 1995. "From the Paperwork Empire to the Paperless Office: Testing the Limits of the 'Science of Tradition'." In *Folklore Interpreted: Essays in Honor of Alan Dundes*, ed. Regina Bendix and Rosemary Levy Zumwalt, 69–92. New York: Garland.

Klein, Barbro. 2000. "The Moral Content of Tradition: Homecraft. Ethnology, and Swedish Life in the Twentieth Century." *Western Folklore* 59 (2): 171–95. http://dx.doi.org/10.2307/1500158.

Laws, G. Malcolm, Jr. 1964. *Native American Balladry*. Philadelphia: American Folklore Society.

Linton, Ralph. 1937. "One Hundred Per-Cent American." *American Mercury* 40: 427–29.

Lord, Albert. 1960. *The Singer of Tales*. New York: Atheneum.

McDonald, Barry M. 1997. "Tradition as a Personal Relationship." *Journal of American Folklore* 110 (435): 47–67. http://dx.doi.org/10.2307/541585.

McDowell, John Holmes. 2010. "Coaxing the Corrido: Centering Song in Performance." *Journal of American Folklore* 123 (488): 127–49. http://dx.doi.org/10.1353/jaf.0.0130.

McKeon, Michael. 2004. "Tacit Knowledge: Tradition and Its Aftermath." In *Questions of Tradition*, ed. Mark Salber Phillips and Gordon Schochet, 171–202. Toronto: University of Toronto Press.

Montell, William Lynwood. 1986. *Killings: Folk Justice in the Upper South*. Lexington: University Press of Kentucky.

Neulander, Judith S. 1998. "Jewish Oral Traditions." In *Teaching Oral Traditions*, ed. John Miles Foley, 225–38. New York: Modern Language Association.

Newman, Philip L. 1965. *Knowing the Gururumba*. New York: Holt, Rinehart, and Winston.

Noyes, Dorothy. 2009. "Tradition: Three Traditions." *Journal of Folklore Research* 46 (3): 233–68. http://dx.doi.org/10.2979/JFR.2009.46.3.233.

Opie, Peter. 1963. "The Tentacles of Tradition." *Folklore* 74 (4): 507–26. http://dx.doi.org/10.1080/0015587X.1963.9716929.

Oring, Elliott. 1978. "Transmission and Degeneration." *Fabula* 19 (3/4): 193–210. http://dx.doi.org/10.1515/fabl.1978.19.1.193.

Oring, Elliott. 1994. "The Interests of Identity." *Journal of American Folklore* 107 (424): 242–47. http://dx.doi.org/10.2307/541202.

Radin, Max. 1935. "Tradition." In *Encyclopaedia of the Social Sciences*, ed. Edwin R. A. Seligman, 15: 62–67. New York: Macmillan.

Rodriguez, Sylvia. 1998. "Fiesta Time and Plaza Space: Resistance and Accommodation in a Tourist Town." *Journal of American Folklore* 111 (439): 39–56. http://dx.doi.org/10.2307/541319.

Rubin, David C. 1995. *Memory in Oral Traditions: The Cognitive Psychology of Epic, Ballads, and Counting-out Rhymes*. New York: Oxford University Press.

Russell, Ian. 1987. "Stability and Change in a Sheffield Singing Tradition." *Folk Music Journal* 593: 317–58.

Shils, Edward. 1981. *Tradition*. Chicago: University of Chicago Press.

Sims, Martha C., and Martine Stephens. 2005. *Living Folklore: An Introduction to the Study of People and Their Traditions*. Logan: Utah State University Press.

Smith, Paul. 1974. "Tradition—A Perspective: Part I, Introduction." *Lore and Language* 2 (1): 15–17.

Smith, Paul. 1975. "Tradition—A Perspective: Part II, Transmission." *Lore and Language* 2 (3): 5–14.

Smith, Paul. 1978. "Tradition—A Perspective: Part III, Information, Perception and Performance." *Lore and Language* 2 (8): 1–10.

Smith, Paul. 1986. "Tradition—A Perspective: Part IV, Variation on the Prospective Adopter's Access to Information." *Lore and Language* 5 (1): 3–38.

Thompson, Stith. 1953. "Advances in Folklore Studies." In *Anthropology Today*, ed. A. L. Kroeber. Chicago: University of Chicago Press.

Toelken, Barre. 1996. *The Dynamics of Folklore*. Rev ed. Logan: Utah State University Press.

Tylor, Edward Burnett. 1871. *Primitive Culture: Researches into the Development of Mythology, Philosophy, Religion, Art, and Custom*. 2 vols. London: John Murray.

Vansina, Jan. 1985. *Oral Tradition as History*. Madison: University of Wisconsin Press.

Voigt, Vilmos. 1983. "Folklore Function in the Development of Creativity." *Ethnologia Europaea* 13: 180–88.

Wilson, William A. 1989. "Herder, Folklore, and Romantic Nationalism." In *Folk Groups and Folklore Genres: A Reader*, ed. Elliott Oring, 21–37. Logan: Utah State University Press.

Wissler, Clark. 1926. *The Relation of Nature to Man in Aboriginal America*. New York: Oxford University Press.

2

Critical Folklore Studies and the Revaluation of Tradition

Stephen Olbrys Gencarella

What characterizes the free spirit is not that his opinions are more correct but that he has liberated himself from tradition . . .

—Friedrich Nietzsche (1996), *Human, All Too Human*

IF WE ACCEPT THE PROPOSITION, AS HENRY GLASSIE asked us to do nearly a generation ago, that tradition is "the creation of the future out of the past" (Glassie 1995, 395), we benefit in turn by questioning how strongly a commitment to that-which-came-before motivates contemporary folklore studies. Glassie offered this contribution in the well-known special issue of the *Journal of American Folklore* on keywords for the study of expressive culture. It is arguably the most important statement on the concept in the 1990s, a culminating and encouraging depiction of tradition (and traditionality and practices of traditionalizing) as still essential to the discipline.

Glassie's description itself was anything but essentializing. Responsive to and adaptive of earlier statements (such as Dan Ben-Amos's 1984 article on the seven strands of tradition), Glassie explored tradition as a process of continuity and change and readily assured that its relationship to history marked a relationship to the "artful assemblies of materials from the past, designed for usefulness in the future" (Glassie 1995, 395). Nevertheless, lurking in this statement is a very precise positioning of the past to the present: *the past comes first*. We may understand this as chronological representation—the past occurs before the future. But we may also wonder if, for most folklorists, the past

DOI: 10.7330/9780874218992.c02

matters more than the future. As I argue in this essay, neither presumption about the past would necessarily illuminate a critical folklore studies.

In a series of articles to date, I have presented a case for the development of an overtly critical folklore studies (Gencarella 2009, 2010, 2011). Akin to other critical scholarship, a critical folklore studies differs from conventional folklore studies in advocating certain political perspectives, critiquing and challenging others, and advancing policies and values consistent with the promotion of social justice. It compels folklore studies to move from a more descriptive to a more intercessory mode of scholarship and in so doing forge alliances with critical cultural studies, critical ethnography and pedagogy, and critical rhetorical studies (or more precisely, the activist-scholarship of the critical rhetoric movement). Further, it reverses the polarity of folklore studies so that above all, *the future comes first*. In an attempt to foster a more equitable world, a critical folklore studies seeks to redress some of the most pernicious expressions of tradition still thriving today, including racism, sexism, classism, ageism, homophobia, and xenophobia.

This does not mean that a critical folklore studies must abandon the concept of tradition as hopelessly tied to the past. Quite the contrary, a critical turn demands keen attention to tradition, understanding it—and specific traditions—as a rhetorical and political resource for promoting certain values and motives (as Robert Glenn Howard details in this volume), as a point of intersection between ideology and agency, and as a constituent of common sense and practical judgment. However, a critical turn requires a revaluation of tradition: a recognition of traditions often excluded from folklore scholarship, an understanding of tradition as always already haunted by betrayal and vice versa, an appreciation of counter-traditions useful as resources for revolutionary action, and a determination to challenge certain traditions of conventional folklore scholarship at the appropriate times.

Some might claim that a critical turn in folklore studies would occupy that space which Glassie saw as the single true opposition to tradition: a change of such complete disruption that it bears no resemblance to its predecessor (Glassie 1995, 395). I think such a characterization would be egregious. Indeed, as I have noted elsewhere, any overtly critical folklore studies owes a debt to cultural activists, LGBT and feminist and Marxist folklore scholars, and many public folklorists, all of whom have long struggled for a more just world both inside and outside academia. Understood in this way, a critical folklore studies is not a rupture but rather another adaptation of the discipline, a complement and not a competitor to conventional folklore studies, one that creates space for overtly political engagements in academic scholarship and the projects folklorists undertake.

A critical folklore studies would likely forefront an observation that Glassie only notes in passing—namely, that tradition implicates the creation and destruction of values. Recognizing the role that intellectuals (traditional, organic, and vernacular) serve in such activity, critical folklorists could unabashedly commit to cultural production and the constitution of political and social values through scholarship, teaching, and other forms of research. While such a commitment might signify the end of any pretense of folklore studies as a science—even as the science of tradition—it might also encourage the next generations of folklorists to embrace what William Wilson (1988) called "the deeper necessity" of the humanities.

To consider this heavy task, let us move momentarily beyond traditional folklore scholarship. In *Daybreak*, Friedrich Nietzsche defined tradition as "a higher authority which one obeys, not because it commands what is *useful* to us, but simply because it *commands*" (Nietzsche 1997, 11; italics in the original). Such obedience, he continues, is the foundation for any morality; hence, the immoral person is one who is "*determined* to depend upon himself and not a tradition" (10; italics in the original). Nietzsche (2005) offered similar claims about tradition and its relationship to the concept of the law in his earlier *Human, All Too Human* (1876) and his later *Twilight of the Idols* (1889), wherein he announced his life's project as a revaluation of all values. Whether successful or not in this goal, his assertions mark two significant points, often understated in folklore studies. First, any set of traditions—or even the concept of tradition itself—may only be understood in reference to the values in whose constitution they participate. Second, any set of traditions must also be understood in reference to the production of their own antagonisms.

Nietzsche's observations draw attention to the intimate link between *tradition* and *betrayal*, both derivative of the Latin word *tradere* (to hand over or to pass on and hence to unconceal and concealment). This chapter will expand upon the connection between tradition and betrayal and the implications for the development of a critical folklore studies in this century. Specifically, I explore that relationship with reference to the Italian philosopher and social critic Giorgio Agamben, a scholar who has not yet enjoyed considerable influence in American folklore studies.[1] I will argue

---

1   The recent contribution by Sarah Gordon (2009) to *Folklore Forum*, "Testimony and

that any study of folklore (whether conventional or critical) that examines specific traditions without also examining their exclusions and possibilities of betrayal is in some way incomplete.

I will then explore the conceptualization of community that follows from Agamben's discussion of tradition and advocate for folklorists to challenge moralistic formations of dominance, such as hegemonic masculinity. By noting that a critic always runs the risk of betrayal (since she or he must judge whether to pass something on to the future or not), this chapter also demonstrates how any move toward a critical folklore studies might need to betray several values and scholarly practices of conventional folklore studies, but in so doing restore a long (if underappreciated) tradition of activism in the discipline.

TRADITION, BETRAYAL, AND FOLKLORE

Several explications of tradition in folklore studies (including those in this volume) begin with the etymological roots of the word. While some have noticed the correspondence of *tradition* with *betrayal* (or *treason* or *traitor*), most usually pass over this observation quickly or relegate it to a footnote. I think this is regrettable; folklorists have not thought enough about betrayal and its relation—etymological, ethical, and political—with tradition.

This myopia is understandable in the context of our disciplinary history. Once the concept of tradition was freed from the more static presentation of early folklore studies and made copasetic with innovation—one of the gifts of the performance turn in the 1960s and 1970s—folklorists themselves had no need to betray the idea altogether. When tradition was given new life—conceptualized both as a fluid process and as a rhetorical practice in which those in the present reconstruct the past—its utility for folklore studies was also renewed. (More than one scholar has noted, for example, that Ben-Amos's (1971) definition of folklore as "artistic communication in small groups" did not include reference to tradition but that he returned to the concept a decade later in his seminal article on tradition's seven strands.) Given this productive evolution, it is not surprising that alternative (even negative) valences of its etymology would be overlooked.

Moreover, contemporary folklore studies often operate in a celebratory mode; folklorists routinely report on the activities of groups whose company

---

Truth after Auschwitz," is an encouraging sign of Agamben's inclusion in the conversation about the political stakes of folklore and folklore studies.

they enjoy and with whom they share trust or friendship. Even in an activist mode indicative of some of the finest contributions of folklore studies, the folklorist usually seeks to assist marginalized people raise their voices rather than critique pernicious behaviors of a community. In these cases, the reasons why a folklorist would not betray the group at hand are obvious and, likely, judicious. A critical folklore studies need not overturn practices of solidarity but would promote explicit resistance to traditions such as sexism or homophobia and might warrant direct confrontation with groups who uphold them.

I propose, then, that an important task of any critical folklore studies is to rectify this scholarly incompleteness by drawing attention to the intimate relationship between tradition and betrayal. I further contend that while the two may appear to be different phenomena, they are in actuality two elements of the same act, insofar as every opportunity to pass something on is also an opportunity to betray that passing. As constitutional law and rhetoric scholar Jack M. Balkin observes, to respect a tradition is also to enact a betrayal in at least three ways (Balkin 1989–1990, 1620). First, the citation of any tradition is a betrayal of alternative modes of expression and thought. Second, it is a betrayal of other available traditions. And third, it is a betrayal of itself to the degree to which it lays the ground for a counter-tradition. I shall later return to Balkin's observations but for now wish to agree that tradition and betrayal are not two distinct events.

Although folklorists have not regularly considered betrayal—or tradition—in this manner, recent developments in the philosophy of language suggest the timing is right for doing so. Giorgio Agamben's (2000) essay "Tradition of the Immemorial" is instructive in modeling a way toward a more politically engaged notion of tradition than currently exists in conventional folklore studies. Admittedly, Agamben asserts from the outset that his concern is not any specific tradition per se but rather the tradition of tradition itself—the very possibility that something may be transmitted at all. In this, he may distinguish his project of philosophy from that of folklore studies to a distance that may seem impassable.[2] I would hope, however, that folklorists are not exclusively interested in specific

---

2   That point made, his work is replete with references to folklore, especially of European ilk. Agamben frequently draws upon folkloric practices of the ancient Greeks and Romans to engage contemporary political ideas such as the state of exception; and in works such as *Homo Sacer: Sovereign Power and Bare Life* (Agamben 1998), he examines the lore of werewolves and outlaws in medieval society.

traditions at the expense of tradition itself and that there is something to be gained by seeing how a different perspective frames the keystone concept of our discipline.

For Agamben, the potential of transmissibility lies at the root of human language, and with it, thinking. Tradition is not ancillary to philosophy but occupies its core and has done so since antiquity. He opens his essay thusly:

> Every reflection on tradition must begin with the assertion that before trans-
> mitting anything else, human beings must first of all transmit language to
> themselves. Every specific tradition, every determinate cultural patrimony,
> presupposes the transmission of that alone through which something like a
> tradition is possible. *But what do humans transmit in transmitting language to
> themselves? What is the meaning of the transmission of language, independent of
> what is transmitted in language?* Far from being of no importance for thinking,
> these questions have constituted the subject of philosophy from its inception.
> Philosophy concerns itself with what is at issue not in this or that meaningful
> statement but in the very fact that human beings speak, that there is language
> and opening to sense, beyond, before, or rather, *in* every determinate event
> of signification. What has always already been transmitted in every tradition,
> the *archi-traditum* and the *primum* of every tradition, is the thing of thinking.
> (Agamben 2000, 104; italics in the original)

We may be tempted to leave it at that, secure in an obvious alliance between philosophers and folklorists—the one concerned with the tradition of tradition and the other with specific traditions, both meeting in a concern with language and discourse. Agamben has furthermore done folklore studies a favor in demonstrating the importance of tradition, and thereby justifying the overcoming of any lingering anxieties that the concept is stale or irrel-evant to a postmodern world.

But let us press further. "What do these considerations imply," Agamben soon asks, "for the constitutive structure of all human tradition?" (Agamben 2000, 105). His response is far reaching. He contends that in any act of tradition—including language—what is passed on is not a thing (a *traditum*), nor a truth, but rather unconcealment itself, the "opening in which something like a tradition is possible" (105). In other words, every act of tradition reminds the interactants not only of the specific tradition itself but of the very possibility of a tradition in the first place.[3] Even when

---

3   As I have argued comparably elsewhere, any formalized folkloric utterance such as a
     proverb reiterates the existence of and need for common sense itself, not just the con-
     tent of a specific body of common sense.

something material is passed down, such as an heirloom, what matters more poignantly is not the thing (for each interactant will interpret the meanings of the thing differently, and in the case of an heirloom, the interpretations of at least one interactant are missing on account of death) but rather the common experiences of the openness of transmission.

Allow me to present one example to bridge the implications of Agamben's assertion with folklore studies. In the three years prior to my writing this article, my grandmother and uncle (by marriage to my grandmother's sister) passed away. More recently, the state of Rhode Island revoked my grandfather's license to drive due to his own health problems, and I inherited his car, a white Buick LeSabre he purchased for my grandmother two decades ago. When I combed through the vehicle, I discovered typical markers of Italian American religiosity: several palms from Palm Sundays, laminated prayer cards, and a plastic statue of the Holy Family. I also uncovered, under several layers of floor mats, a cache of coins: pennies, dimes, nickels, and a quarter, some just greening from age. The coins dated mostly from the 1980s and no later than 1992, the year the car was purchased. They were the original coins tossed into the vehicle by my uncle as a good luck blessing, a typical tradition of southern Italian Americans. Few discoveries could have excited me more. Once gifts and expressions of fidelity and solidarity between the living, they were now literal gifts from the dead.

The interactants who first experienced and interpreted the meanings of these coins and the ritual of their exchange are gone. Their memories cannot be recalled, nor their impressions returned to discourse. But what these coins can still do—and with them, the people now passed—is remind an observant future of an openness that was once used and encourage a future openness by witnessing to it. This is what Agamben hints at when he invokes the "immemorial" aspect of tradition: "The tradition of transmissibility is therefore immemorially contained in every specific tradition, and this immemorial legacy, this transmission of unconcealment, constitutes human language as such" (Agamben 2000, 111). This approaches, perhaps, what Glassie implies by defining tradition as the creation of the future from the past, but it is not nostalgic. It does not assume the "nothingness of the present" (Glassie 1995, 395) because it is concerned with making present the openness of transmission over time.[4] In this way, the future is not

---

4   To be clear, I deeply appreciate Glassie's commentary, even as I decline the request to consider the future as a creation of the past on the grounds that this assumption may too readily fall prey to a nostalgic and conservative disciplining of potentialities.

contingent upon or indebted to the past. The future and the past share a potentiality for openness, as dictated by those in the present—in the flesh and in discourse—who protect or shut down that openness through the formative rhetorical act of speaking to the past and the future and the present. And I would add that in a critical perspective, there exists not only recognition of a potential for openness but a responsibility to it, and to a making of possibilities for the future.

Although optimistic about the openness established by transmissibility, Agamben also recognizes a corollary to the tradition of tradition implicated by all specific acts of tradition. That corollary is betrayal, which he depicts as an inherent aspect of communication in several ways. First, as any discourse may be used to conceal, it simultaneously reveals—"betrays"—its capacity to unconcealment. Concealment implies unconcealment. (Agamben considers this philosophically, but it is also the defining feature of rhetoric, the significance about which ancient philosophers and sophists debated.) Second, Agamben here follows Plato: for a discourse to be remembered it must betray its endless openness and be "closed," as it were, as a memory. Third, all communication presupposes that language exists; yet such a statement cannot be expressed without signification. Hence, the first human tradition—language—is also the first betrayal, the possibility of language betraying its own impossibility.

There is another order, which Agamben does not address directly but that is akin to the same processes of concealment and unconcealment that occupy his meditation: as one produces discourse, one inevitably betrays other discourses. Any performance of actual utterances constitutive of the social world and of identities for navigating that world is simultaneously a closing and an opening of perspectives. This is very closely related to what Kenneth Burke called the "terministic screen" of language. As Burke suggests, any given terminology is at once a reflection, a selection, and a deflection of reality, a way to direct attention (Burke 1989, 115). To call a group of people "folklorists" is to not call them something else, perhaps "philosophers" or "scientists" or "folk." Understood thusly, politics is the rhetorical act of name-calling, fought in the nuances of connotations taken as denotations. And as Burke further notes, "we *must* use terministic screens, since we can't say anything without the use of terms" (Burke 1989, 121; italics in the original). To become human is to enter this game of concealment and unconcealment: "The human animal, as we know it, *emerges into personality* by first mastering whatever tribal speech happens to be its particular symbolic environment" (Burke 1989, 124; italics in the original). Bringing the insights of Agamben and Burke together, we may perceive our species as contradictory in the best sense, bound mutually to the openness of language and to closing that openness for the sake of actually speaking. In this way, there is nothing more natural than betrayal and tradition, and perhaps no relationship more pressing for understanding the human condition itself.

If I may again rely upon a personal anecdote for illustration: recent to the writing of this essay, my four-year-old son spotted a rogue mushroom in a meal we brought home from a take-out Chinese restaurant. This sight prompted him to explain, "You can't eat mushrooms that you find in the woods, but you can eat ones that are in food." My wife and I were taken aback by this declaration, for neither of us had ever spoken to him about mushrooms, and we had no idea where he had gathered this information (a haunting epistemological aporia typical of parenting). His prompting nevertheless called for a response, some form of ratification or correction.

We decided to agree with his very simplistic division between the wild and the cooked. For fear of how he might interpret and act upon a more sophisticated and scientifically precise answer, we chose not to explain that there are ample mushrooms in the woods that may be consumed safely. We also did not report that the mushrooms on one's plate may be quite dangerous under certain circumstances. And I certainly did not inform him that at that very moment, I was caught in the grips of crippling mycophobia at the sight of the slimy fungus. Although trembling, I was hopeful that if he did not sense my visceral nausea, he would not carry on this debilitating habit and indulge in traditions reliant upon those questionably gilled things, including the cuisine of his extended family and our Italian American heritage.

In this specific case, a binary seemed like the best judgment and explanation to guide potential future actions, especially with our awareness as parental figures that opportunities will eventually arise to recalibrate. That said, we do not always choose the most expeditious path of binary divisions. At times when one of our children has declared matter-of-factly that boys have a penis and girls have a vagina, we have tried to complicate matters, assuring that that is often or usually the case but not always so. And when one has asserted that only boys may become firemen—again, a statement the origins of which we can only speculate—we disagree, even without wondering whether the child is making a gendered comment about labor or trying to determine if there is a semantic game at play by which to distinguish fire*men* from fire*women*.

Hence, even for one's own offspring, there is ample need for betrayal, just as there is ample need for tradition. It is through these communicative actions that knowledge is forged and values are constituted. I mention these mundane examples, then, to demonstrate that betrayal is not necessarily abnormal or abhorrent; it is imperative to human communication and a necessary component of all rhetorical expression that shapes human motives and action. And while specific performances may heighten expectations of tradition or betrayal (such as culturally salient political speech or the practice of *omertà*), this dual-process characterizes any act of communication, as any utterance is simultaneously a concealment and an unconcealment.

Although I do not mean to rely upon academic cliché, this point also underscores that any act of communication is also an exercise of power, a political and ethical action. Admission of this may be one of the features that most distinguishes a critical folklore study from a conventional one. Both forms of scholarship recognize an act of transmissibility in tradition and the importance of that transmission for the interactants. But whereas a conventional folklore study may be content to ask only what is transmitted, a critical folklore study must also ask what is *not* transmitted and what is betrayed in the transmission. Another way to express this distinction is that a critical perspective, in being attentive to what is silenced or absent, is more concerned with openness and opening possibilities by attending to that which was not allowed. This may occur at the level of the utterance or at the level of a worldview; the critic is one who pays attention to possibilities excluded in discourse.

What are the implications of this perspective for folklore studies and for a critical turn in the discipline? On the most basic order, this suggests that folklorists benefit from paying closer attention to betrayals, both overtly enacted ones (such as those in which innovation is interpreted as betrayal in the eyes of participants, or when participants refuse to meet the expectations of a traditional performance) and more subtle ones (such as marginalization processes or specific rituals of abjection and absolution). Certainly, a conventional approach may consider emic perceptions of betrayal at the contours of tradition, ascertaining the importance of one for the survival of the other.

Although consideration of the emic boundaries constituting tradition and betrayal provides a good step toward a more complete appreciation of any given community, it is not enough for a fully critical perspective grounded in deconstructive scholarship. For this emphasis, one must also consider the role of betrayal in the political constitution of community, even as community itself is an expression of dual nature of concealment and unconcealment and the impossibility of communication. Again, permit me to illustrate with what may initially seem a petulantly jejune example: bread crumbs.

"Don't be afraid to use a lot of breadcrumbs." This statement is written on a card I prepared, many years ago, when I asked my aforementioned grandmother to teach me her recipe for meatballs. The abundance of bread crumbs was indeed the secret to getting meatballs as close as possible in texture—although not in taste—to her artwork. It was also a trick she learned from her mother to stretch a meal and the reason most members of my extended family consider any compact meatball to be a culinary travesty, even as it is the norm in finer cuisine. Moreover, the referent signified a mass-produced bread crumb such as Progresso, or perhaps something made locally at McQuades or Ritacco's or Dunns Corners Market, but not done by hand. Although no one in my family would speak of it in a direct manner, the purchase of such a simple commodity was a small marker of having made it beyond immigrant working-class experience.

In the year prior to my grandmother's death, several members of our family were gathered in her kitchen, and the discussion turned to the plethora of new foodstuffs now available. The arrival of panko, the Japanese-style bread crumb, meant that a conversation was necessary to recalibrate whether they were acceptable for a meatball recipe that honored the family tradition. Perhaps not surprisingly, the decision split along generational lines, with the younger more accepting than the older of this change. Quinoa, however, was simply out of the question for the majority, even as some of us tried in vain to reframe the grain as a healthier version of acini di pepe.

Surely the reader of this essay will see in this example a repetition of the perennial exchange between tradition and innovation; there are countless examples of similar family conversations in the vast literature of folklore studies. But to move from a conventional to a critical perspective, one must deconstruct dimensions not obvious or clearly articulated in this interaction and enter those considerations for practical judgment. Whether or not a given community acts upon an openness presented to it is a pressing political and ethical question, a reminder that everyday life and the vernacular is a locus of politics more pressing than formal elections, and worthy of a critical response.

Certainly, traditional foodstuffs matter in order to continue the illusion of shared ethnic identity. But from a critical perspective, a conversation about bread crumbs is much more than an opportunity to renew and reinvigorate solidarity; it is also an opportunity to exclude and betray potentialities. The rejection of panko and quinoa may be harmless if it is simply an issue of desired taste on the tongue; but if the rejection signifies a fear of foreignness or an unworthiness of alien things, it may reveal well-anchored traditions of xenophobia or associations bordering on racism. And, said bluntly, such compromising traditions of rejecting the Other are unnecessary for the continuation of benefits in the fiction of ethnicity or family bonds. In drawing attention to these more subtle social figurations, the critical folklorist may serve as a friend to a given community by calling it to more noble aspirations.

COMMUNITY, TREASON, AND CRITICISM IN FOLKLORE STUDIES

As we both reveal and conceal in discourse, we simultaneously approach and distance ourselves from interlocutors. The instability, impossibility, and dual nature of language drives the desire for unity through communication. Kenneth Burke long ago made this eloquent observation in *A Rhetoric of Motives*:

> Identification is compensatory to division. If men were not apart from one another, there would be no need for the rhetorician to proclaim their unity. If men were wholly and truly of one substance, absolute communication would be of man's very essence. It would not be an ideal, as it now is, partly embodied in material conditions and partly frustrated by those same conditions; rather, it would be as natural, spontaneous, and total as with those ideal prototypes of communication, the theologian's angels, or "messengers." (Burke 1969, 22)

"Tradition" may be shorthand for a desire to communicate fully, to achieve revelation and nearness. But it, too, is also an impossibility. From this perspective, any specific tradition that participates in the construction of a morality pretends to a stability that does not exist. In the most extreme examples, proponents of a particular illusion of stability demand obedience and punish violation. Hence, for Burke, war becomes the ultimate disease of cooperation, not only because countless cooperative acts must go into producing conflict but because large groups of people must elect to cooperate in closing down—in killing, figuratively and literally—the possibility of the Other and of coexistence, all in the name of a singular morality and worldview.

In noting our fundamental division and in admonishing that too much cooperation in a singular moral vision may result in very dire circumstances, Burke foreshadows Agamben's concern in the second half of "Tradition of the Immemorial" that community is *not* a shared identity and that a politics predicated on such a closed perspective runs the risk of injustice. Although I will not chart every move Agamben makes through Plato and Aristotle and eventually Hegel (to whom Agamben assigns the honor of being the thinker who "most vigorously posed the problem of tradition and its destruction"; Agamben 2000, 111), I would draw attention to the seemingly abrupt change of tempo he offers in citing Carl Schmitt's recognition of "division" as one of the three fundamental categories of the political ("taking" and "pastoring" being the other two) (112). Agamben's point is that as we become increasingly aware of the dual nature of language, we confront the absence of a foundation for truth; this is what he calls the "radical crisis of the presupposition" (111).

Such crisis is characteristic of post-modernity, in no small measure on account of mass communication and globalization that change the way we understand ourselves by fostering the presence of others (and other worldviews and moralities) in an unprecedented manner. As an economic system that thrives upon selling to all regardless of moral conviction and identity, late capitalism demolishes divisions between consumers; yet its spread necessitates rapid cultural contact that previous periods and communities did not experience.[5] This is the dilemma of the contemporary world: that which partially makes possible more attention to the openness and potentiality of human expression (as well as to panko and quinoa and, further, to Internet technologies that fueled the Arab Spring) also creates the conditions for injustice and sets the stage for reactionary attempts to stabilize boundaries of collective identity by excluding possibilities.

Agamben's solution to this formidable dilemma (akin to Burke's) is to find ways to accept division, starting with an honest assessment that community is not actually a shared existence and that, to the contrary, division is the hallmark of community:

---

5   This is not a defense of late capitalism, a position I would never take. It is a recognition that a global economy predicated on the spread of capitalism inevitably creates challenges to stable political identities—folk, if you will—as it opens new markets. Unlike the spread of a philosophy or critical perspective that attends to openness in a more responsible and acclimating manner, capitalism's alacrity to open markets and exploit labor and consumption often exacerbates cultural tensions and contributes to fueling conflicts that a philosophy or critical perspective would mitigate.

We are united only through our common participation in an Unparticipated; we are anticipated by a presupposition, but one without an origin; we are divided, without any inheritance. *This is why everything we can take is always already divided*, and why the community that binds us—or, rather, the community into which we are thrown—cannot be a community of something into which we are appropriated and from which we are subsequently separated. Community is from the beginning a community *of parts and parties*. (Agamben 2000, 112; italics in the original)

Only by recognizing what Richard Bauman (1971) and other performance-oriented folklorists long ago identified as differential identities at the social base, the *division* that community implies (because any community responds to the originating division of language, the dual nature of communication that allows an openness of transmissibility and thereby tradition and betrayal) may we move forward toward the rhetorical production of social organizations that accommodate *difference* and tolerance of the Other.

The irony, of course, is that to accomplish this critical task of opening communities to difference we may need to betray traditions that reject disagreement with their underlying moral ideologies. Moralists are politically problematic precisely because they are not committed to opening potentialities and new rhetorical constructions of community and are often dangerously well organized in their opposition to such alternatives. Moralists are adept at hiding the fragmentary nature of community in order to exclude those who do not adhere to the traditional values or traditional appearances of their particular fiction of community taken for reality.

We need only a cursory examination of the formal political situation in the contemporary United States to see, yet again, the forces of right-wing moralists gathering to combat signs of openness—from the election of an African American to the presidency to the rising populations of Latinas and Latinos tipping the national ethnic composition, to the sprouting of legalized gay marriage, to the ever-growing admiration for hip-hop and punk aesthetics among the young. The attacks upon immigration, labor, women's rights, the impoverished, and social services assisting the elderly and students—attacks against the future—are themselves a venerable political tradition, one whose fervor is now excited by the multiple possibilities threatening to destabilize dominant order and hegemonic masculinity. The good news is that, to borrow a line from Woody Guthrie, these moralists are bound to lose because they are fighting an impossible enemy, the root of all tradition and expression itself.

That does not mean, however, that those of us on the side of openness should lazily wait out the change moralists guarantee by their recalcitrance. We have work to do in the form of resistance and revolutionary action in order to move our local and national communities toward social justice. That preparatory attitude well may be the primary difference between a conventional and a critical perspective in folklore studies. If we take seriously the division that Agamben and Burke (and countless others—I do not suggest that only their views matter) envision as a resource for accommodating difference and openness, we must continually ask what formations of the world best suit this accommodation and utilize our scholarship to advance them when possible.

We may take stock in and rigorously adapt, for example, Agamben's depiction of a "community without presuppositions" as the guiding term for this pursuit of justice. We may understand the conundrum of our contemporary experience as warranting a community without presuppositions, even as we contradictorily demand sterner foundations. And with Agamben, we may see in the contradiction of these two needs "the root of our discomfort and, at the same time, our only hope" (Agamben 2000, 113). A reason for hopefulness exists if the openness of language itself serves as inspiration for the creation of an open society. Imagine, if you will, a community that maximizes openness for the most people, a community that recognizes it is always already divided and does not perceive such knowledge as a threat, a community that is willing to betray traditions in order to allow for the importation of new traditions and the bodies that bring them.

To pursue such a sense of community, folklorists would need to more readily accept that not all traditions are good—or interesting—simply because they are traditions. Some traditions should be handed down, others should be betrayed, and folklorists are well qualified to speak critically to this judgment in specific situations. Such an assertion does not demand that critical folklorists attempt to betray all traditions (in the way Nietzsche imagined his project of the revaluation of all values) but encourages their examination for hidden motives of intolerance and injustice. And in cases of the most pernicious traditions formative of a community, a critical folklore study must work to dismantle them. A critical folklorist may accordingly need to become *treasonous,* in sense that the anti-racist activist Tim Wise utilizes the term:

First, in the traditional sense of national betrayal, for indeed, although the nature of white supremacy in the United States has changed, the substantive fact of white racial power and privilege remains real enough as to suggest that at many levels, the nation's culture, politics, and many of its people are still committed to the maintenance of racial inequality. So, to speak against such forces is to commit treason, in so far as those purposes remain so intimately bound up with the national direction of the United States . . . But I am also thinking of treason in a different way: as a betrayal of one's expected allegiance to one's *race*. Although race treason may not be a concept as immediately recognizable to many, it is simply undeniable that over the course of USAmerican history, whites have been expected to fall in line, to accept the contours of racism, to remain quiet in the face of Indian genocide, the enslavement of African-Americans, the conquest of half of Mexico, and any number of racist depravities meted out against people of color. We were supposed to put allegiance to race, to whiteness, above allegiance to humanity. So, to speak against the prerogatives of whiteness, or merely to break the silence about white racism, is, at some level, to engage in "race treason." (Wise 2008, 4–5; italics in the original)[6]

Wise's primary concern is racism, but his description is fitting for all other expressions of social and economic injustice. As an educator, Wise's proposed counter-movement is the introduction and practice of a vocabulary of resistance, one designed to thwart customary discourses of collaboration with racial inequality. He is unapologetic in his aim, and he is also remarkably consistent in his judgment, adhering to a standard in which he supports formations marked by tolerance and openness and excoriates those that are not. I can imagine the unease with which some readers may encounter this advocacy of treason, but it is consistent with the earlier described approaches toward emancipatory action.

We have now reached a time to consider the role of folklore studies in this pursuit. For Agamben, the philosopher's critical agenda lies in attending to the tradition of tradition so as to keep open the possibility of possibilities. For Burke, the rhetorical critic similarly maintains openness by preventing rhetorical constitutions from being taken too seriously as reality at the

---

6   Wise is adamant that treason against *whiteness* is not the same thing as treason against white *people*, who are also harmed by the destructiveness of white privilege. Length constrains commentary here, but I should note that much folklore itself comments upon and even celebrates betrayal, treason, and the traitor. The folkloric concept of the outlaw and the trickster, for example, demonstrates that everyday critics and vernacular criticism often address the tradition-betrayal relationship in fruitful ways that should be emulated by folklore scholars.

exclusion of alternatives. And what of the critical folklorist? Allow me to review some principles a critical folklore studies might utilize in pursuit of communities without presupposition, ever moving toward more realization of social justice and emancipation from pernicious traditions of domination.

First and foremost is the notion that lore constitutes folk. This proposition does not deny that actual people perform lore but recognizes folklore's rhetorical capacity to constitute collective identities and common sense, which, although ultimately fictional, become politically consequential. This assertion resonates with several folklorists who have argued that society is constituted in communication (Bauman 1992, xiv) and that groups only exist "because its members create communications that call it together bring it to order" (Glassie 1995, 400) and most closely links critical folklore studies with the critical rhetoric movement. This observation also echoes Ernesto Laclau's (2006) claim that the creation of a people—a folk, if you will—is the primary task of a radical politics. Hence, any critical endeavor must concern itself with constitutional performances.

Second is a claim that *any* lore constituting a folk be considered folklore, not just the genres traditionally assigned in the previous centuries. On the one hand, this dismisses distinctions between orality and mediated experience, or between folklore and fakelore, as simply irrelevant; what is more important are the aesthetic and ethical visions that participants in a given lore share or contest. On the other hand, this declaration means that traditional systemic expressions themselves (such as racism and homophobia) should be conceptualized as folklore rather than limiting classification to specific racist jokes or homophobic folk tales.

Third is the obvious aim of this scholarship to be *critical*, for which another brief etymological explanation is helpful. As Roland Barthes reminds us, the purpose of criticism is to call into crisis (Barthes 1982, 379)—or as Roland Champagne translates Barthes, "*criticizing* (performing criticism) is inciting a crisis" (Champagne 1984, 20; italics in the original). Critical folklorists must turn their attention to inciting crises in traditions that prohibit social justice. They are responsible to crisis—or better still, to *krisis*, the originating Greek word meaning (among other things), a calling forth for judgment.[7] In this manner, a critical perspective heightens the

---

7   I would be remiss not to mention an alternative suggestion by Michael McGee (1998, 36–44), who depicts the responsible rhetorician as seeking *stasis*, not the krisis pro- moted by a critic; by this he means mutual understanding and respect rather than judg- ments made in order to win a political argument. While I respect McGee's position and

human capacity to betray traditions for a political purpose. The critic is one who has the stomach to betray even those traditions whose fictional nature has long been forgotten.

Hence, critical folklore scholarship would attempt an interruption of certain fictions taken for reality in order to forge new realities and offer new articulations through perspectives by incongruity, comic correctives, or overt criticism and critique (each discursive situation calling for a different rhetorical response). In producing critical work, the folklorist would recognize criticism as natural—indeed ordinary—to the human condition, even as such criticism might create the extraordinary event of a crisis. Accordingly, taking sides is a necessary step in the pursuit of social justice. Silence about domination and the dominant's attempt to maintain power is a form of compliance with such hegemony. A critical folklore study might therefore ignore Glassie's otherwise good advice for historians and history-minded folklorists to avoid dichotomizing human beings into the angelic and the bestial (Glassie 1995, 396), when humans perform bestial actions of injustice upon one another. And in so doing, they might grasp what Balkin calls, quite refreshing in its honesty, an ax to grind (Balkin 1989–1990, 1627).

It is my hope for folklore studies that this century will see the discipline (regardless of what it is called or what departments it is housed in) provide opportunities not only for new and more voices currently excluded from academia but for new scholarly practices admitted to our journals, conferences, and other forms of research and outreach. In other words, I hope that we have the courage to betray academic conventions and make ever more room for alternative expressions and experiments. This does not require the end of conventional folklore studies. It does, however, demand that we raise the political stakes of our scholarship by reconsidering the scholarly traditions we obey simply because they command.

Let me also insist that this hope is not purely idealistic, in the way much conventional folklore studies is idealistic in its nostalgia. Rather, I imagine a robust critical folklore studies as partially idealistic and partially

---

his concern that a krisis-model might fail feminism in its patriarchal competitiveness, I also think it is politically naïve to ignore the determination that some groups demonstrate in their zeal to eradicate openness and potentiality for others. Ideally, I desire the stasis that McGee (and Burke) recommends, but I do not regard it as the always appropriate goal to inform political strategies. This is one of the reasons I have encouraged folklorists to engage the work of Antonio Gramsci, who has no qualms in advocating revolutionary social change against those who resist it for their exclusive benefit.

pragmatic. It would not seek utopia but rather struggle to make the future better, redress past injustices, and improve the present for as many people as possible. Presuming with Agamben and Burke that we humans are not unified, such an approach may recognize the comfort of unity and community but would not uphold those manifestations to their extremes, whereupon only those who seek perfect obedience to prescribed moralities are admitted membership.

In bringing this section to a close, I would like to proffer several practices that would greatly benefit a critical folklore studies and a more complete and politically purposeful scholarship of tradition. The first is the employment of artistically engaging, activist models of scholarship that push against the traditions of domination that currently exist. I specifically have in mind the work associated with the "transgressive tales" project led by Pauline Greenhill and Kay Turner, which promises to queer the Grimm's fairy tales and thereby resist hegemonic masculinity and heteronormativity. I would also note here (as I have elsewhere) the contribution of Stetson Kennedy (republished in 2011) in busting the Ku Klux Klan and petition for the increased acceptance of publications by autoethnographers and other performative critics in the journals of folklore studies.

The second practice is the adaptation of folklore scholarship for progressive political purposes, even if the research was not originally meant for such an agenda. Christine Garlough's (2008) study of street theater among feminist activists in India, for example, should be required reading for anyone trying to build a similar movement. Simon J. Bronner's (2000) history of the role of traditionin the culture wars of the 1980s and 1990s provides ample examples that are useful to those who craft public policy, such as the decision by Bill Clinton and Al Gore to assume the mantle of traditional values rather than yield them to the Republicans. There are potentially countless other forms of conventional scholarship that might inspire more critical perspectives, and it would behoove our discipline to encourage such adaptations.

By way of anecdotal support for this claim, I would like to mention a few of the final projects produced by students in two classes of mine dedicated to critical folklore studies. None of the enrolled students had prior coursework in folklore, but the questions of social justice and political activism informed their anticipated careers. The contributions of David Shuldiner and Deborah Kodish and Archie Green were, not surprisingly, guideposts throughout the semester. Most striking, however, was the ease with which students found critical applications of methodologically conventional scholarship. Joseph P. Goodwin's study of gay folklore served as the inspiration for one student's project on "fuck-lore," a performance that served both as a scholarly study and a means to spread the word about homophobia still rampant in a liberal community that claimed to be accepting of homosexuality. Wolfgang Mieder's analysis of the proverbs of Harry Truman similarly led another student to critique the use of maxims in the speeches of leading Tea Party figures. Elaine Lawless's copious work on myths of femininity inspired several students to projects critical of suffocating patriarchal religious expression. I could continue but will summarize by noting that in the call for a critical folklore studies, all I am doing is following the wisdom of outsiders and neophytes who so clearly see how folklore studies may help resist traditions of domination.

This leads me to another locus for collaboration: the law. The publication of the two-volume *Folk Law: Essays in the Theory and Practice of Lex Non Scripta* (Renteln and Dundes 1994) nearly two decades ago was a promising start, but uptake on further developments has been slow.[8] This is regrettable, because tradition plays an essential role in the legal system of the United States (and elsewhere), and the law bears an essential role as a lore constitutive of folk as citizens. Balkin's deconstruction of the Supreme Court's majority decision in *Michael H. v. Gerald D.*, one predicated on Justice Antonin Scalia's particular appeal to tradition, demonstrates the possibility for scholarly conversation and public activism around legal issues by scholars from both fields working together. And akin to folklore studies, critical legal studies emphasizes that betrayal of tradition may be necessary for the pursuit of social justice. As Balkin notes, *Brown v. Board of Education of Topeka* is "from one perspective, the beginning of a great tradition of protecting civil rights. But from another perspective, it was a betrayal of the Court's proper institutional role, and of the intentions of the framers of the fourteenth amendment" (Balkin 1989–1990, 1622).

Lest this essay become repetitive, I will not explore the myriad ways this statement echoes with the concerns outlined above. I do wish, however, to remark one final time that this example evidences the intimate relationship between tradition and betrayal and the subsequent necessity for a critical scholar to support a political perspective without apology. In

---

8   As an encouraging example of renewed interest, see Robert Glenn Howard's essay in this volume on vernacular authority and the force of law.

an era when legislation may move quickly—and unjustly—to determine a range of issues concerning the marginalized in US society, and when the right's solution to virtually any political problem is to destroy decades of progressive social and economic programs and roll back civil and labor rights, the luxury of presumed neutrality is not only shortsighted, it is potentially irresponsible.

CONCLUSION: THE REVALUATION OF TRADITION

Throughout this essay, I have argued that the concept of tradition remains essential to the development of a critical folklore studies but that it must be more completely understood in relation to betrayal. Tradition and betrayal lie at the root of human communication and any attempts to forge community (even as the instantiation of community implies further division), and thus responding to both and encouraging one or the other in a politically salient and ethically consistent manner is, simply, recognizing that scholars do what everyone else does and do not need to pretend otherwise. A critical folklore studies would not shy away from conversations about whether specific traditions should be passed on or brought to an end. Critical folklorists would, of course, need to debate the standards by which they betray and advise handing on traditions, but such action itself is consistent with those who seek social justice as an ever-widening opening of possibilities and potentialities in advocating communities without presuppositions. While this may require critical folklorists to openly engage the latest incarnation of the culture wars, struggle over traditional values, make room in our scholarly apparatuses for such criticism, and build academic and intellectual allegiances with other critical movements, it may also honor the legacy of work by folklorists and vernacular intellectuals who have, often without support or gratitude, toiled to redress economic, political, and social injustices. That, surely, is a tradition worth handing on.

ACKNOWLEDGMENTS

This essay is dedicated to the memory of Charles Angelo Gencarella, a beloved grandfather and scoundrel.

REFERENCES

Agamben, Giorgio. 1998. *Homo Sacer: Sovereign Power and Bare Life.* Trans. Daniel Heller-Roazan. Stanford, CA: Stanford University Press.

Agamben, Giorgio. 2000. "Tradition of the Immemorial." In *Potentialities: Collected Essays in Philosophy*, ed. Daniel Heller-Roazan, 104–15. Stanford, CA: Stanford University Press.

Balkin, J. M. 1989–1990. "Tradition, Betrayal, and the Politics of Deconstruction." *Cardozo Law Review* 11:1623–30.

Barthes, Roland. 1982. "Writers, Intellectuals, Teachers." In *A Barthes Reader*, ed. Susan Sontag, 378–403. London: Vintage.

Bauman, Richard. 1971. "Differential Identity and the Social Base of Folklore." *Journal of American Folklore* 84 (331): 31–41. http://dx.doi.org/10.2307/539731.

Bauman, Richard. 1992. "Introduction." In *Folklore, Cultural Performances, and Popular Entertainments: A Communications-Centered Handbook*, ed. Richard Bauman, xiii–xxi. New York: Oxford University Press.

Ben-Amos, Dan. 1971. "Towards a Definition of Folklore in Context." *Journal of American Folklore* 84 (331): 3–15. http://dx.doi.org/10.2307/539729.

Ben-Amos, Dan. 1984. "The Seven Strands of *Tradition*: Varieties in Its Meaning in American Folklore Studies." *Journal of Folklore Research* 21 (2/3): 97–131.

Bronner, Simon J. 2000. "The American Concept of Tradition: Folklore in the Discourse of Traditional Values." *Western Folklore* 59 (2): 143–70. http://dx.doi.org/10.2307/1500157.

Burke, Kenneth. 1969. *A Rhetoric of Motives.* Berkeley: University of California Press.

Burke, Kenneth. 1989. "Language as Action: Terministic Screens." In *On Symbols and Society*, ed. Joseph Gusfield, 114–25. Chicago: University of Chicago Press.

Champagne, Roland. 1984. *Literary History in the Wake of Roland Barthes: Re-Defining the Myths of Reading.* Birmingham, AL: Summa Publications.

Garlough, Christine. 2008. "On the Political Uses of Folklore: Performance and Grassroots Feminist Activism in India." *Journal of American Folklore* 121 (480): 167–91. http://dx.doi.org/10.1353/jaf.0.0010.

Gencarella, Stephen Olbrys. 2009. "Constituting Folklore: A Case for Critical Folklore Studies." *Journal of American Folklore* 122 (484): 172–96. http://dx.doi.org/10.1353/jaf.0.0086.

Gencarella, Stephen Olbrys. 2010. "Gramsci, Good Sense, and Critical Folklore Studies." *Journal of Folklore Research* 47 (3): 221–52. http://dx.doi.org/10.2979/jfolkrese.2010.47.3.221.

Gencarella, Stephen Olbrys. 2011. "Folk Criticism and the Art of Critical Folklore Studies." *Journal of American Folklore* 124 (494): 251–71. http://dx.doi.org/10.5406/jamerfolk.124.494.0251.

Glassie, Henry. 1995. "Tradition." *Journal of American Folklore* 108 (430): 395–412. http://dx.doi.org/10.2307/541653.

Gordon, Sarah. 2009. "Testimony and Truth after Auschwitz." *Folklore Forum* 39 (1). http://folkloreforum.net/2009/09/28/testimony-and-truth-after-auschwitz/#more-296.

Kennedy, Stetson. 2011. *The Klan Unmasked.* Tuscaloosa: University of Alabama Press.

Laclau, Ernesto. 2006. "Why Constructing a People Is the Main Task of Radical Politics." *Critical Inquiry* 32 (4): 646–80. http://dx.doi.org/10.1086/508086.

McGee, Michael. 1998. *Rhetoric in Postmodern America: Conversations with Michael Calvin McGee.* Ed. Carol Corbin. New York: Guilford Press.

Nietzsche, Friedrich. 1996. *Human, All Too Human.* Trans. R. J. Hollingdale. New York: Cambridge University Press.

Nietzsche, Friedrich. 1997. *Daybreak: Thoughts on the Prejudices of Morality*. Ed. Maude-marie Clark and Brian Leiter. New York: Cambridge University Press. http://dx.doi.org/10.1017/CBO9780511812040

Nietzsche, Friedrich. 2005. *The Anti-Christ, Ecce Homo, Twilight of the Idols and Other Writings*. Ed. Aaron Ridley and Judith Norman. New York: Cambridge University Press.

Renteln, Alison Dundes, and Alan Dundes, eds. 1994. *Folk Law: Essays in the Theory and Practice of Lex Non Scripta*. Madison: University of Wisconsin Press.

Wilson, William. 1988. "The Deeper Necessity: Folklore and the Humanities." *Journal of American Folklore* 101 (400): 156–67. http://dx.doi.org/10.2307/540106.

Wise, Tim. 2008. *Speaking Treason Fluently: Anti-Racist Reflections from an Angry White Male*. Berkeley, CA: Soft Skull Press.

3

Vernacular Authority
Critically Engaging "Tradition"

Robert Glenn Howard

INTRODUCTION: VERNACULAR AUTHORITY IN EVERYDAY CONVERSATION

At a wedding reception I once attended, a banquet-style midday dinner of steaks, potatoes, and more traditional Filipino dishes gave way to wine, mahjong, and conversation. "Joan," recounted stories of her childhood in the rural Philippines.[1] She described her "Auntie Loling" who had a "spirit friend." Joan's animated storytelling had commanded the attention of most of the players at the mahjong table when her daughter asked her: "How did [the spirit] exist? Did it used to be human before?" Joan responded to the whole group, booming in her typically authoritative tone:

> They call it "*espiritista!*" In Filipino folklore there are good fairies and the bad fairies . . . The good spirit will befriend you, will give you a good harvest on your farm or will give wild pigs for dinner meat . . . [But] the bad spirit will possess you and later you go crazy. (Joan 1994a)

In her response, Joan referred to "folklore" as an authorizing force in her assertion that Filipino sorcery is real. Later she made it clear that this folklore was a source of power alternate to any offered by the dominant institution in her family's public life at that time: the Catholic Church.

Joan recounted how her Auntie Loling worked with a spirit friend to help find a significant sum of money that had disappeared. Based on the

---

1   The names of the respondents have been changed to protect their identities.

DOI: 10.7330/9780874218992.c03

spirit's advice, Loling sent relatives to retrieve the cash. When the excited group returned to the house to report their success, Joan and her mother happened to be there, sharing a cup of coffee with the local priest who had unexpectedly dropped by for a visit. Joan smiled as she relished the memory of his disapproval: "My mom invited him [in] for coffee—so the priest was there. And the priest was just shaking his head. Because he said, ya know, 'that's the work of the spirits.'" (Joan 1994b)

As both a Filipino immigrant to the United States and a devout Catholic, Joan's recounted experiences become expressions of a specifically Filipino traditional authority that stands alongside but apart from the institutional authority of the Catholic Church. As such, Joan's everyday storytelling points to an important tension in the concept of tradition. On the one hand, *tradition* can refer to the empirical quality of an act as having been handed down, while on the other hand, it can refer to a noninstitutional or vernacular authorizing force perceived by those participating in an act.

The empirical sense of "tradition" comes into sharp focus when folklore studies are imagined in terms of a "science of tradition." Here, calling something traditional is the empirically verifiable claim that a specific component of expressive culture has continuities and consistencies through space and time (Georges and Jones 1995). Because *empiricism* is a term for the broad idea that scientific knowledge must be based on the replicability of evidentiary experiences through observation or under the controlled conditions of experiments, the published documentation of cognate forms of Filipino sorcery starting in the sixteenth century empirically verifies that Joan's beliefs are traditional (Cale 1973, 112; Fansler 1965, 214–17; Lieban 1967, 20–21; Pajo 1954, 110–14). In this sense, Joan's "folklore" has the quality of being handed down over several hundred years at least. On a strictly etic or analytic level, an external expert can document, classify, and verify that quality in her stories.

The sense of tradition as an authorizing force, however, is more sharply in focus when researchers approach folklore as performed expressive behavior or "discourse." Approached as discourse, the quality of being traditional is a perception among participants that their action is the result of social connections that have endured through space and across time. Focusing on Joan's deployment of the term *folklore*, we can see this second sense of tradition operating. For Joan, the use of the word *folklore* asserts that there are continuities and consistencies that she asks her audience to accept as evidence of the reality of Filipino spirits. In subsequent interviews, Joan proudly recounted many tales of her youth in the rural Philippines featuring her powerful aunt using a male spirit to subvert husbands and thieves—as well as priests. Spending time with Joan and her family, I garnered a richer sense of the context for Joan's storytelling when, on one occasion, I heard her husband refer to these narratives of magically empowered women as "crazy superstitions."

In the case of Joan's statement about "Filipino folklore," these two aspects of tradition (the empirical and the authorizing) happen to coincide. However, this is not necessarily always the case. Take, for example, a very different kind of communication: the influential book by political activist and feminist theologian Starhawk (1979), *The Spiral Dance: A Rebirth of the Ancient Religion of the Great Goddess*, a work that has become foundational for many pagans. In the first chapter, Starhawk claims, "According to our legends, Witchcraft began more than 35 thousand years ago, when the temperature of Europe began to drop and the great sheets of ice crept slowly south in their last advance" (Starhawk 1979, 3). Here she authorizes her form of pagan belief by combining her description of the Old Religion with the assertion of a continuous practice of European witchcraft dating back to the last Ice Age. While some pagans accept this claim, historians have shown that there is no empirical basis for such a continuous tradition (Magliocco 2004, 46–47). The fact that these two aspects of tradition—its empirical verifiability and its vernacular authority—are not yoked together creates an important opportunity and places a significant responsibility on the shoulders of researchers.

While the discipline of folklore has long sought to accurately document traditional elements of culture, many folklorists have shied away from the critical assessment of folkloric expression. Meanwhile, the rise of critical studies has made social critique a dominant mode of expression in the humanities and interpretative social sciences. Stephen Olbrys Gencarella writes, "If folklore—its performance, exhibition, and analysis—faces a crisis today, it may lie not simply in questions of its academic survival but in its critical contribution to the politics of interpretation" (Gencarella 2009, 172). In chapter 2 of this volume, Gencarella aggressively imagines a "critical folklore studies" that goes beyond description to advocate for social justice: rejecting bigotry in traditions of all kinds even to the point of calling for folkloristic activism. In chapter 1, Elliott Oring also notes the tendency for folklorists to avoid the traditions that include bigotry. Oring, however, is interested in those problematic traditions for more scientific than critical reasons. For Oring, leaving any evidence out of the science of tradition yields a biased data sample and a biased sample yields less generalizable discoveries. For Gencarella, on the other hand, folklore research may be of dubious value without what he terms an "ax to grind" in the service of a specific social cause.[2] Gencarella seems much less interested in the empirical assessment of tradition.

A discursive approach to communication events offers a middle way between these two perspectives because it values the social aspects of the performance separately from any empirical traditionality. This approach begins by acknowledging that the empirical and the authorizing aspects of any deployment of tradition are not necessarily related. From that acknowledgment, the researcher can approach any real-world discursive action recognizing that its empirical traditionality is often minor and sometimes irrelevant to its social value. From a discursive perspective, any individual's deployment of her or his own construction of tradition seeks some outcome in the moment of the communication event.

Whether the handed-down nature of the tradition is empirically verifiable or not, the researcher can locate the empowering force of the discursive deployment of vernacular authority in the specific context of one or of a related series of communication events. Once that force is located and contextualized, the researcher may assess if the particular use of vernacular authority is problematic or if it suggests some positive outcome. This critical assessment is possible because the value of the traditional is not located outside of its discursive function. Instead, its value is located in its deployment as part of real human expressive behavior, and that value may or may not coincide with any empirical quality of being "traditional."

Attempting to critically assess specific communication events—such as Joan's use of the term *folklore* or Starhawk's appeal to the Old Religion—the

---

2   Though Oring notes well-known studies of bigoted jokes—and there are feminist and other critiques of folktales to be sure—the ongoing ethnographic engagement with individuals who hold a problematic tradition is very difficult, at least because thickly descriptive interpretive ethnography requires ongoing and (at least somewhat) functional personal relationships between the researcher and her or his local consultants. As a result, these types of studies present unique difficulties. These difficulties are themselves under-discussed in ethnographic circles, and there are few examples to look to when engaging such a study. One example of a multi-decade engagement with just such a tradition can be found in my work on vernacular apocalyptic belief among fundamentalist Christians that appears in its fullest form in the book *Digital Jesus: The Making of a New Christian Fundamentalist Community on the Internet* (Howard 2011).

researcher is less engaged with the facts or aesthetics of the traditional expression as he or she is with the social impact that such expression might have. Considering the social impact, the folklorist is both the documenter of what is traditional and a commentator on the role the concept of tradition plays. Not merely calling out the bigoted nature of an anti-Semitic joke or the limited roles for young people offered by fairy tales, a discursive approach asks: "How is Joan empowered or disempowered when she appeals to folklore? Are contemporary believers empowered or disempowered by creatively imagining their new religious movement as ancient? What about Catholics who don't believe in folklore or politically active feminists who reject the ancient authority of 'Witches?'"

In the globally interconnected worlds of many individuals today, it is important that folklorists make critical moves to engage a politics of interpretation in ways that responsibly represent vernacular voices. Communication and travel technologies have increased many people's ability to actively choose what and with whom they engage in their everyday discourse. This increased agency has increased the power of vernacular authority in comparison to its role during the late print and broadcast ages because today's participatory media allow individuals to express themselves often right alongside powerful institutions. While scholars of media have long been adept at engaging the power adhering in mass media, they are in need of the folklorist's perspective on the power of everyday expression as they attempt to engage participatory media (Howard 2012). One way to help bring that perspective to bear is for folklorists to approach everyday participatory discourse through the concept of vernacular authority.

Accordingly, in the next sections of this chapter, I consider *tradition* as a discursive formation. Then I define *vernacular authority* as a central way tradition functions discursively. Then I apply the concept of vernacular authority to two examples of everyday expression online, in which this authority is elevated above that of institutions. The concept allows me to critically assess the role that elevated authority plays in the ideologies these media users are constructing for themselves. My first example explores how vernacular authority empowers gay Catholic individuals to stand up to a hegemony that rejects their very identities. In the second example, I analyze how proponents of "natural family living" employ vernacular authority to dismiss potentially valuable sources of information about their health and their children's health. In both cases, I treat the concept of vernacular authority as a specific kind of attempt to garner power through discourse that emerges whenever there is a suggestion that noninstitutional processes have participated in the emergence of conditions that support current beliefs, values, or practices. In this sense, "institutions" are (in line with the Latin origins of the word) social formations that have been founded through a formal speech act, usually in the form of a written document. I argue that by critically assessing the role of vernacular authority in these kinds of communications, folklorists can bring our field's values and tools to researchers grappling with the surge of everyday communication now possible in an age of network communication technologies.

Then, in the final paragraphs of this chapter, I reconsider Starhawk's claim to a continuous tradition of European witchcraft. While it might be easy for a folklore researcher to simply debunk the claim, it would be equally easy to unreflexively praise the empowerment it seems to offer believers. A responsible analysis requires that the researcher seek to understand vernacular authority both on its own terms and in terms of the twenty-first-century globalized and transnational modernity we now all inhabit together. In the case of Starhawk, the critical researcher must seek to assess her claims in light of the creative power of metaphor that she values above the "stories" told by empirical research (Starhawk 1979, 192). A discursive approach to this traditional communication must assess Starhawk's claim to authority by considering what impact such a claim has or might have on the wider social formations in which we all share a stake.

TRADITION

As Simon J. Bronner notes, "the philosophy of folklore study and its relation to public ideas of culture reside in the keyword of tradition" (Bronner 1998, 5). As other chapters in this volume have already shown, previous scholars considering the history and meanings of "tradition" have documented how the term came from the Latin *traditum* meaning "something handed over." Less often noted, however, is that some of the earliest English usages of the word carry not the force of the everyday but the force of law. This is clear in its earliest definition as "an ordinance or institution orally delivered."[3] John Wycliffe's 1388 translation of Paul's Letter to the Colossians (Cooper 2002) contains one the earliest written examples of "tradition" in English. In Wycliffe's translation, the line reads,

---

3   *Oxford English Dictionary*, 1989, 2nd. ed., s.v. "tradition."

"See ye that no man deceive you by philosophy and vain fallacy, after the tradition of men, after the elements of the world, and not after Christ" (Colossians 2:8). Here, Wycliffe's concern (via Paul) is specifically about the Colossian Christians giving authority to "an ordinance or institution orally delivered" (a "human tradition") instead of the Holy Spirit made manifest during the individual experience of God's Word read or heard in the vernacular language of the everyday believer.

As a forerunner of the Reformation's rejection of papal authority, Wycliffe specifically argued for individual access to the Bible so everyday people could experience God's words themselves instead of relying on "human tradition." This definitive early use of the word in English associates it with the spiritually "deceitful fallacy" of institutional power and sets it in opposition to the vernacular alternate to the church made available when individuals could hear or read the Bible in their own (vernacular) language (see Howard 2011, 4–6). In this early form, "tradition" referred to the oral dispensation of *institutional* power.

The English word *institution* is derived from the Latin verb *institutio* meaning "to establish." While some definitions of "institutions" have shifted to include things like "custom," the defining characteristic of an institution is that it has been instituted or founded by some formal act that is typically linguistic, either oral or in writing. Institutions, often with complex apparatus such as that of the Catholic Church, function as powerful authorities. Wycliffe sought to break away from that authority in his argument against tradition. Wycliffe's early association of the two suggests that (historically at least) institutional elements are more central to the idea of tradition than are the folkloric, the vernacular, or the everyday.

In chapter 8 of this volume, Simon J. Bronner articulates the more common, current understanding of tradition as a noninstitutional authority when he suggests that the "handiness" of tradition serves as a basic starting point from where individuals sort out the situations they confront in their daily lives. Individuals' sense of "tradition" (their common knowledge handed on by their culture) gives them cultural maps showing where they are and helps guide them on how to proceed. In this sense, tradition is fundamentally "handy" because it is the first tool people reach for when confronted with the need to make a decision.

Extending this modern understanding of tradition a little, we can give Bronner's formulation a slightly more critical inflection when we imagine "tradition" not as just "handy" but as a handy *authority* to which individuals can appeal while adjudicating between the possibilities offered them by everyday living. When "handiness" functions as an authoritative "shorthand" that individuals deploy in their daily lives, it is functioning as a tool. Twentieth-century social critic Kenneth Burke famously termed such tool-like ideas "equipments for living" (Burke 1973, 304). Imagined as equipment, these ideas can be viewed in the terms made famous by sociologist Langdon Winner's (1986, 19) insight that "artifacts have politics." Just like material artifacts, the qualities of the idea-tool shape the products (material and otherwise) it creates.

Imagined as equipment that shapes social formations, the handiness of tradition is open to social criticism because more than just any one individual has a stake in the social aspects of their group. In a weakly critical form, the social critic could limit herself or himself to an empirical investigation of the facts behind the tradition: "How far back can it be traced in documents? Where has it migrated over time? Does it make claims that are supported by scientific investigations?" And so on. From this perspective, the value of the tradition is limited to its verifiable continuities and consistencies over space and time. In a stronger form, the social critic asks: "How well suited is this specific 'tradition' for use as basic equipment for living? Who does it empower? Who does it disempower?"

To make this move toward a stronger critical engagement with expressions of tradition, a rigorous accounting of vernacular authority shifts the analytical focus from the empirically verifiable background of the expression to the social impacts of its assertions. From this discursive perspective, vernacular authority emerges in a specific individual or series of related communication events where there is a suggestion (overt or implicit, consciously considered or not) that noninstitutional processes occurring over space and time have participated in the emergence of conditions that support the assertions, beliefs, or practices advocated by the communication.

In this sense, vernacular authority reimagines Bronner's concept of "handiness" in a way that accounts for Dorothy Noyes's important observation that the groups who foster any tradition can be (like tradition itself) conceived in two fundamentally different ways: as scientifically verifiable "empirical networks of interaction" or as "the community of the social imaginary," like that made famous by Benedict Anderson (Noyes 2003, 11; see also Anderson 1991). A discursive approach leans more toward the critical than the empirical by focusing on the value of the "social imaginary" of a tradition and less on the "empirical networks" from where it may or may not emanate. While this perspective assumes that vernacular discourse has power that the researcher can document, it does not assume that power is necessarily fair or just.

To critically engage vernacular discourse, the researcher seeks to make value judgments based on the social impact of claims authorized by a sense of tradition instead of empirical "discoveries" about its historical or current networks (Walzer 1987, 3). As philosopher Michael Walzer describes it, social criticism occurs when members of a specific social group speak "in public to other members who join in the speaking and whose speech constitutes a collective reflection upon the conditions of the collective life" (Walzer 1987, 35). While the discovery of existential facts may become important (even decisive) to this critical activity, it remains a means to the end of collective reflection on the social itself. A critical approach to "tradition" would specifically seek to understand claims to vernacular authority as assertions of power in specific contextualized communication events and then seek to evaluate those claims in terms of their impact on broader social formations. In the final move, the critic must communicate her or his judgments to the broader community involved in that social formation through teaching, exhibitions, video, writing, or other public discourse.

VERNACULAR AUTHORITY

The concept of vernacular authority is based on the idea that any claim to being supported by tradition asserts power because it seeks to garner trust from an audience by appealing to the aggregate volition of other individuals across space and through time. This sort of authority is similar to what Erika Brady has termed "relational authority," Sabina Magliocco has explored as "participatory consciousness," or what I have documented extensively among online fundamentalist Christians as "aggregate authority" (Brady 2001, 7; Magliocco 2012, 19; Howard 2011, 20–21). As imagined aggregate volition, this "lore" manifests as a perceived tradition. A trust in the aggregating of volition through informal social processes (the "handed-down" nature of a tradition) marks this particular authority as noninstitutional or vernacular.

As I have discussed in relation to Wycliffe's translation of Paul, institutions also have handed-down or aggregated authority, and individuals can also attempt to garner trust based on their position in relation to an institution: a priest is sometimes trusted to make judgments about the state of an individual's soul based on his authorization to act on behalf of the institution of the Catholic Church; a journalist writing for *The New York Times* gains trust based on her or his presumed adherence to rules monitored by accomplished editors; or an academic researcher publishing in *Nature* earns trust for her or his publication based on the perception of the rigorous peer review associated with that publication.

Alternate to institutional authority, however, vernacular authority emerges when an individual makes appeals that rely on trust specifically because they are *not* institutional. Trust is justified by the assertion *because* the claim does not rely on any authority arising from formally instituted social formations like a church, a newspaper company, or an academic journal. As Oring has already noted in chapter 1, traditions can very well be institutional. The vernacular, however, is specifically set apart from the institutional.

Based in its classical definitions, "vernacular" can best be defined dialectically as that which is opposed to its alternate term "institutional" (Howard 2011, 7–10). An appeal to vernacular authority is an appeal to trust in what is handed down *outside* of any formally instituted social formation. Although it is possible for vernacular authority to be based on something other than the handed-down quality of tradition (in, for example, an individual's personal revelation from God), folklorists tend to focus on instances where it appeals to a trust in some shared "common sense" or, to use the Classical Greek term for it, *doxa:* informally aggregated communal wisdom (Isocrates 2000, 291ff; Poulakos 2001). In terms of "equipment for living," tradition's role as common sense compels researchers to consider the "politics of interpretation" by reflecting on the trust we and others place in a tradition.

Today, critically assessing tradition is increasingly important because global communication technologies have changed the dynamics between institutional and vernacular authority. At the dawn of the age of print, the control of the capability to manufacture inexpensive books destabilized the manuscript-based authority of the priest class in Europe and, ultimately, contributed to the Protestant Reformation (Eisenstein, 1979; 336ff). However, the rise of both public and private institutions that could provide the means to physically distribute large numbers of books across vast geographic spaces created a publishing industry that produced texts not easily imagined as "artistic communications in small groups" (Ben-Amos 1971, 13). When broadcast media arose to displace publishing, there still seemed to be a bright and easily discerned distinction between a small group and the institutional mechanisms 'that made the movie *Star Wars* or the television show *MASH*.

However, Internet media (particularly "participatory media" like Facebook, Twitter, or any WordPress blog) blur the more physical distinctions between mass media and the small group that characterized earlier eras (Howard 2008b, 490–91). When *The New York Times* allows its readers to comment on their institutional articles in a text box just below the published piece, the vernacular and the institutional stand side by side in the same medium. Both are marked, but they are marked in distinction from each other: one as an institutional product and one as the vernacular commentary. Unlike a book or a television broadcast (that has not been placed online anyway), there is the opportunity for a small group to informally comment in a way that accesses the same audience as the institutional communication.

Mass media locates the decision making involved in the creation of global communication in the hands of institutionally empowered actors like writers, producers, and editors, whereas participatory media offers everyday individuals more choice both in the media they consume and in the globally accessible communication they enact. With more access to both institutional and vernacular expression, individuals can now choose to move beyond the communication delivered in print-, broadcast-, or cable-based media and consume homemade videos of freestyle biking teenagers, digitally modified photos that enact political commentary, or blogged texts describing the daily experiences of a stay-at-home mom.

The increased freedom of choice in what individuals can consume, combined with more opportunities to consume vernacular expression more quickly, increases vernacular authority because individuals can choose to consume ideas based on their already accepted values (or "traditions," in Bronner's sense of the term). When they do this, the continuities and consistencies that are the source of much vernacular authority are seemingly increased because the individuals are consuming media premised on their already-held values. When individuals frequent specific online locations that are linked by a shared value or interest, they enact what I have previously termed "vernacular webs" (Howard 2008a, 2008b). As a result, communicating in vernacular webs increases the perception of continuities and consistencies and thus increases vernacular authority.

As optimistic researchers like Harvard law professor Yochai Benkler (2008) and media theorist Henry Jenkins (2006) have demonstrated, creating these vernacular webs can be very empowering because individuals can seek out, compare, and assess large amounts of information before they make decisions. Similarly, it can create new opportunities for transformation as individuals access and are influenced by ideas with which they might not have otherwise come into contact (Howard 1997). On the other hand, there are less optimistic researchers, such as the administrator of the White House Office of Information and Regulatory Affairs, Cass Sunstein, who has demonstrated how vernacular webs can be disempowering if individuals allow them to reify into communication enclaves that "filter" out ideas which might give them access to useful information or challenge them to think in new ways (Sunstein 2007, 138).

In the next section, I apply the concept of vernacular authority to two very different kinds of online discourse to explore both the optimistic and pessimistic possibilities of participatory media. First, I look at the authority created by self-identifying "gay Catholics." Here we find a clear example of individuals being empowered by vernacular authority to contradict the Catholic Church's institutional authority on who is a Catholic. In other cases, however, vernacular webs can disempower individuals if they choose to repeatedly seek out media that supports their already-held beliefs. To examine this sort of vernacular authority, I compare the case of gay Catholics online to some vernacular webs formed around the ideology of natural family living.

TWO VERNACULAR WEBS: GAY CATHOLICISM AND NATURAL FAMILY LIVING

Gay Catholicism

While vernacular webs have probably existed as long as communication, network media have extended the ability to communicate across space and through time. As a result, network media functions to magnify vernacular authority. In some cases, this is empowering. Among gay Catholics online, for example, there is a clear case of individuals being empowered. But in the case of some individuals heavily influenced by the ideology of natural family living, this authority can be so overwhelming that it functions to disempower the participants in the web. Exploring these two cases demonstrates how imagining vernacular authority as a discursive construction allows researchers to critically assess the social impact of individuals choosing to make claims from vernacular authority.

In order to document gay Catholic discourse online, I conducted a series of searches on common Internet search sites for the terms "gay" and

"Catholic." Then I followed the links created by individuals whose pages appeared in the search returns in and across a variety of network media. Exploring this discourse, with the help of research assistants, we developed a catalog of topics that were most often discussed. We noted the exact terms used to reference the three most prevalent topics. Then we executed multi-termed keyword searches within six major participatory media. We archived the specific pages we found and organized them by both topic and medium.

The three most common topics we found suggest that this vernacular web centers its discourse on real-world activities that are central to the participants' identities. Specifically, they included sharing stories and advice about finding a friendly parish and the challenges of interacting with local church officials; the temptation, pressure, and challenges of leaving an official Catholic parish for some sort of alternative religious community; and the need and challenge of taking communion even when it is explicitly forbidden for people who are regularly engaging in same-sex sexual activity.

Among hundreds of returns to searches of terms associated with these topics, I found "John's" Myspace page. John has enjoyed a lifelong and intense relationship with the divine. This relationship was solidified when, at fourteen years old, he watched his mother die from a misdiagnosed stroke. During the quickening illness, he called out for God—and he had a revelation. As he describes it:

> I had a sense that a voice had spoken to me inside my head, or as if a thought had been inserted in my consciousness. This was "Whatever happens, [John], I will always be with you" . . . I have never experienced anything positive like this ever again. Somehow, I don't need to. The promise was so absolute and uncompromising that it has always been enough for me to fall back on in all my later troubles. (John 2010)

As a result of his intense faith, John eventually converted to Catholicism and worked as a lay minister but finally left the mainline church to follow what he terms a "radical orthodox traditionalism" (John 2010). John is not just a Catholic; he is a very conservative Catholic—at least in some ways.

John first accepted he was gay as an undergraduate studying theoretical physics at Cambridge University. Through a series of intense romantic engagements, he has lived with his current same-sex partner for over fifteen years. John's Myspace page and other participatory media resulted from one of his early romantic engagements: his (eventually) successful attempts to convert a former love interest, "Paul," to Catholicism. In a sad irony, once

Paul accepted John's Catholic faith, he rejected homosexuality and refused further contact.

During this dramatic period of John's life, he started posting web-based media about his struggles as a gay Catholic. Soon individuals sharing this identity found John's online expression, and he slowly developed an ongoing web of correspondence with other gay Catholics. John acts as a mentor in that community, often offering advice to others who share his identity.

In November 2009, John published a blog entry titled "How to have yourself unexcomunicated" [*sic*]. In the entry, John posted a letter he received from another gay Catholic that echoed an experience shared among many of John's readers. Seeking John's advice, the sender revealed that he had recently come out to his local priest; and in response, the priest forbade him from taking communion. After the text of the letter, John typed his response. The aggregate volition of individuals sharing the fundamental belief that they are, in fact, gay Catholics emerges both in the posted document and the responding comments beneath it.

The letter John posted described the interaction between the priest and the gay parishioner this way:

> [My pastor's] gentle and compassionate nature led me to think he might at least respect my conscience in the matter. I was mistaken . . . He was very clear that if I could not obey the Church in this matter that I had to refrain from receiving the Sacraments . . . Not being able to receive the Eucharist is proving to be spiritually harmful. After much thought and prayer, I decided the best thing would be to leave. (John 2009)

The letter goes on to describe how the priest, after noticing the man missed church for a few weeks, called to enquire after him and insisted they have coffee together. Worried about the impending meeting, the man explained to John, "I don't know what to expect. I don't know if he will reconsider his position about denying me the Sacraments or challenge me with Scripture and Church teaching" (John 2009).

John's response offered a powerful and sustained twelve-point argument that culminated in the claim that the honesty inherent in coming out meant, "[The priest] should return the honour by respecting your conscience in this matter by not judging you and not refusing you sacramental absolution." In this response, John repeated a series of ideas common throughout this discourse. In particular, he made the argument that it would be hypocritical (and thus a sin) to profess that gay sexual activity is unethical if an individual feels in her or his heart that God would not have created people with an innate tendency to sin. As it is often put, God would not create people who are innately "evil." Both creating and recreating these common arguments, John's claims simultaneously appeal to and enact the aggregated vernacular authority of gay Catholics, of which John is an important figure (John 2009).

In response to this post, John received public comments supporting and admiring the courage of his e-mailer. Acting together, these individuals generate a shared authority for the validity of their identity as well as the valuation of courage in the face of institutional rejection. In this discourse, one commenter wondered if individuals should really be so committed to being a member of a community that institutionally rejects their core identity. The commenter wrote, "why bother trying to get the Church to love Gays . . . when it's not the Church's love you are after; it's God's love" (John 2009).

John responded, "Obviously, [yours] is not a Catholic outlook on matters" (John 2009). Clearly, John feels his outlook *is* a Catholic one—a gay Catholic one. In light of John's final assertion here, this example presents a particularly clear case of individuals using a vernacular authority that they dynamically enact in online discourse to counter a very powerful institutional authority.

The Catholic Church claims to be the final arbitrator of who is "Catholic." In Catholic theology, an individual must be a "communicant" to be a practicing Catholic. To be a communicant, individuals must enact the ritual of Holy Communion at least once a year. The ritual can only be successfully administered to individuals who have attained a temporary state of grace by seeking forgiveness for their sinful acts from a priest authorized by the church or in an individual Rite of Penance and Reconciliation at the beginning of the liturgy. In 1986, however, the church specifically asserted that individuals who habitually choose to live gay lifestyles cannot be reconciled to the church (Vatican 1986). While the position of the church will continue to evolve over time, and the application of this idea by specific religious practitioners varies widely, the church is commonly held to assert the idea that while gay people are not "innately evil" (as John accused the priest of believing above), the choice to habitually engage in same-sex relations renders the individual leading a typical gay lifestyle unable to attain the spiritual state necessary to take yearly communion. This means that individuals living a LGBT lifestyle cannot be Catholic in the terms established by the church.

The online enclave formed by these individuals, however, generates an alternate authority for who is Catholic. As Leonard Norman Primiano notes, this sort of gay Catholic identity is a particularly clear case of vernacular religion (Primiano 1993, 1995, 2001, 2004). From a critical perspective on tradition, this individual deployment of vernacular authority seems to have the social impact of connecting individuals and empowering them to form an identity that has been denied by the hegemonic claims of one of the most powerful religious institutions in history.

While the case of vernacular Catholicism online demonstrates how vernacular authority can be empowering, the case of natural family living complicates any generalized critical assessment of vernacular authority. In the vernacular web surrounding discourse about natural family living, some individuals exhibit such an intense distrust for institutions that they discount the possible benefits offered by institutional medicine to their children and themselves (Kitta 2012). As Charles Briggs and Clara Mantini-Briggs have powerfully demonstrated in their research on cholera in the Delta Amacuro region, "[s]tories are just as real as germs," and both can undermine our efforts to reduce human suffering (Briggs and Mantini-Briggs 2004, 7). While certainly a healthy distrust for institutions is warranted (Goldstein 2008), and many aspects of Internet communication can function therapeutically for the sick (Goldstein 2004), when vernacular authority is so magnified by the online proliferation of rumors that it limits individuals' abilities to access health benefits, the social impact of that authority needs to be carefully considered. The next set of examples in this section engages in that consideration.

Natural Family Living

The ideology of natural family living was popularized by a periodical titled *Mothering Magazine*. Founded in 1976, the magazine focused on natural mothering processes. Associated with the feminist movements of that time, the magazine sought to provide women with an alternative to heavily medicalized practices by functioning as resource for information about birthing and childcare. Expanding its focus over time, the ideology has become associated with discourses such as that surrounding the home birth movement that advocates for nonclinical birthing environments; "attachment parenting," which argues that mothers or other adults should be in constant physical contact with young children; and "unschooling," which suggests that children learn best through everyday experiences and that such experiences are hampered by the formal educational practices of schools. All these discourses share a reverence for what is perceived as "natural" and distaste for what is perceived as artificial human intervention into biology and psychology.

In the digital age, scientific research, popular books, and periodicals available on these topics can now be easily accessed through Internet searches for the key terms associated with them. Some of the most well-known sites include Nature Moms, Natural Family Online, and Earthy Family. However, the largest overall site is hosted by the online version of *Mothering Magazine*. Like most of these sites, Mothering offers professional journalism to its readership. The site is much larger than similar online magazines, however, because it hosts a massive public forum where individuals post and exchange their own ideas about natural family living. Formerly called "Mothering Dot Commune," the forum changed its name in 2008 to "Mothering Dot Community" and is generally referred to as "MDC."

On MDC, over 150,000 registered users post their beliefs and respond to each other's posts. At the time of this research, these users had written over 5.4 million posts. Taken together, these posts create a huge enclave of communication premised on the idea of natural family living.

The forums are broken into nearly fifty subforums that focus their discussions on specific topics. These topics range from "Gentle Discipline" to "I'm Pregnant!" and from "Lactivism" to "The Case against Circumcision." Each of these topics is discussed in terms of how human biology dictates particular practices. "Gentle Discipline" suggests that children can be led into good behavior by gently channeling their problematic impulses. "Lactivism" focuses on the idea that social norms push women away from their natural role as breast-feeders. Circumcision is strongly discouraged in this community because it is thought to inhibit natural immune response and sexual function and causes traumatic memories in adult males. Surrounding all of these topics, the forum can be seen to elevate vernacular authority over institutional authority by the repetition of specific claims among its everyday users. The forum powerfully pits the vernacular against the institutional by repeatedly expressing distrust at three levels: medical practitioners, the institutional structures that empower them, and (in its most extreme form) the belief in a wide-ranging conspiracy between media, government, and the medical industry.

Participating in the community since 2007, I have observed that one of the most commonly repeated challenges to institutional authority is in the expression of distrust and hostility to actual medical practitioners on the ground. These kinds of statements can become more extreme when individuals swap stories about experiences they have had with doctors. In a discussion of what to do if a doctor recommends inducing labor during a difficult pregnancy, one user states, "Trust yourself and your body and your baby before you let them get their hands on you" (MegBoz 2009). While recounting how a doctor treated a yeast infection on a male infant's penis by pulling back the foreskin and applying an antibiotic cream, a user wrote, "Why isn't this sexual assault?" (PuppyFluffer 2007). During a discussion about a doctor's recommendation to circumcise an infant who was having repeated infections, a user wrote, "Odds are high that if you do take him to a urologist they will recommend circ[umcision]. After all they make their big money from surgery" (MCatvrMom2A&X 2007).

The idea that individual doctors are corrupt is supported by the repeated expression of distrust for the institutional structures that empower those medical practitioners. This is common in discussions of the "birth industry," circumcision, and elsewhere, but it is maybe most prevalent in the discussion of vaccines. One user exemplifies the attitude that vaccines are "unnatural" when she states, "I believe that all vaccines are 100% harmful and 100% ineffective and have always been a big scam. Vaccines are blood poisoning and are completely toxic garbage and do not belong in the human bloodstream" (MyLilPwny 2009).

The idea that vaccines are a "big scam" is a common one. In another post, a user links the medical field's advocating of vaccines to a fundamental misunderstanding of human biology that pervades modern Western medicine: "Most people in the health field, even if they are more 'natural[,]' buy into Germ Theory" (MyLittleWonders 2006). By far, the most common explanation for doctors buying into "Germ Theory" is clearly expressed when one user writes: "IMO [in my opinion], it's all about the pharm[aceutical] industry. Hmmm . . . how do we get people to buy stock in the company that produces Tamiflu(sp?)? Scare people!" (NaomiLoreli 2006).

In the most extreme assertions I have found commonly repeated, the distrust of specific medical practitioners evolves from a disregard for the institutional structures that have generated their expertise to a belief in a broad conspiracy between medical practitioners, pharmaceutical companies, media institutions, and governments.

Exchanging conspiracy theories has been common in the forum since I have been observing it, and it can occur in discussions about almost any topic. Discussing a particular episode of the television show *Law and Order*, a user describes how the show depicted a mother being convicted of murder after not vaccinating her child. Another user comments, "These kinds of plots are introduced by vaccine makers to Hollywood. Big pharma is very much in control of the film industry" (Gitti 2009b).

The media attention to the movement of an H1N1 flu pandemic from Asia to North America in fall 2009 became a major catalyst for these kinds of discussions. Generally a conspiracy is imagined between the government and the pharmaceutical industry, where companies that stand to make money from the purchase of vaccines by the government will pay kickbacks. A user wrote, "Because of the politics involved, it makes me even more sure that our kids shouldn't be injected with any vaccine because it's all just money, greed, politics, and disregard for human life" (AllyRae 2009). The specific allegation that the H1N1 virus was actually manufactured by drug companies and then released in Asia is often repeated. One user wrote, "Personally, not to look for the black helicopters or anything, but I think it [H1N1] is a man-made strain, tested overseas to see what would happen on a population too uneducated to realize what was going on" (Grahamsmom98 2005). These kinds of discussions often lead to worries that the government will force individuals to take the H1N1 vaccine. One user reported that her husband "learned today that the state of MA has legally deputized doctors and dentists in preparation for mass vaccinations . . . I sometimes sound like a conspiracy theory nut but my state is sure passing a lot of laws about it lately for some reason" (laohaire 2009).

Another user worried about the potential malevolent motives for the manufacture of swine flu and the forced vaccinations she expected to follow: "I do hope people wake up soon and see what is really happening" (Gitti 2009c). In another thread, someone suggested everybody put an anti-vaccination bumper sticker on her or his car. But another user warned against it: "I can't express my fear of this enough. I already live in fear of the government as is . . . I just want to curl up and die so President Obama's death squads don't get to me first" (Minarai 2009).

At its most extreme, more traditional conspiracy claims crop up in support of the vaccine conspiracy theories. One user suggests that a book she read might be relevant. According to her, the book posits that vaccines are designed to use nanotechnology to, as she puts it, "inject people with a transmitter" (honeybuch2k8 2009). In another thread, a user takes it to the furthest extreme when she advocates for political suicide: "If an injection means a rotten life or death afterward, why would you ever subject to it? *Even at gunpoint I will refuse.* Let them shoot me" (Gitti 2009a; italics in the original).

As an example of a critical approach to tradition, I have engaged these two cases by exploring how these individuals construct vernacular authority. In terms of the social impact of individuals choosing to make these claims, the case of gay Catholics shows how increased access to the expression of others who share a very specific identity seems to be improving the daily lives of these individuals by harnessing vernacular authority to the end of creating more inclusive ways of imagining what it means to be a Catholic. While this might be threatening to some non-gay Catholics, it seems to be playing a very positive role in the lives of these individuals. We should value this deployment of vernacular authority because it opens an avenue to act against the hegemonic assertions of an institution hostile to a significant number of individuals in our society.

Considering the social impacts of some of the natural family living discourse, on the other hand, presents a more difficult case. By seeking out the MDC Forum and locating like-minded others, some of these individuals may magnify their perception of continuities and consistencies in personal experience narratives and rumors. As Diane Goldstein notes, online vernacular communication about health issues has some clear dangers in its potential for the "perpetuation of health rumors, hoaxes, and disinformation" (Goldstein 2004, 39). Recently, folklore researcher Andrea Kitta (2012) has completed a full ethnographic study of the negative impacts associated with legend and rumor in relation to the perception of health risks. She concludes: "Vaccination will continue to be an issue in years to come. With new vaccines being developed, more celebrity involvement, and great access to the media and Internet, people will continue to question if vaccination is right for them" (Kitta 2012, 137). In some cases, that questioning can be so powerfully magnified by vernacular authority that these dangers swell beyond the specific cases of information-seeking users finding inaccurate information into a generalized authoritative force that may limit the ability of individuals to judge information they are receiving online.

The perception created by personal experience narratives and rumors repeatedly shared by like-minded forum users could then encourage them to choose to avoid medical treatment for their children or themselves. Here there is a potentially negative social impact of vernacular authority.

It is no doubt empowering for these individuals to be able to question a medical establishment they have had little chance to engage in previous generations. However, it is potentially disempowering if their aggregated expression overwhelms their desire to access care or their ability to judge the massive amount of medical research and opinions made available to them online. This disempowerment should be worrisome to us all because a rejection of preventative care for children unjustly and unnecessarily places those children at increased risks for health conditions that might lessen their participation in social activities as well as increase the costs of an already overtaxed health care system.

While these two cases present extremes of the possibility of vernacular authority, I will conclude in the next section by returning to the example of Starhawk's claim to a continuous European tradition of witches dating back to the Ice Age to suggest that most cases, like that of Starhawk, necessitate a far more nuanced consideration of the complex interpretative politics of vernacular authority—and such nuance must be the goal of any responsible critical engagement of human expressive discourse.

PURELY EMPIRICAL OPTIONS

At the beginning of this chapter, I asserted that considering how specific communication events discursively imagine "tradition" allows researchers to consider to what ends individuals are deploying their claims to vernacular authority. Because tradition in this sense is considered a handy tool (equipment for living), the careful observer can critically assess its social impacts. Expanding on Gencarella's suggestion that folklore studies should have an explicitly critical component, I have offered the concept of vernacular authority as one way to engage discursive deployments of tradition more critically by considering the politics of interpretation inherent in any appeal to the vernacular.

Even more than media, literary, or political criticism, the critically minded folklorist must remain extremely aware of her or his institutional power as a representative of an academic or professional institution because that power has its own social impacts. We can see this in chapter 4 of this volume, where Casey R. Schmitt uses his institutional voice to question the University of Illinois's Chief Illiniwek tradition as being "worth" the insult some feel it makes to their heritage. We can also see it in chapter 5 where Merrill Kaplan implores academics to consider the vast implications of the fact that Internet traditions are largely curated by "the folk" instead of researchers.

Folklore studies have long valorized the everyday, and often they have sought to preserve what they imagine as fragile. While that outmoded perspective on folklore may underestimate the actual power of *das Volk*, it remains true that the institutional authority folklorists wield in terms of adjudicating what is "traditional" (or what has a "positive social impact") may in some cases have significant repercussions for the actual traditions we document and analyze. One such case is in the "empirical" response to Starhawk's 1979 pagan theological text, *The Spiral Dance*.

As I recounted at the outset, Starhawk made a claim to vernacular authority by imagining a continuous tradition of European witchcraft. She wrote, "According to our legends, Witchcraft began more than 35 thousand years ago" (Starhawk 1979, 3). An empirically minded thinker who is familiar with theories of human migration might immediately suspect that this is not true because it does not comport with previously accepted scientific knowledge. She or he might begin to formulate a plan to demonstrate how either the evidence offered by Starhawk is based in error or such overwhelming documentary evidence exists contrary to her claim that she should be disregarded. If the researcher imagines "tradition" as a simple issue of "empirical" truth in the form of scientific knowledge based on the replicability of evidentiary experiences, this would seem like a satisfactory kind of study to undertake. This purely empirical option seems reasonable and useful because it seeks to discover the facts of evidence and not enact any critical judgment about the folkloric expression.

Recognizing the institutional power of the researcher, however, brings to light how any attempt to opt out of a critical perspective necessarily fails. If a researcher publishes a study that documents the lack of empirical evidence for a continuous tradition of witchcraft in a rebuttal to Starhawk but does not engage the important appeal to vernacular authority she makes when she modifies her claim with "according to our legends," then that researcher has failed to engage the pagan worldview Starhawk is articulating on its own terms. The researcher would be cherry-picking a particular detail (the empirical evidence of a continuous tradition) at the expense of grappling with the meaning of "our legends" for Starhawk and her followers. If a more bold researcher specifically understood that Starhawk is making a claim about the creative power of storytelling, but asserted that an empirically verified story is *more* true, then that researcher would be explicitly reducing the value of this tradition to its supposedly neutral empirical existence across space and time. In either case, these purely empirical options are, intentionally or not, also blunt advocacy for an ideology that Starhawk specifically opposes because they elevate empirical knowledge over creative magic. And Starhawk expected this. In 1979 she wrote,

> In the eighteenth century, came the age of disbelief. Memory of the true Craft had faded; the hideous stereotypes that remained seemed ludicrous, laughable, or tragic. Only in this century have Witches been able to "come out of the broom closet," so to speak, and counter the imagery of evil with truth. The word "Witch" carries so many negative connotations that many people wonder why we use the word at all. Yet to reclaim the word "Witch" is to reclaim our right, as women, to be powerful; as men, to know the feminine within as divine. (Starhawk 1979, 7)

Well documented in Magliocco's definitive study of contemporary paganism, *Witching Culture*, there actually was a systematic academic rejection of claims to a continuous European tradition of witchcraft (Magliocco 2004, 193). These researchers took an empirical option. However, as Magliocco notes, a central tenet of many pagan beliefs is a rejection of what Starhawk calls "the age of disbelief." For many pagans today, opting only for empirically verifiable stories reduces the individual person's ability to magically engage (to construct) their worlds in ways that are empowering.

Starhawk anticipated the empirical option by giving its perspective a place in her worldview: "without discarding science, we can recognize its limitations" (Starhawk 1979, 191). Distinct from empirical knowledge, "magical systems are highly elaborate metaphors, not truths." It is precisely from their metaphoric nature that they gain power beyond that of the empirical: "The value of magical metaphors is that through them we identify ourselves and connect with larger forces; we partake of the elements, the cosmic processes, and the movement of the stars" (Starhawk 1979, 192).

At the level of interpretive politics, this magical perspective seems to be an empowering way that some people assert a vernacular authority. This may be appealing and powerful even if the tradition undergirding that authority rests on a "magical metaphor" of contemporary pagan "legends" instead of empirical scientific methods. As equipment for living a pagan life, these stories may be far more valuable than those of the academic historian. However, as Walzer (1987) suggests, a critical approach to vernacular authority cannot simply address the empowerment of the individual deploying the authority. A truly responsible social criticism must be an ongoing "collective reflection" on "the collective life." Just as the researcher cannot exclusively focus on the seemingly neutral argument that something is "empirically" traditional, she or he cannot simply advocate for the empowerment of one group without attempting to explore the nuanced ways that empowerment might interact with others.

The role of the social critic is fulfilled when she or he engages in this responsible exploration in public communication. This is more important today than ever before because all of us in this globally connected world create tools for living that shape not just our lives but also the social situations through we engage each other. This fact becomes particularly clear in the pagan example when we consider that some contemporary pagans are demanding the reburial of pre-Christian archaeological artifacts. Paul Davies, of the pagan group Council of British Druid Orders, told the British newspaper *The Guardian,* "We view them [pre-Christian human remains] as living people and therefore they have rights as people. Because the ancestors can't give their consent in this way, the council [of British Druid Orders] speaks for the ancestors" (Randerson 2007). While it may be empowering for individuals to imagine that their religious group has the ability to speak for the dead, making such a bold claim about potentially valuable archaeological artifacts necessitates a critical engagement with the collective social impact this aggressive appeal to vernacular authority could have.

Interrogating such complexities is essential in an age of global communication because the current diversity of belief, practice, and authority will only continue to expand. While cultural studies scholars of media have long addressed institutional communication in critical terms, the criticism of vernacular expression requires a more nuanced approach because expert researchers are specifically empowered to place an institutional stamp of authority on "traditions." In those moments, the cultural critic has a significant responsibility that requires we pay close attention to the politics even of the most empirical claims we make because those claims interact with and can alter the existing trust that empowers both traditions and institutions. Folklorists have long recognized this, and so today's expansion of vernacular authority in the rapidly multiplying array of network communication technologies opens the door for critical folklore studies to assert the field's long experience with research on everyday expression.

ACKNOWLEDGMENTS

I would like to thank Marie Stolzenburg and Jillian Alpire for their tireless efforts in the collection and archiving of the research contained in this article. I would like to thank Megan Zuelsdorff for her ongoing input on vaccines and children's health from an epidemiological perspective. I would also like to thank Sabina Magliocco and Merrill Kaplan for the discussions of pagans and paganism that pointed me toward both the problems and power of that magical worldview; and I would like to thank the folklore students of the University of California, Berkeley for their important insights on my (mis)conception of the "institutional." I would like to thank the Wisconsin Alumni Research Foundation and the Hamel family for the funding that has made this research possible. Finally, a special thanks to Trevor Blank for a careful editorial eye, insightful commentary, and his ongoing attention to our schedule.

REFERENCES

AllyRae. 2009. "Fine and Jail time for not taking swine flu in MA????!!!!" Mothering-DotCommunity Forums. http://www.mothering.com/community/discussions/showthread.php?p=14283818. Accessed July 15, 2010.

Anderson, Benedict. 1991. *Imagined Communities: Reflections on the Origin and Spread of Nationalism*. London: Verso.

Ben-Amos, Dan. 1971. "Toward a Definition of Folklore in Context." *Journal of American Folklore* 84 (331): 3–15. http://dx.doi.org/10.2307/539729.

Benkler, Yochai. 2008. *The Wealth of Networks: How Social Production Transforms Markets and Freedom*. New Haven, CT: Yale University Press. http://yupnet.org/benkler/archives/8.

Brady, Erika. 2001. "Introduction." In *Healing Logics: Culture and Medicine in Modern Health Belief Systems*, ed. Erika Brady, 3–14. Logan: Utah State University Press.

Briggs, Charles L., and Clara Mantini-Briggs. 2004. *Stories in the Time of Cholera: Racial Profiling during a Medical Nightmare*. Berkeley: University of California Press.

Bronner, Simon. J. 1998. *Following Tradition: Folklore in the Discourse of American Culture*. Logan: Utah State University Press.

Burke, Kenneth. 1973 [1941]. *The Philosophy of Literary Form*. Berkeley: University of California Press.

Cale, Alejandro M. 1973. "A Critical Study of the Superstitious Beliefs of Misamis Occidental." Master's thesis, Far Eastern University, Manilla, Philippines.

Cooper, William. 2002. *Wycliffe New Testament 1388: An Edition in Modern Spelling, with an Introduction, the Original Prologues and the Epistle to the Laodiceans*. London: The British Library.

Eisenstein, Elizabeth L. 1979. *The Printing Press as an Agent of Change: Communications and Cultural Transformations in Early-Modern Europe*. Cambridge: Cambridge University Press.

Fansler, Dean S. 1965. *Filipino Popular Tales*. Hatboro, PA: Folklore Associates.

Gencarella, Stephen Olbrys. 2009. "Constituting Folklore: A Case for Critical Folklore Studies." *Journal of American Folklore* 122 (484): 172–96. http://dx.doi.org/10.1353/jaf.0.0086.

Georges, Robert A., and Michael Owen Jones. 1995. *Folkloristics: An Introduction.* Bloomington: Indiana University Press.

Gitti. 2009a. "Anyone else totally creeped out?" MotheringDotCommunity Forums. http://www.mothering.com/community/discussions/showthread.php?p=13999035. Accessed July 15, 2010.

Gitti. 2009b. "Could this really happen?" MotheringDotCommunity Forums. http://www.mothering.com/community/discussions/showthread.php?t=1078249. Accessed July 15, 2010.

Gitti. 2009c. "Freaking out about swine flu vaccine, can anyone make me feel better?" MotheringDotCommunity Forums. http://www.mothering.com/community/discussions/showthread.php?t=1111153. Accessed July 15, 2010.

Goldstein, Diane. 2004. "Communities of Suffering and the Internet." In *Emerging Illnesses and Society: Negotiating the Public Health Agenda*, ed. Randall M. Packard, Ruth L. Berkelman, Howard Frumkin, and Peter J. Brown, 121–39. Baltimore: Johns Hopkins University Press.

Goldstein, Diane. 2008. "Imagined Lay People and Imagined Experts: Women's Use of Health Information on the Internet." In *Global Science/Women's Health*, ed. Cindy Patton and Helen Loshny, 25–49. Youngstown, NY: Teneo Press.

Grahamsmom98. 2005. "Avian flu." MotheringDotCommunity Forums. http://www.mothering.com/community/discussions/showthread.php?t=351849. Accessed July 15, 2010.

honeybunch2k8. 2009. "Another reason to avoid swine flu vax . . ." MotheringDotCommunity Forums. http://www.mothering.com/community/discussions/showthread.php?t=1121063. Accessed September 6, 2009.

Howard, Robert Glenn. 1997. "Apocalypse in Your Inbox: End Times Communication on the Internet." *Western Folklore* 56 (3/4): 295–315. http://dx.doi.org/10.2307/1500281.

Howard, Robert Glenn. 2008a. "Electronic Hybridity: The Persistent Processes of the Vernacular Web." *Journal of American Folklore* 121 (480): 192–218. http://dx.doi.org/10.1353/jaf.0.0012.

Howard, Robert Glenn. 2008b. "The Vernacular Web of Participatory Media." *Critical Studies in Media Communication* 25 (5): 490–513. http://dx.doi.org/10.1080/15295030802468065.

Howard, Robert Glenn. 2011. *Digital Jesus: The Making of a New Christian Fundamentalist Community on the Internet.* New York: New York University Press.

Howard, Robert Glenn. 2012. "'The Homo Depot' and Other Works: Critiquing Vernacular Video." *Cinema Journal* 51 (4): 191–97. http://dx.doi.org/10.1353/cj.2012.0080.

Isocrates. 2000. *Isocrates II.* Ed. Jeffery Henderson. Cambridge, MA: Harvard University Press.

Jenkins, Henry. 2006. *Convergence Culture: Where Old and New Media Collide.* New York: New York University Press.

Joan. 1994a. Personal Interview. January 14, 1994.

Joan. 1994b. Personal Interview. March 1, 1994.

John. 2009. "How to Have Yourself Unexcommunicated." *Faithful to the Truth.* http://blogs.myspace.com/index.cfm?fuseaction=blog.view&friendId=#####&blogId=519#####8. Accessed July 15, 2010.

John. 2010. "My Life Story." P####'s home page. http://######/pharseas.world/story.html. Accessed July 15, 2010.

laohaire. 2009. "Do I have to worry about the school administering vaccines?" Mothering-DotCommunity Forums. http://www.mothering.com/community/discussions/showthread.php?t=1125154. Accessed July 15, 2010.

Kitta, Andrea. 2012. *Vaccines and Public Concern in History: Legend, Rumor, and Risk Perception.* New York: Routledge.

Lieban, Richard W. 1967. *Cebuano Sorcery: Malign Magic in the Philippines.* Berkeley: University of California Press.

Magliocco, Sabina. 2004. *Witching Culture: Folklore and Neo-Paganism in America.* Philadelphia: University of Pennsylvania Press.

Magliocco, Sabina. 2012. "Beyond Belief: Context, Rationality and Participatory Consciousness." *Western Folklore* 71: 5–24.

MCatvrMom2A&X. 2007. "Dr wants to circ my boys sore pee pee!" MotheringDotCommunity Forums. http://www.mothering.com/community/discussions/archive/index.php/t–684379.html. Accessed July 15, 2010.

MegBoz. 2009. "What exactly causes labor to naturally begin." MotheringDotCommunity Forums. http://www.mothering.com/community/discussions/showthread.php?p=13920022. Accessed July 15, 2010.

Minarai. 2009. "Free bumper sticker! 'say 'no!' to forced vaccinations." MotheringDotCommunity Forums. http://www.mothering.com/community/discussions/showthread.php?p=14162965. Accessed July 15, 2010.

MyLilPwny. 2009. "Vaccination for worse living conditions?" MotheringDotCommunity Forums. http://www.mothering.com/community/discussions/showthread.php?t=1141695&highlight=. Accessed July 15, 2010.

MyLittleWonders. 2006. "Former neighbor (picu nurse) told me to vax . . ." MotheringDotCommunity Forums. http://www.mothering.com/community/discussions/archive/index.php/t–428052.html. Accessed July 15, 2010.

NaomiLoreli. 2006. "If you were stocking up on NT foods due to Bird Flu what would you stock up on??" MotheringDotCommunity Forums. https://www.mothering.com/community/discussions/showthread.php?p=4779332. Accessed July 26, 2009.

Noyes, Dorothy. 2003. "Group." In *Eight Words for the Study of Expressive Culture*, ed. Burt Feintuch, 7–41. Urbana: University of Illinois Press.

Pajo, Maria Caseñas. 1954. "Bohol Folklore." Master's thesis, University of San Carlos, Ceba City, Philippines.

Poulakos, Takis. 2001. "Isocrates' Use of Doxa." *Philosophy and Rhetoric* 34 (1): 61–78. http://dx.doi.org/10.1353/par.2001.0004.

Primiano, Leonard Norman. 1993. "'I Would Rather Be Fixated On the Lord': Women's Religion, Men's Power, and the 'Dignity' Problem." *New York Folklore* 19: 89–103.

Primiano, Leonard Norman. 1995. "Vernacular Religion and the Search for Method in Religious Folklife." *Western Folklore* 54 (1): 37–56. http://dx.doi.org/10.2307/1499910.

Primiano, Leonard Norman. 2001. "What Is Vernacular Catholicism? The 'Dignity' Example." *Acta Ethnographica Hungarica* 46 (1): 51–58. http://dx.doi.org/10.1556/AEthn.46.2001.1-2.6.

Primiano, Leonard Norman. 2004. "The Gay God of the City: The Emergence of the Gay and Lesbian Ethnic Parish." In *Gay Religion: Continuity and Innovation in Spiritual Practice*, ed. Scott Thumma and Edward R. Gray, 7–30. Lanham, MD: AltaMira Press.

PuppyFluffer. 2007. "Yeast infection on penis dr said *after* retracting him!" Mothering-DotCommunity Forums. http://www.mothering.com/community/discussions/showthread.php?t=658462. Accessed July 15, 2010.

Randerson, James. 2007. "Give us back our bones, pagans tell museums." *The Guardian.* http://www.guardian.co.uk/science/2007/feb/05/religion.artnews. Accessed July 15, 2010.

Starhawk. 1979. *The Spiral Dance: A Rebirth of the Ancient Religion of the Great Goddess.* San Francisco: Harper and Row.

Sunstein, Cass. 2007. *Republic.com 2.0.* Princeton, NJ: Princeton University Press.

Vatican. 1986. "Letter to The Bishops of The Catholic Church on The Pastoral Care of Homosexual Persons." Congregation for the Doctrine of the Faith. http://www.vatican.va/roman_curia/congregations/cfaith/documents/rc_con_cfaith_doc_19861001_homosexual-persons_en.html. Accessed July 15, 2010.

Walzer, Michael. 1987. *Interpretation and Social Criticism.* Cambridge, MA: Harvard University Press.

Winner, Langdon. 1986. *The Whale and the Reactor: A Search for Limits in an Age of High Technology.* Chicago: University of Chicago Press.

4

Asserting Tradition
Rhetoric of Tradition and the Defense of Chief Illiniwek

Casey R. Schmitt

*T*RADITION IS A POWERFUL WORD. IT CALLS AUTHORITY and emotion and personal investment into being; it creates socially recognized realities, drawing ostensibly on the past, but is not necessarily grounded in anything but the community and discourse of the present. I first recognized this power at only ten or eleven years old, sitting at the kitchen table with my younger brother and sister, frosting sugar cookies in the shape of snowmen and preparing for an annual visit from Saint Nick. Performing seasonal actions each year, like frosting cookies and singing carols, was a point of pride and genuine, joyful satisfaction—to recreate the Christmas holiday in full each year, somehow magically conquering the calendar and reanimating the past. The repeated action was an opportunity to recapture—to relive—a special moment in time marked by symbols, sensations, and songs, but most of all, tradition: a concept that was suddenly shaken when my little sister posed a curious question.

Along with the cookies and milk for Saint Nick, she wanted to know where had we placed the carrots for his flying reindeer friends. When we shrugged, she insisted that Christmas would not be Christmas if we neglected to leave carrots on the roof, as we had always done in years before. She was quite adamant about this point, as perhaps only a self-assured six-year-old can be. However, my brother and I were confused. You see, our family had never left carrots on the roof before. Not once. There had been cookies and milk, quite certainly, but no carrots. Never. We tried to explain this to her, but her pleas only grew more urgent. Carrots, she contested,

DOI: 10.7330/9780874218992.c04

were part of the holiday. In her mind, we had always left them out—and on the roof of the house, no less, so that the flying reindeer could easily reach them. Neglecting to leave carrots would disrupt the day's very meaning and would be tantamount to skipping the Christmas tree, the exchange of gifts, or the Christmas Day mass.

At this early age I first hit upon the same conclusion Richard Handler and Jocelyn Linnekin (1984) articulated so well—that tradition is interpretive. It is defined not necessarily by historical or cultural precedent but by the *perception* of that precedent. To declare and believe a practice to be traditional—as my sister had done, attributing to the carrots a deep historical, cultural, and personal significance—is oftentimes enough to make it so. Once deemed "traditional," the practice takes on the symbolic meaning of tradition, demanding the same respect and evoking the same passionate emotion and devotion of other like "traditions." In my family's kitchen, arguing with my siblings, I accepted this discovery, and (with a bit of compromise when it came to climbing onto the roof in mid-December) my family began leaving carrots for Santa's reindeer along with cookies and milk on every Christmas Eve. Wherever my sister had gotten the idea—whatever its actual origins happened to be—it became part of our annual family practice. Spurious tradition, as Handler and Linnekin might say, became genuine. To me, at the time, none of this seemed to be all that problematic.

However, in recent years we have seen more unsettling developments in the assertion of tradition. Not all arguments over historical practice and proper performance are settled between siblings or within the confines of a single home. In fact, in a world where access to information spreads every day—where people from not only the same family in the same kitchen, but from all global locations and cultures can easily and instantaneously interact with and learn from each other—the misattribution of "traditional" origins spreads across populations and into the digital realm. When opposing parties make contradictory claims or appeals by invoking the term *tradition*, and the reverence it affords, friction and animosity can result. As information and intercultural understanding spread, what are we to make of assertions of tradition that misrepresent and sometimes even outwardly threaten the cultures and traditions of others? This seems to be a key question for the discussion of tradition in a rapidly globalizing world, and one that I will address in this chapter. I am again thinking specifically of a particularly vivid occasion in my own memory.

In late fall 2010, I arrived on the University of Wisconsin–Madison campus and saw several student newspaper reports about the city's annual weekend Halloween celebration, known in recent years as "Freakfest." The cover of one student paper, *The Badger Herald*, featured a young white male, dressed in buckskins and war paint, wearing a headdress and dancing to a boom box. As a folklorist and a humanist, I was a bit taken aback. Rather than comment on the potentially racist and culturally disrespectful nature of the costume, the accompanying caption and article merely touted the annual festival's success, calling the offensive costume "spooky and creative" (Rainey 2010). Unsurprisingly, the controversial image prompted a slew of online protests decrying the cultural insensitivity of both the reveler and the *Herald* itself. Then something interesting happened. Defenders of the costume and the newspaper fired back on these comment boards with seemingly righteous anger, sarcasm, and ridicule; they stressed that the Freakfest celebration was merely meant in fun, that it represented a tradition in its own right, and that the costume itself was, in fact, traditional and therefore meant no disrespect (Rainey 2010). These defenses of Freakfest's ludic and often intentionally tabooed nature asserted a grounds of tradition, condoning the defenders' claim to be champions of maintaining tradition and allowing them to strike back—at times quite venomously—at those who would question the racially insensitive costume as anything but a bit of good-natured Halloween fun.

While interesting in its own right, the controversy surrounding the *Badger Herald*'s coverage of Freakfest is by no means an isolated case. Even in a world with increasing global access to multiple media that facilitate intercultural discourse on a level never before attained (not to mention near-universal access to information that is capable of unequivocally debunking cultural misconceptions and racial stereotypes), the evocation of "tradition" in similar cases ensures that intercultural tensions and misunderstandings persist. Despite allowing audiences to see ethnic minorities in film and television or interact with people unlike themselves on Internet forums and chat boards, these newfangled expressive media outlets have also allowed blackface and redface, offensive, divisive, and hurtful traditions to not only endure but thrive in becoming flashpoints for heated, discordant argument that might not otherwise take place. In other words, as global media technologies spread, the evocation of "tradition" as a grounds of justification for practices becomes a potentially dangerous and hurtful rhetorical move, encouraging global media audiences not to accept and engage one another in dialogue but rather to emphasize their own differences and move further apart. It is no revelation to note that Internet chat boards have often supported and facilitated bickering, baiting, and caustic confrontation; but the evocation of "tradition" itself leads to contention by endowing each side of any debate with a deep sense of authority and authenticity (see Ben-Amos 1984; Howard 2008, 2010).

Asserting tradition online and through mass media is fundamentally different from asserting tradition face-to-face in small communities. While emergent technologies encourage people from divergent backgrounds to interact, asserting "tradition" works as a kind of rhetorical gambit, halting further discourse and delegitimizing claims that question practices and positions as themselves culturally insensitive. In the twenty-first century, it seems, tradition and global technology collide to foster for customs a space for appropriation, continuation, dissemination, and, ultimately, an inherent form of folk community self-defense, regardless of the customs' actual origins or intersocial transgressions.

This chapter addresses the problem of competing traditions (those which are established in opposition to one another and are thus hindering or outright preventing the intercultural understanding that many hoped would come with the spread of information and communication technologies) by engaging the label of tradition and its social implications in a global media world. What happens, it asks, when one group offends another with some practice while both claim legitimacy through tradition? What happens when an offending party and an offended party both claim traditional affiliation to a dance, song, or fashion of dress? What happens when, as I observed in the wake of Freakfest 2010, both white revelers and actual Native Americans claim the authority to represent American Indians through community "tradition?"

Building upon Robert Glenn Howard's (2008) concept of "vernacular authority," I explore how the simple evocation of "tradition," or insistence upon a certain practice's place within a line of other practices, creates an air of unassailable authenticity. This unassailable authenticity may spark debate, but it also draws adherents and defenders; and once "tradition" has been asserted, identified, and adopted, it can no longer be "not traditional" ever again.

In order to examine this vernacular assertion of tradition in the modern era as a potentially problematic development, I turn attention to a more well-known case example: that of Chief Illiniwek, the (until recently) official mascot and symbol of the University of Illinois. The case of "The Chief," of course, illuminates an understanding of the Freakfest Indian costume controversy, but it also provides a well-documented case of the persistent role of "tradition" and discourse in the early digital age. During the 1990s and early 2000s, Native American activists and others singled out the Chief as a racially and culturally insensitive stereotype. In response to intense public pressure and scrutiny, the university officially "retired" the Chief and his public dance performances in 2007. And yet, in the Internet age, the Chief tradition lives on, dismissed institutionally but still embraced by the "Illini Nation" alumni folk community and supported through websites and uploaded video files featuring his celebrated dance. The Chief, to his fans, is touted online as a tradition, and this label inspires emotion, devotion, and continued adherence—not entirely different from the emotion and devotion of my six-year-old sister at Christmastime, but certainly with more pertinent social repercussions. The online discourse surrounding Chief Illiniwek parallels the online discourse surrounding the Freakfest Indian, but on a much larger scale. It is bitter and contentious, but it again reveals that the term *tradition* in the twenty-first century is an avenue toward (1) appropriation of practices across cultural groups; (2) persistent continuation of practice where continuation may not have happened before; (3) dissemination of practice and the spread of both information and misinformation; and, ultimately, (4) a line of defense for folk groups or enclaves that feel criticized in the public eye.

Many have considered Chief Illiniwek from analytical, critical, and socially scientific perspectives (Connolly 2000; Delacruz 2003; Black 2002; Clark 2005; Edmunds 2007), but I take a discursive approach and gear my analysis toward the implications for the continued online folk treatment of the Chief. I treat each of the four aspects listed here separately in the hopes of exposing how, in a multimedia, multicultural world, we must carefully reexamine issues of legitimacy in declaring "tradition," rhetorical power in that legitimacy, and the ways in which people come to believe what has and has not been inherited or "handed down" from the past.

CHIEF ILLINIWEK AND TRADITION

Chief Illiniwek first appeared in 1926, during the halftime of a football game between the University of Illinois and the University of Pennsylvania. Illinois student Lester Leutwiler, a former Eagle Scout, created a costume and dance for his performance as the fictional American Indian representing the Illini people of central Illinois. The crowd met the event with great enthusiasm and, as Leutwiler handed the role over to other students through the years, the prominence of the Chief at sporting events and on campus grew with great speed. By the late 1980s, the Chief and his celebrated dance were an emblematic source of pride for University of Illinois alumni and fans across the state and nation. At this same time, however, the Chief also became a focus of harsh criticism—from both Illinois students and activist onlookers in other parts of the world.

Spokane Indian and University of Illinois graduate student Charlene Teters spoke out against the Chief's portrayal of Native American peoples. The Chief, she argued, was an open mockery of sacred aspects of Native American culture—an appropriation of Native identity comingled with comic exaggeration, inaccurate aesthetics, and unjustified claims to Native American authority that ultimately reduced American Indian culture to a Hollywood-influenced gymnastics routine with no acknowledgment of actual Native concerns. The Chief's supporters initially dismissed, rebuffed, and ridiculed Teters and her allies. But the release of a documentary film titled "In Whose Honor? American Indian Mascots in Sports," by Illinois alumnus Jay Rosenstein, coupled with steadily greater news coverage, drew more national attention to the controversy. University officials reconsidered the situation, gradually reducing the Chief's presence on campus despite vehement counterprotests from thousands of his supporters.

In 2007, the Chief made his last official appearance, performing his "Last Dance" before a full crowd of cheering Illini fans during a men's basketball game against Michigan in the University of Illinois at Urbana-Champaign's Assembly Hall. At that time, the traditions that were symbolically encoded and decoded within the Chief seemingly came to an end. The recurrent performance of young white men who dressed as stylized Indian chiefs and danced in exaggerated leaps before University of Illinois fans also appeared to be gone forever. The university had effectively halted the "handing down" of the practice—so crucial to many definitions of "tradition" (Handler and Linnekin 1984, 274). Yet within twenty-four hours of the Chief's "Last Dance," a video of the performance had been posted to the popular online video-sharing website YouTube. Soon enough, other videos joined it. Below the video postings, viewers could leave comments, stating their support for the Chief tradition and voicing their anger over its suppression. Others posted messages decried the Chief and his dance as offensive and ridiculous, but supporters seemed only fueled by this engagement and argued that their traditions were being stolen away.[1]

Despite vehement protests from Native Americans who found the Chief insulting and debasing, several new websites dedicated to the maintenance and revival of the Chief tradition quickly surfaced, including Students for Chief Illiniwek, the Honor the Chief Society, and The Chief Lives. These websites (and others like them) openly invoked a rhetoric of "tradition," featuring the word prominently in their title bars and dedicating whole pages and Frequently Asked Questions sections toward establishing and explaining the Chief's role as tradition. In the twenty-first century era of uploaded film and online folk communities, the Chief's stifled practice found a means of continuation never before available, which evoked tradition in an unprecedented, uniquely twenty-first century fashion.

The case of Chief Illiniwek provides several new questions in the study of tradition. First and foremost, while it reifies Handler and Linnekin's premise that tradition is interpretive and not inherent, it forces us to reassess whether some traditions are (or should be) more inherently valued than others. While the Chief and his dance were traceably and artificially created, the University of Illinois alumni and fan community quickly came to embrace both as meaningful to its personal history and identity—but does this make them equal in our eyes to the traditions of actual Native American peoples and actual descendents of Illinois Indians? It seems unjust that one people's tradition, created just over eighty years ago, should have precedence over the protests of the people it claims to represent—with a tradition tracing back to a time before recorded history. Yet, at the same time, it also seems unfair to simply dismiss the cherished customs and values of any group of people simply because we disagree with them. The battle over the Chief presents a moral and ethical paradox for the compassionate ethnographer. It also requires us to rethink the ways in which tradition is "invented" and why.

Hobsbawm and Ranger, perhaps the most cited authorities on the topic, explain that "invented traditions" are meant to "inculcate certain values and norms of behaviour by repetition, which automatically implies continuity with the past" and that such perceived continuity aims to create social cohesion in real or imagined communities, legitimize institutions, or promote value systems, beliefs, or behaviors (Hobsbawm and Ranger 2002,

---

1   The YouTube clip of "Chief's Last Dance on ESPN" can be found at http://tinyurl. com/yka9p7s. Accessed February 19, 2011.

1, 9). What does it mean for the Hobsbawm and Ranger model when it is the vernacular authority (and not the institutional authority) that works to create a tradition? What does it mean when the institution ceases to promote a tradition, but the people themselves fight for its continuation? Robert Glenn Howard's (2008, 2010) work on vernacular authority provides us with some initial answers.

In chapter 3 of this volume, Howard notes that tradition is based upon a vernacular assertion and that the resulting air of vernacular authority is "a specific kind of attempt to garner power through discourse that emerges whenever there is a suggestion that noninstitutional processes have participated in the emergence of conditions that support current beliefs, values, or practices." These claims to authority can be imagined as a larger category that encompasses the idea of an emically perceived (though not necessarily empirically factual) "tradition," and they appear readily traceable in participatory media such as online comment boards and discussion pages, as "communicating in vernacular webs increases the perception of continuities and consistencies." Tradition, in these terms, remains as Handler and Linnekin described it: a wholly symbolic construction by and for the people who label it so and an interpretive process that relies much more heavily on present ideas and opinions than on the imagined past it seeks or claims to represent (Handler and Linnekin 1984, 273). Building on Howard's conception, we can tackle the ethical implications of an online vernacular authority in the context of a globalized world.

In an age of heavily mediated communication, in which those customs identified as traditions are increasingly influenced by what we see on film, television, and computer screens, we must also carefully heed the words of anthropologist Anthony Buckley. He recognized that the act of labeling a practice as "tradition" is, in fact, a rhetorical move and that "when people identify themselves with a tradition, in the sense of stating that it represents what they believe, usually they are trying to define their group identity either to assert its importance or to defend it against another" (quoted in Gailey 1989, 146). We must not conceptualize tradition in the twenty-first century exclusively in the same terms as small group folk culture and custom but rather recognize it as an inextricable aspect of global communication and intercultural interaction. As such, in discussing tradition in the modern day, we must look beyond philosophy, folklore, and cultural anthropology to include communications, media studies, and social sciences in our work and discourse.

The concept of tradition as invention of a particular history, so well described by Hobsbawm and Ranger (2002), finds new dimensions when the driving forces behind modern media—whether they be commercial, ideological, informational, or vernacular—are more closely considered. If we define history, in the words of Henry Glassie, as "an artful assembly of materials from the past, designed for usefulness in the future" (Glassie 1995, 395), invented tradition shares a significant overlap with those messages and memories constructed and popularized not only in folk culture but in commercial and popular media like film, literature, television, and song.[2]

The ethical dilemmas faced through communication and interaction in a global media world are complex and troublesome for the scholar who seeks to remain objective in his or her judgment of culture, but folk communities and bearers of tradition themselves increasingly articulate their concerns over these dilemmas. The widespread attention and ongoing, heated debate over the Chief Illiniwek tradition is a clear example of this development. When one group's tradition openly competes with another in the same globalized arena, there are no easy answers, but for an intelligent discussion of tradition in the twenty-first century to take place, the questions must be addressed. Thus, we arrive at the true heart of this chapter, and the terms—or "aspects" of tradition—that I hope will

---

2   As folklorists, we can and should consider the work of researchers such as communications scholar Greg Dickinson (2006) or historian Stephanie Coontz, both of whom examine in detail how television successfully established a "traditional" image of the nuclear family that was an ahistorical and "qualitatively new phenomenon" (Coontz 2000, 25). Similarly, historian Alison Landsberg (2003) researches the ability of popular film to establish a "prosthetic memory" of events that audience members never experienced and, at times, never even happened at all. These scholars' works illustrate that popular media increasingly drives and intermingles with tradition. In traditions that set one group of people against another, like the Chief Illiniwek tradition, we might start with literary scholarship such as Homi K. Bhabha's (1990) work on nation and narration and Edward W. Said's (1978) work on Orientalism; we may also expand our scope to include David Morley (2000) and his discussion of media's abilities to exclude perceived Others; Helen Tiffin's (1997) discussion of how literature often allows one people to speak for another; or Chinua Achebe's (1988) arguments about how harmful such media-driven assertions about peoples and the past can be. Traditions and popular media retellings of the past can bring people together, rousing unlike people in unlike situations to cooperate and co-identify (Bhabha 1990, 45), but they can also drive people apart, benefitting one group at the expense of others, and, as Linnekin notes, undercutting "the cultural authority of indigenous peoples by calling into question their authenticity" (Linnekin 1991, 446). Ultimately, considering multiple fields and interdisciplinary approaches encourages folklorists to better understand the power relationships implicit in labels of "tradition."

inform our next steps as scholars, ethnographers, communicators, and individuals. I will highlight four key aspects of the Chief tradition and the discourse surrounding it in an effort to deepen our understanding of how modern media outlets have fundamentally altered the processes of tradition in the world today.

ASPECT 1: APPROPRIATION

Among the greatest insults perceived by opponents of the Chief during the height of protest and debate was the University of Illinois's (primarily white) appropriation of Native American traditions and identity (Rosenstein 1997). The university had taken on the identity of the Illini "Nation," and the Chief appropriated and adapted supposed Native American styles of dress and dance. Charlene Teters and others protested that white Americans and the university had no claim to Native identity or culture and that their interpretations of American Indian traditions were actually gross perversions (see King and Springwood 2001; Spindel 2002).

Predictably, supporters of the Chief felt otherwise. They saw themselves as bearers of a tradition that would vanish without their efforts, justifying their unsolicited appropriation of Native American identity. The interviewees in Jay Rosenstein's documentary repeatedly stressed this sentiment. Jeff Beckham, who portrayed the Chief in 1994, explained that his performance held a twofold purpose: first, "to help us remember the . . . people who were here, on the land, before this University was ever dreamed of," and second, "to honor those people" (Rosenstein 1997). University of Illinois alum and state legislator Richard J. Winkel claimed, "It's an attempt that people try to remember a vanished tribe, the Illini tribe of the 1760s" (Rosenstein 1997). From the perspective of supporters, the Chief is not an insult but a sign of respect and honor. Historian R. David Edmunds notes that to Chief supporters, "the spirit of these noble martyrs [the original Illini Indians] now manifested itself in 'the Chief,' who rallied the new Illinois faithful to pigskin splendor" (Edmunds 2007, 238).

Communication scholar Jason Edward Black explains that by using a Native American as a symbol, schools like the University of Illinois have "appropriated the Indian to mean honorable, brave, and courageous" (Black 2002, 610); they use American Indian culture as "a truly admirable synecdoche for what remains 'good' in society and on the playing field: strength, determination, obstinacy, and courage" (607).[3] Nevertheless, the statements from both sides of the argument—however earnest—hearken uncomfortably close to the narratives of noble savagery and vanishing Indians that plagued the 1800s and much of the twentieth century. Supporters of the Chief who claim to be protecting Native American tradition assert a knowledge of tradition based not on study or science but on popular representation in dominant white culture and imply a lack of agency (or even existence) in those true descendents of the Native people of Illinois.

Educator Elizabeth M. Delacruz explains what ought not need to be explicitly stated: "in reality, most Anglo-Americans actually know little if anything about the beliefs, values, cosmology, or cultural practices of any Native Americans, past or present" (Delacruz 2003, 18). Instead, they are inventing a tradition of the Indian—symbolically creating a past to foster group identity while implying that other claims to the traditions are feeble and fading. Historian Mark Connolly also cites evidence for this claim by arguing that when inaccuracies in university representations of Native American culture are exposed supporters respond by "imbuing them with a false, manufactured authenticity" (Connolly 2000, 534). The appropriation of Native American images and cultural elements, he argues, is primarily concerned with boosting pride and communal identity for college "booster culture" (538–39). The result of such appropriation and alteration, Black claims, is not a tradition of preservation and respect (as exemplified by the mere existence at one time of a university-sanctioned Chief Illiniwek toilet paper) but of identity building for the dominant group. University and fan appropriation of Native identity encourages transformation mimesis, in which the dominant culture merges itself with marginalized identity, ultimately perpetuating white hegemony and promoting cultural imperialism by seizing authority to speak for marginal traditions and then remaking them as dominant groups see fit (Black 2002, 611–15).

Even after the Chief was officially retired, online supporters defended (and continue to defend) the practice as a continuation of Native tradition for Native Americans' sake. In the comments section in response to a

---

3   As evidence, Black cites the University of Illinois at Urbana-Champaign's *Honor the Chief Society*, which claims in its charter that "the tradition of our Chief is a great link to our great past, a tangible symbol of an intangible spirit, filled with qualities to which a person of any background can aspire" (Black 2002, 612–13).

YouTube posting of Chief Illiniwek's "Last Dance," for instance, one poster writes, "it's not about cultures it's about tradition. and they're not making fun of them. they're doing real native american dances."[4] Another poster on the same page writes in response to comments from angry Native protestors, "would you rather your history be forgotten? Would you rather nobody ever teach what happened to your people[?]" and adds, "What you are proposing will only ensure that the cycle of history repeats itself. While your people were wronged, that history does not belong solely to you. It belongs to mankind in the hopes that one day the world will be a better place."

These types of arguments contribute to online vernacular authority and assert that appropriation is fully justified for the sake of preserving tradition. The defense of appropriation smacks of paternalism and, in this case, defends the unauthorized reinterpretation and simplification of a practice as preservation; but it seems nonetheless convincing for those who celebrate the Chief. This type of appropriation is an increasing concern in a globalized world, as dominant culture and access to simplified knowledge about marginalized peoples simultaneously spread. In a media-saturated age, non-native University of Illinois students and alumni may, in fact, have grown up with access to much of the same information about and images of Native Americans as have American Indians themselves The Internet age forces us to rethink, in this light, who exactly can be the true and/or valid heir.

ASPECT 2: CONTINUATION

Alongside arguments claiming that the Chief maintains and preserves Native culture, the Chief tradition is itself being maintained and preserved online. Internet videos, websites, and chat boards have allowed an officially suppressed custom to continue to thrive and inspire support. Video and web technologies are allowing "traditional" customs to survive in a way never possible before the twentieth century. Whereas, in other eras, an officially prohibited custom might continue behind closed doors or on private, sanctioned grounds, the Chief and his dance are still readily available to the public through the Internet, and supporters may continue to view and celebrate him in spite of the tradition's physical non-existence.

---

4   The comments section in response to the YouTube clip of "Chief Illiniwek Last Dance, Tribute - Official Vid" can be found at http://tinyurl.com/3rwq7zd (accessed February 19, 2011).

Other supportive comments on the Chief's "Last Dance" YouTube page stress the need for and faith in the continuation of the performance. One site patron writes, "i grew up knowing what the chief was and how i truly enjoyed seeing him[.] its just too bad it takes just a few whinny ass people to screw up an 83 year tradition . . . I SAY ROCK ON TO THE CHIEF[.] HE WILL BE BACK."[5] Another writes, "I cannot believe, nor will I ever believe, that this tradition is finished. The Orwellian/Bradburian facist censors will ultimately tire on this issue and find some other cause to pollute with its leftist propaganda . . . In time, [the University of Illinois at Urbana-Champaign] will get the hint and change course."[6]

Websites dedicated to the Chief also tout online continuation as a victory for tradition. The Chief Lives, the self-proclaimed "Official Website for the Chief Tradition," was created and is supported by the Council of Chiefs, an organization of University of Illinois alumni who have previously portrayed Chief Illiniwek. The website stresses that the Chief has been a "great tradition for more than 80 years" and explains, "Although the last official dance took place in February, 2007, 'The Chief Lives' and his spirit is alive and well in the hearts and minds of thousands and thousands of alumni, students, Chief supporters and members of the Illini Nation on campus and throughout the country." The organization's stated mission is "to keep the Chief, his image and the Tradition visible to those who support the Chief tradition over the years and who are interested in finding ways to continue and build the tradition moving forward."[7]

Without question, the Internet has made these goals unprecedentedly simple to achieve. While the Chief remains a hotly contested, detested, and maligned symbol, and while many continue to agree that he is a racially and culturally insensitive figure, Internet accessibility and free speech laws have ensured that the Chief tradition remains.

ASPECT 3: DISSEMINATION (AND MISINFORMATION)

A third aspect of twenty-first-century tradition illuminated by the example of Chief Illiniwek is increased dissemination. In an age of global media, the

---

5   Ibid. All user-generated commentaries have been reproduced throughout this chapter without spelling or grammatical alterations and reflect their appearance in online discourses.

6   Ibid.

7   *The Chief Lives,* accessed February 19, 2011, http://thechieflives.com.

images and narratives of the Chief can spread at incredible speeds and over incredible distances. A story told online can find audiences well beyond a story told between friends. In the best of times, the speed of and access to communication can serve to educate and inform, but the Internet is also a site of widespread and hyper-sped misinformation as well. As a tradition, Chief Illiniwek and his origins are now available to a global audience, ensuring that more individuals will be attracted to them, but they are also more open to misrepresentation and misconstruction than ever before.

Websites dedicated to the Chief also often detail his history and origins. The Students for Chief Illiniwek website (which has since migrated to Facebook) and the Honor the Chief website tell similar stories of a time "centuries ago," when French explorers encountered a group of people called the "Illini," or some variation thereof. The sites claim that that Chief Illiniwek represents these people. Furthermore, the sites stress how the Chief's costume and dance have developed out of careful study of Native American customs, often conducted under the aid and instruction of Native American peoples themselves.

The Honor the Chief site explains, "Although the original Illini disappeared from the region long ago, one way that they are remembered [is] through the Chief Illiniwek tradition at the University of Illinois at Urbana-Champaign." The site further details how Lester Leutwiler based his original dance on his studies as an Eagle Scout and how in recent years it has evolved to approximate Native American fancy dancing. Despite charges that "the dance of Chief Illiniwek burlesques Native American religion and, thus, is demeaning," the site maintains that the dance is similar to fancy dances and counters, "It would be wrong to call the art of Native American dancing inherently demeaning if performed by a non-Native American, even in a more public venue." The site also stresses the authenticity of the Chief's regalia, given to the university by the Oglala Sioux. These stories, in turn, ultimately find their way onto online comment and discussion boards in defense of the Chief—only, problematically, they are not entirely true. That is not to say that they are entirely false either, but rather that the history of the Chief is more murky and, at the least, heavily contested.

R. David Edmunds explains at length how the history of the Illini people, their bravery, their association with the Chief, and a legendary siege at Starved Rock "were not based upon fact, but upon fancy" (Edmunds 2007, 238). "As Illinoisans," he writes, "we reveled in the romantic glory of the tale" (238). Recognizing that there was never, historically, a single

"Illini tribe"; that Natives in Illinois did not wear Sioux regalia and, in fact, were their habitual enemies; and that despite online protests to the contrary, the Chief's dance held more in common with Hollywood B-Westerns and stage musicals than Native American fancy dancing, Edmunds writes, "For many Illinoisans, this is all 'beside the point'" (239). What matters instead, he notes, is the legend—the symbol of what supporters want and believe the Chief to be. Mark Connolly notes that at both the University of Illinois and elsewhere, "universities made no effort to portray the tribes realistically or authentically; rather, these institutions' symbols were nothing more than virtually interchangeable amalgams of headdresses, war paint, fringed buckskin suits, and red-skinned faces" (Connolly 2000, 533).

While modern communication technologies might sometimes allow us to discourage the spread of misinformation, in the case of the Chief, we see that they often perpetuate and disseminate stories regardless of their scientific or historical accuracy. Vernacular authority again steers the acceptance of one story over another, or, at the very least, it sets one story in irreconcilable contrast with another. One poster to a YouTube comment thread attempts to silence opponents of the Chief by explaining, "back in the day [the Illini Chief dancers] were real native americans . . . they were showing off what the ancestors of the land did when they went to war."[8] Another writes, "This dance is based on the Native American Fancy Dance, which is a dance of self expression, so there is no way that it could be non-authentic."[9] Supporters repeat the story of the extinguished Illini tribe: "the school has an interview with the last living illini indian which states that having the university of illinois represent the illini indians in this way was a great honor."[10] One poster asks rhetorically, "didnt the Illiniwek tribe actually sell the rights of their indian tribe name to the university[?] correct me if im mistaking but i believe that there were only a couple surviving members of that tribe and the university payed them pretty good money for the rights to that name."[11]

These posters defend the authenticity of the Chief's costume and dance as well: "Its not mocking any religon at all," one poster argues, "the dance

---

8   Comments, *YouTube*, "Chief Illiniwek Last Dance, Tribute," accessed February 19, 2011, http://www.youtube.com/all_comments?v=Oq4KpDhFZVM.

9   The comments section in response to the YouTube clip of "Chief Illiniwek" can be found at http://tinyurl.com/3rwj77v (accessed February 19, 2011).

10   Ibid.

11   Comments, *YouTube*, "Chief Illiniwek Last Dance, Tribute," accessed February 19, 2011, http://www.youtube.com/all_comments?v=Oq4KpDhFZVM.

was proven authentic." Another writes, "the outfit is traditional (the original was actually made by women from an Indian tribe)." A third argues, "If the Native Americans found it offensive then they would have never agreed to make the regalia for this and to teach each person who was the chief how to do the dances. It was done to show respect of the Natives of the land that the school was built on. And not all of the people who have been the chief where white, many in the past have been Native American."[12]

These stories and claims are questionable at best, but they are nevertheless asserted and disseminated online as fact. The dance was never "proven authentic." The Chief's dance is created by individual Chiefs, not taught to them by Native American instructors. The vast majority of Chief portrayers have been white males—except in the case of one white female. Yet those who tell the stories assert them vehemently. One poster, boldly defending the authenticity of the costume, writes, "dont comment unless you know the facts . . . you just make yourself look like a jackass" while another, responding to the criticism of a self-identified Native American, writes, "whatever tribe you part of has nothing to do with this."[13] On a subject of heated public debate, it is difficult to resist making a judgment call, but the contestation surrounding the Chief Illiniwek saga clearly demonstrates (for better or worse) that the consideration of tradition in an era of network communication must also equally consider the spread of misinformation.

ASPECT 4: DEFENSE

As debate over the Chief continues online—even years after the University of Illinois officially retired him—support and opposition parties seem to dig in their heels more and more deeply. In defending the use of Native American symbols and mascots, Mark Connolly notes that university booster groups tend fall back on one of three main defensive arguments: 1) that Native Americans have no grounds to protest when other groups portrayed as sporting mascots don't seem offended; 2) that not all Native Americans find the mascots offensive and therefore those opposing the mascots are overly sensitive, and 3) that the mascots themselves are symbols of honor, respect, cultural sustenance, and tradition (Connolly 2000).

---

12   Ibid.
13   Ibid.

While the first two defenses waver under scrutiny, the third argument—the "tradition defense"—proves more difficult to rebut.

Tradition is, after all, what a people say it is. Defending the Chief as a valued tradition gives the practice an aura of authenticity and validity; and, in a balanced democratic society defending free speech—as long as something is not a demonstrable hate crime—we have no means of fairly prioritizing the values of one tradition over another. If the descendents of the Native people of Illinois hold one tradition and the Illini Nation of University of Illinois fans hold another, the "tradition defense" seems to ask how we can claim that one is more important than the other when they come into direct conflict? Both represent sizable populations with distinct values and concerns. Certainly, one might argue, American Indian traditions are older, but staying true to Handler and Linnekin or Hobsbawm and Ranger requires us to accept that, in reality, the documented age of a tradition does not intrinsically promote or negate its validity. Thus, the evocation of tradition in the debate over conflicting or competing symbols and customs creates a kind of stalemate, at which both sides lay claim to the unassailable authority of that mystical term *tradition*.

The online rhetoric in defense of the Chief abounds with "tradition" language. The Students for Chief Illiniwek website stresses that the Chief is a "beloved 80-year symbol" and that his dance is "the greatest tradition in college athletics." The site goes on to explain, "The tradition of the Chief is a link to our great past, a tangible symbol of an intangible spirit, filled with qualities to which a person of any background can aspire: goodness, strength, bravery, truthfulness, courage, and dignity." The Honor the Chief website goes further, subtitling its "Frequently Asked Questions" page "The Tradition" and stressing the importance of the Chief Illiniwek symbol:

> For 80 years, the Chief has been the symbol of the spirit of a great university and of our intercollegiate athletic teams, and as such is loved by the people of Illinois. The University considers the symbol to be dignified and has treated it with respect . . . The Chief Illiniwek tradition can be transformed into an educational asset, to both the University and to the Native American community . . . Together, we can utilize our considerable strengths and resources to celebrate diversity—our growth as a human race—and create a true consensus for the future.[14]

---

14   "FAQ: The Tradition," *Honor the Chief Society*, accessed February 19, 2011, "http://www.honorthechief.com/Tradition/index.html.

As with the legend of the Chief's origin, individual Chief supporters adopt these sentiments. "It's quite unfortunate," writes one YouTube poster, "that our universities are under assail from the progressive politically correct haters. They'll do anything to deteriorate history and tradition."[15] Another writes in defense, "the chief is not racist . . . outsiders just make it seem so . . . they dont understand the tradition, pride, respect the Chief brings to ILLINOIS and all tribal nations.. CHief will live on!!! OSKEE WOW WOW!!"[16] Building on these sentiments, some posters then return to the claim that the Chief is preserving Native traditions—not perverting them. After stressing that portrayers of the Chief "must go through an extensive selection process and learn TONS of info about the tribe," one poster claims the end of the Chief tradition is a threat to actual Native American traditions and adds, "Now i bet less than half of the children born will even know Illinois was inhabited by Native Americans at one point. Way to go make it so they never fucking existed[.] that makes since."[17]

Of course, these kinds of arguments, websites, and web postings are met with abundant criticism and protest. The same discussion and comment boards featuring support for the Chief and defense of the tradition are flooded with responses from those who find the Chief racist, ridiculous, and offensive. After one Chief defender wrote, "It doesn't matter how stupid you think it is, its an 81 year old tradition that represents the U of I. think about that," an opponent wrote back, "81 years of tradition doesn't amount to horseshit for our traditions go back eons."[18] A third asked, "how can you care about an 81 year old tradition when thousands of native americans died to keep their traditions sacred[?] this has got to be at the top of the list of the most disrepectful things i have seen in my life."[19]

These online forums could have been (and perhaps still could be) a place for intercultural dialogue, fostering understanding. Alongside support for the Chief, opponents and Native Americans post their perspectives on the

15   Comments, *YouTube*, "Chief Illiniwek Last Dance, Tribute," accessed February 19, 2011, http://www.youtube.com/all_comments?v=Oq4KpDhFZVM.

16   Comments, *YouTube*, "Chief Illiniwek," accessed February 19, 2011, http://www.you-tube.com/all_comments?v=jCiSbWXo77M.

17   Ibid.

18   Ibid.

19   Ibid.

dance. One explains, "there is no Illini Nation who taught anybody at the U of I the dance . . . that is a Lie . . . There only remains the Peoria Nation in Miami Oklahoma."[20] Another writes, "hahaha, funny the university of illinois has a lot to learn about dancing, regalia and much more about the native people, ive been dancing grass and fancy and this dance 'chief illiniwek' does is nothing close to any dance done at powwows."[21] Still, the dialogue seems blocked. Tempers rise. Discussion turns to profanity and name-calling. And both sides inevitably return to claims to authenticity, validity, and authority through tradition. "This video is not honoring natives," one poster writes, "it is criticing us . . . this white person who is dancing doesn't know the tradition behind our dancing[.] you think you do but you DON'T!"[22] Another complains, "So this tradition that started in the twentieth century outweighs the culture and spiritual beliefs of these natives who had been around for hundreds of years before Europeans set foot here? It's a mockery, and the native's aren't asking for much. Don't abuse the dignity of their religion, and the debate is over."[23] But, of course, the debate is *not* over—at least, not as long as both sides center their arguments upon appeals to tradition.

As Hobsbawm and Ranger note, traditions are very often invented in the first place to stir group or nationalistic sentiment, rally people for a communal cause, and distinguish one people's set of concerns from another's (Hobsbawm and Ranger 2002, 124). Alternately defined as product and process, tradition is ultimately a label, an idea, a word with unusual rhetorical weight and the power to invoke pride, dedication, and steadfast identification with a group or cause. When two groups turn to tradition for justification of competing practices and values, neither can convincingly persuade the other. Camps are formed and meaningful intercultural action is stunted. The example of the Chief shows that, with the spread of global media networks, tradition might, at times, be more of an impediment than a boon.

---

20   Comments, *YouTube*, "Chief Illiniwek Last Dance, Tribute," accessed February 19, 2011, http://www.youtube.com/all_comments?v=Oq4KpDhFZVM.

21   Comments, *YouTube*, "Chief Illiniwek," accessed February 19, 2011, http://www.youtube.com/all_comments?v=jCiSbWXo77M.

22   The comments section in response to the YouTube clip of "Chief Illiniwek University of Illinois" can be found at http://tinyurl.com/3teplnb (accessed February 19, 2011).

23   Comments, *YouTube*, "Chief Illiniwek Last Dance, Tribute," accessed February 19, 2011, http://www.youtube.com/all_comments?v=Oq4KpDhFZVM.

CONCLUSIONS

Admittedly, in addressing these four aspects of the Chief Illiniwek tradition in the twenty-first century, I have to this point avoided answering what is perhaps a fundamental question of the case: whether scholarly analysis should actually worry itself about the promotion of intercultural dialogue. Certainly, we could argue that it should not. Our jobs as documentarians and researchers are not necessarily aimed at fostering global harmony. Traditions have always sat in conflict and competition with one another. The discord documented here is certainly not a new development in history. Yet it is, however, amplified by the spread of communications technologies and globalization. At the very least, we must be wary of the modern era's influence on patterns of appropriation, continuation, dissemination, and tradition-reliant defense if we are to track and analyze the evocation of tradition in a socially and academically useful manner. The world in the twenty-first century is changing, and we ought all be aware of it.

When the practices, symbols, and identities of minority populations and marginalized peoples are appropriated by more dominant cultures with more social and economic capital, I cringe. When these more dominant groups claim the authority to promote the continuation or dissemination of these practices and symbols, even through alteration and misinformation, we should all grow uneasy. It reeks of paternalism and of whitewashing complex intercultural histories. It takes from some people the basic rights of agency and self-representation. It seems to place what are sometimes frivolous objects and activities over simple efforts toward tolerance, pluralism, and respect. Yet when the group labeled as the offending party protests that it is merely adhering to and celebrating its own traditions, I hesitate in my critical judgment. Why is this?

It is because "tradition" remains a tricky and amorphous term, valid in its application nearly from the moment of that application. Its strength as a term works only within the community that deploys it, is only fully respected and understood by those who already agree with it. In labeling an event or symbol or practice "traditional," a community solidifies its importance within the community, regardless of outside criticisms. And when two communities value so-called traditions that conflict openly with or offend one another, tradition is perhaps no longer a practical, useful, or even relevant term for intercultural dialogue. Appeals to tradition can sometimes lead to nowhere when striving to boost intercultural understanding and respect.

Perhaps the answer to the question is that while different scholars come from different perspectives, and that some will choose to engage through scholarly activism while others will opt not to pass judgment in the pursuit of empirical objectivity, "tradition" is truly not a relevant term when analyzing or encouraging discourse between any two opposing groups. Rather, it is a term that inspires sentiment and communal identity within any given group so powerfully that it also spills over into how that group defines itself to outsiders in spite of its inefficacy in that arena.

A tradition is always a valid cultural rallying point, but under any other name, it is not immune to scrutiny or critique. Violence remains violence. Insult remains insult. All that changes is the frame. Perhaps those working toward healthy intercultural dialogue should search for and promote a different set of terms.

Meanwhile, and until then, the emic deployment of the term *tradition* seems bound to continue, often on both ends of any given subject. That emic deployment remains relevant to our study and fascinating in its potency. It keeps practices alive in ever new and evolving ways, even under pressure and through periods of change. Once a year, at an annual "Next Dance," an unofficial Chief Illiniwek continues to perform for an officially non-university-affiliated crowd. The online folk community both fuels and celebrates these gatherings. That community is itself fueled and celebrated by the evocation of "tradition." The term establishes and encourages continued authority for those who use it and, in the new millennium, demonstrates that authority can spread more quickly and more widely than ever before. In other words, the mere word *tradition* is a powerful tool; we must be wary of the many different ways and reasons for which people might use it.

I think back, one more time, to that Christmas with my siblings so many years ago. When my little sister claimed that Christmas wasn't Christmas without carrots, she convinced us how that was so—and a tradition was born. I wonder now, what if she had had the power then to spread this belief beyond our family kitchen and onto computer screens across the nation? What if others repeated her words, reposted them, and discussed them? And what if her call for Christmas carrots somehow came into direct conflict with the holiday traditions of another group of people, with their own claims to tradition? Who has the authority to legitimately claim tradition over another person? How do those claims influence inter-social relationships and power? Who invents the tradition; who follows it without protest; and who comes to actually believe in its culturally crucial truths? It is a playful, even silly example to consider, I suppose, but these questions should remain valid for thoughts of any tradition when moving forward in a new millennium.

REFERENCES

"2010 Students for Chief Illiniwek Presents: The Next Dance." *YouTube.com.* http://www.youtube.com/all_comments?v=OK-49LWQdkQ. Accessed February 19, 2011.

Achebe, Chinua. 1988. "An Image of Africa: Racism in Conrad's *Heart of Darkness.*" In *Hopes and Impediments: Selected Essays, 1965–1987,* ed. Chinua Achebe, 1–13. Portsmouth, NH: Heinemann.

Ben-Amos, Dan. 1984. "The Seven Strands of *Tradition*: Varieties in Its Meaning in American Folklore Studies." *Journal of Folklore Research* 21 (2/3): 97–131.

Bhabha, Homi K., ed. 1990. *Nation and Narration.* London: Routledge.

Black, Jason Edward. 2002. "The 'Mascotting' of Native America: Construction, Commodity, and Assimilation." *American Indian Quarterly* 26 (4): 605–22. http://dx.doi.org/10.1353/aiq.2004.0003.

"Chief Illiniwek." *YouTube.* http://www.youtube.com/all_comments?v=jCiSbWXo77M. Accessed February 19, 2011.

"Chief Illiniwek Last Dance, Tribute - Official Vid." *YouTube.* http://www.youtube.com/watch?v=O7tyfQu4QJo http://www.youtube.com/all_comments?v=Oq4KpDhFZVM. Accessed February 19, 2011.

"Chief Illiniwek University of Illinois." *YouTube.* http://www.youtube.com/all_comments?v=TaYYzfdjoGw. Accessed February 19, 2011.

Clark, D. Anthony Tyeeme. 2005. "Indigenous Voice and Vision as Commodity in a Mass-Consumption Society: The Colonial Politics of Public Opinion Polling." *American Indian Quarterly* 29 (1): 228–38. http://dx.doi.org/10.1353/aiq.2005.0039.

Connolly, Mark R. 2000. "What's in a Name? A Historical Look at Native American-Related Nicknames and Symbols at Three U.S. Universities." *Journal of Higher Education* 71 (5): 515–47. http://dx.doi.org/10.2307/2649258.

Coontz, Stephanie. 2000. *The Way We Never Were: American Families and the Nostalgia Trap.* New York: Basic Books.

Delacruz, Elizabeth M. 2003. "Racism American Style and Resistance to Change: Art Education's Role in the Indian Mascot Issue." *Art Education* 56 (3): 13–20.

Dickinson, Greg. 2006. "The *Pleasantville* Effect: Nostalgia and the Visual Framing of (White) Suburbia." *Western Journal of Communication* 70 (3): 212–33. http://dx.doi.org/10.1080/10570310600843504.

Edmunds, R. David. 2007. "Comment: Starving Rocks and Dancing Mascots." *Journal of the Illinois State Historical Society* 100 (3): 237–39.

Gailey, Alan. 1989. "The Nature of Tradition." *Folklore* 100 (2): 143–61. http://dx.doi.org/10.1080/0015587X.1989.9715762.

Glassie, Henry. 1995. "Tradition." *Journal of American Folklore* 108 (430): 395–412. http://dx.doi.org/10.2307/541653.

Handler, Richard, and Jocelyn Linnekin. 1984. "Tradition, Genuine or Spurious." *Journal of American Folklore* 97 (385): 273–90. http://dx.doi.org/10.2307/540610.

Hobsbawm, Eric, and Terence Ranger. 2002. *The Invention of Tradition.* Cambridge, UK: Cambridge University Press.

Honor the Chief Society. *Honor the Chief.* http://www.honorthechief.com. Accessed February 19, 2011.

Howard, Robert Glenn. 2008. "The Vernacular Web of Participatory Media."
    Critical Studies in Media Communication 25 (5): 490–513. http://dx.doi.
    org/10.1080/15295030802468065.
Howard, Robert Glenn. 2010. *Digital Jesus: The Making of a New Christian Fundamentalist
    Community on the Internet.* New York: New York University Press.
Landsberg, Alison. 2003. "Prosthetic Memory: The Ethics and Politics of Memory in an
    Age of Mass Culture." In *Memory and Popular Film*, ed. Paul Grainge, 144–61. Man-
    chester: Manchester University Press.
Linnekin, Jocelyn. 1991. "Cultural Invention and the Dilemma of Authenticity." *American
    Anthropologist* 93 (2): 446–49. http://dx.doi.org/10.1525/aa.1991.93.2.02a00120.
King, C. Richard, and Charles Fruehling Springwood, eds. 2001. *Team Spirits: The Native
    American Mascots Controversy.* Lincoln: University of Nebraska Press.
Morley, David. 2000. *Home Territories: Media, Mobility and Identity.* London: Routledge.
Rainey, Ryan. 2010. "Officials Call Freakfest a Success, Arrest Decrease Again." *The Badger
    Herald*, November 2, 2010. http://badgerherald.com/news/2010/10/31/officials_
    call_freak.php. Accessed March 10, 2011.
Rosenstein, Jay. 1997. *In Whose Honor? American Indian Mascots in Sports.* New Day Films.
Said, Edward W. 1978. *Orientalism.* New York: Pantheon Books.
Spindel, Carol. 2002. *Dancing at Halftime: Sports and the Controversy over American Indian
    Mascots.* New York: New York University Press.
Students for Chief Illiniwek. *Students for Chief Illiniwek.* http://studentsforchief.com.
    Accessed February 19, 2011.
The Council of Chiefs. *The Chief Lives: The Official Website for the Chief Tradition.* 2010.
    http://thechieflives.com. Accessed February 19, 2011.
Tiffin, Helen. 1997. "Colonialist Pretexts and Rites of Reply." *Yearbook of English Studies*
    27: 219–33. http://dx.doi.org/10.2307/3509144.
"Chief's Last Dance on ESPN." *YouTube.* http://www.youtube.com/
    watch?v=O7tyfQu4QJo. Accessed February 19, 2011.

5

Curation and Tradition on Web 2.0

Merrill Kaplan

THE EUROPEAN ROOTS OF FOLKLORE STUDIES LIE WITHIN the nineteenth-century explosion of the collection and publication of traditional expressions. Those expressions were documented, "artifactualized," and made consumable by the curious among the emerging educated middle class and analyzed and discussed by the members of a scholarly community. Something similar to this explosion is happening again. Today, however, it is happening on the World Wide Web. The online folk do not only pass on tradition by electronic means, they also collect and annotate it. Essentially, the curation of tradition has itself become traditional.

In an effort to shed light on these emergent folk processes and reveal their implications for our conceptualizations of tradition in the twenty-first century, this chapter analyzes several influential, popular websites that clearly demonstrate the online curation of folklore. On the whole, these sites are managed, organized, and/or patronized by people whom we do not generally think of as fellow keepers of the discipline of tradition—or heirs to the Grimms' project of documenting and studying that tradition. Nevertheless, nonacademic websites now house vast collections of traditional material, encourage ongoing collection and contribution, and support communities that actively discuss and research collections' contents. If we want to understand the nature and workings of tradition on the Internet in the early twenty-first century, we should take note that among the diverse flora of online tradition—rumors, jokes, legends, forwardables, macros, chatboard games, etc.—the collection, classification, publication, and analysis of folklore has itself become a vernacular practice.

DOI: 10.7330/9780874218992.c05

The word *tradition* is a sticky and contested noun and needs clarification. It has been applied to (1) the process by which cultural goods come to persist through time or exist across physical or virtual space (i.e., the passing-on or passing-around as implied by the word's Latin etymon, *tradere*), (2) the stuff passed on or around in the above manner, and (3) a category of cultural goods (see number 2) not natural but constructed by a particular community. All three kinds of tradition intersect on the World Wide Web.

Despite our continuing tendency to think of tradition in the first sense as the handing-down of material over time, we have increasingly been willing to identify online phenomena with relatively shallow time depth as tradition in the second sense. This is more than reasonable. Long before the Internet, folksong scholars Phillip Barry and Fannie Hardy Eckstorm noted that material distributed across space could be no less traditional for being recent.[1] They distinguished *tradition in time* and *tradition in space* and stressed that a recent song familiar to "an indefinite number of persons, over a large territory" was as traditional as one passed down through the ages (Barry and Eckstorm 1930, 2). Territory now extends into virtual space; and in the high-speed online environment, expressive forms may be widely attested demographically even if new or ephemeral. That folklore—the stuff of tradition—has made the leap to the cyber world and has been pinging around the Internet is old news.

Traditional stuff had already found a home in local networks before today's Internet emerged. Once the Internet did come into being, digitized folkloric forms could be easily found in the text-based world of e-mail and newsgroups that preceded the World Wide Web. After the shift to a graphical user interface and the use of browsers, the same genres and more spread into the newly available virtual real estate of Web 1.0's static webpages. The so-called Web 2.0, home to social media among other things, now provides a more interactive and collaborative environment for yet more expressive forms like Photoshops, image macros, video remixes, and chatboard games while older, purely verbal genres continue to circulate over e-mail.[2] When

---

1   I am indebted to Kimberly Ball for this reference.

2   For work on these genres see Dégh (1999); Fialkova and Yelenevskaya (2001); Foote (2007); Fox (2007 [1983]); Frank (2004); Heyd (2008, 2009); Kibby (2005); Reno (2007); Revak (2010); Shifman (2007). The most international bibliography of works on folklore on the Internet, as well as in mobile electronically mediated communication such as text messages—(Alekseevsky n.d.)—may be, appropriately enough, found online. See also, of course, the bibliography in Blank (2009). The study of fast-changing collaborative electronic environments is a vast field in itself. For its pre-Internet

working with this material, it pays to remember the broader definition of *tradition* as a process that includes handing around as well as handing down.[3]

Understanding tradition as stuff is well and good, but defining it as an objective, natural category of stuff has proved problematic; the work of Hobsbawm and Ranger (1983) and Handler and Linnekin (1984) has done much to make those problems visible. A postmodern turn has saved us, however; for the stuff identified as traditional is always so identified by some community. Tom Mould suggests we understand the stuff of tradition to be those elements of culture to which a community has granted the symbolic quality of "the traditional" in an ongoing interpretive process (Mould 2005, 259). This update of Dell Hymes's term *traditionalization* is easily applied to the processes that construct a community, such as that which the Québécois perform in defining an ethnohistorical identity.[4]

Folklorists, too, construct tradition as a category of stuff by labeling things as traditional. Elliott Oring has quipped that folklorists use the word *folklore* simply to mark territory, as when we toss out the flip (and traditional) assertion that "folklore is what folklorists study" (Oring 2009). Once invoked, this powerful formula turns whatever one is researching at the moment into folklore. The word *tradition* can be used the same way: like the term *folklore*, is it "constitutive of the phenomenon" itself (Kirchenblatt-Gimblett in Franklin 2001, 215). Thus, the folklorist's object of study is created as any object of ethnography is created—"by virtue of being defined, segmented, detached, and carried away by ethnographers" (Kirshenblatt-Gimblett 1998, 17–18). Having created the objects that create the discipline, folklorists also create themselves as experts, keepers of the discipline, masters of a privileged discourse.

Dorothy Noyes's encyclopedic article goes a long way toward bringing coherence to the multiple uses and usages of *tradition*.[5] After surveying some of the vast history of the term, Noyes gives us not a definition but an evocative

---

beginnings, see Grudin (1994).

3   Simon J. Bronner (2009) has pointed out that tradition might also be a handing *up*, especially if it is dependent on electronic media with which children are more proficient than their parents.

4   Properly speaking, Mould is interested in that process as a means of "establishing continuity with the past," historical or imagined. I would replace "the past" with "a larger context of practice and/or expression," to account for the value many online communities place on creativity that draws on the newest (and yet already widespread) jokes, pranks, etc. in preference to those that have become "tired."

5   For more on tradition, see Cashman, Mould, and Shukla (2011, 1–7), with references.

image: "the transfer of . . . [a] practice, a body of knowledge, a genre, a song, anything sufficiently framed and internally structured to be entextualizable or objectified or named: in [Greg] Urban's term, a cultural object" and the "transmission of meta-knowledge along with the practice itself: what it means, how it is to be used, everything that is shaven off when it is packaged as a product or an entry in a database" (Noyes 2009, 248). This is a nice formulation. It avoids unsupportable Hobsbawmian binaries of authenticity and inauthenticity and welcomes goods into the fold regardless of whether they have been "objectified or named" by their users (i.e., traditionalized) or outsiders. It involves stuff, constructedness, and transmission, and it delineates where the handing-on of stuff ceases to be tradition: at the door to the shop and the archive. I understand this to mean the point where, having been segmented, detached, etc., the stuff passed on is carried off into another mode of circulation. The circulation of cultural goods in a capitalist economy is easily discussed as commodification. What, then, to call the ongoing transmission of cultural objects once they have passed out of the scene Noyes paints for us, shorn of meta-knowledge, entered into the archive, and then made to circulate anew in published collections or scholarly works? I call this *curation*, and it is basic to the practice of folkloristics.

I use the word *curation* this way with the knowledge that its semantic range has expanded considerably of late.[6] However, its newer meanings have

---

6   Curation, in media circles, has come to mean the thoughtful gathering of information produced by others for presentation to (yet) others. According to voices in new media, it is the key to new business models that will save the profitability of media in an age of information superabundance (Bruns 2008; Rosenbaum 2009). From there, the word has been extended into, seemingly, every commercial or potentially commercial realm in which the variety of items on offer proliferates. For example, a quick Google search for the terms *selection*, *clothing*, and *curated* results in over 735,000 hits, and, if a sample of fifty is representative, they overwhelmingly represent shops rather than exhibitions. For Steven Rosenbaum, curation more generally "is about adding value from humans who add their qualitative judgment to whatever is being gathered and organized" (Rosenbaum 2011, 3). Even "accidental curation" can emerge from the small, simple actions of large groups of people who click "Like" buttons on Facebook or tag photos on Flickr (Rosenbaum 2011, 202–6; contrast Gehl 2009).

Not everyone is happy with new media's and others' appropriation of the title of "curator" for what is, in the eyes of some, a glorified aggregator and, in the end, only "Someone (Else) to Sort Through This Rubbish" (newcurator 2010). New media–style curation, whether intentional or accidental, does not move the material gathered and organized across a line analogous to the line where tradition ends and meta-knowledge is stripped away. Curated news remains news to be consumed as news. It is not detached from its context of use and made an ethnographic object to be consumed as an example of the genre "news," and it does not become part of a work about news where new less to do with my project than does the more conservative understanding of curation as the preservation, cataloging, interpretation, and exhibition of artifacts to an audience. If those artifacts are intangible and traditional (legends, jokes, practices, etc.), then collecting, cataloging, analyzing, and publishing them in entextualized form is directly analogous to the curation of physical objects in museums. When folklorists publish collections of such artifacts or quote them in their works of scholarship, they continue to transmit them, but we do not usually think of this handing-on as tradition. To do so tends to offend our instinctive feel for the authentic, and Noyes helps us see why. Where the cultural object is detached from use and emic meaning, it ceases to be *performed* in Richard Bauman's sense and is only quoted.[7] Meta-knowledge about how to use it or do it properly is shorn away, but new meta-knowledge is attached to it in the form of indices, interpretations, analyses—meta-knowledge about how to look at it. In this sense, where tradition ends, curation begins.

---

meta-knowledge is attached to it. "Accidental curation" is a form of vernacular catalog-ing, and fascinating as such, but there arises no work from it that we might point to as the catalog, analogous to the edited folklore collection. There is only metadata (e.g., tags, Likes, browsing trails) yet to be mined. While users uploading videos to YouTube may tag them with keywords that, taken together, make up vernacular taxonomies or "folk-sonomies" (see Bruns 2008, 171–98; Vander Wal 2007), YouTube is still primarily a site of expressive communication; "Broadcast Yourself" is its motto, not "Index Your Stuff" or—to take the actual motto of Urban Dictionary, a collectively but quite intentionally curated dictionary of folk speech—"Define Your World."

I am not the first to associate curation and reference works. For Krista A. Kennedy (2009), encyclopedias of any vintage are sites of knowledge curation; she compares the collaborative authorship of Wikipedia and the eighteenth-century *Chambers' Cyclopæ-dia*. What distinguishes Kennedy's curated reference works from published collections of folklore is the amorphous quality of the knowledge collected in encyclopedias (i.e., not sufficiently framed and structured to qualify as a cultural object or objects).

Where curation of one's "life world" (Franklin 2001, 229) fits in, I am not sure. I lean toward seeing it as another form of expressive communication (and often auto-communication), recontextualization more than curation, in the sense used here. Much more remains to be said about the points of connection and disconnection between and among tagging, "accidental curation" (Bruns 2008, 202–6) and tradi-tionalization, folksonomies, and vernacular practices of cataloging (see Vo 2007), pro-dusage (see Bruns 2008) and tradition, crowdsourcing and exploitative appropriation of tradition, and—not least—the emergent vocabulary of computer-mediated com-munication (CMC) studies and the *termini technici* of folkloristics. I hope to return to some of these matters in another venue.

7　In other words, communicated with "an assumption of accountability to an audience for the way in which communication is carried out, above and beyond its referential content" (Bauman 1975, 293).

Folklorists have spent a lot of time looking for the stuff of tradition on the Internet in context, which has generally meant in performance.[8] Some scholars looking for folklore online suffer disappointment—for example, Russell Frank, who seems dissatisfied with having to supplement the forwarded jokes gleaned from his own inbox with others from huge collections to be found on websites. He cites Elliott Oring on the "problem with this kind of website" (Frank 2009, 103)—namely, that it "is more like an archive than a repertoire" (Oring 2003, 139).[9] Many such sites are like archives because they *are* archives, sites of curation more than performance.

The websites profiled throughout this chapter collect material, classify it, and publish it in electronic form instead of print. Many of them also offer analysis of their contents and/or provide the infrastructure for others to analyze it in comment threads, chatboards, or other venues for interactivity; and they cover a wide range of genres, some of which are familiar from face-to-face interactions, with others peculiar to the web environment: legend and rumor, folk speech, and Internet memes. These curatorial websites support communities for whom the material collected is the object of study and discussion. Moreover, their collected materials are both similar to and different from the paperbound collections we associate with the birth of folklore studies.[10] Similar to their nineteenth-century counterparts, they have emerged at a moment of expanding literacy and newly democratic publishing technology. They are signs that another field of folklore studies is coming into being.[11]

---

8   See for example, Fialkova and Yelenevskaya (2001), who write about "storytelling" on chatboards; Roth (2009), who writes about *Erzählen* and *folkloristische Kommunikation* on the Internet; and Linda Dégh (1999, 57), who writes about "the legend conduit of the world wide web" and worries that proper performance will never find a place there.

9   Oring makes a sensitive argument for seeing and analyzing a performance context on one such humor site, one that elicited reader feedback on the quality and content of the jokes rather than their origin and social meaning (Oring 2003, 129–40). This is a very fruitful approach, and I do not mean to argue against its validity in any way.

10   Scholars of computer-mediated communication (CMC) and rhetoric have been very interested in determining which online genres are new and which are reproductions of familiar, offline genres (see, for example, Crowston and Williams 2000). Heyd (2009) notes enthusiasm for discoveries of truly new genres. Kennedy (2009) also stands out, arguing that even the massively collaborative Wikipedia is not so new after all.

11   Theresa Heyd notes the "rich and messy domain of folkloristic creativity" online that produces image macros, jokes, and e-mail forwardables. Looking at sites similar to those discussed here, she calls them the "first attempts at systematizing this field." It is

LEGEND AND INDIVIDUAL CURATION

The Grimms' landmark *Deutsche Sagen* (1816, 1818) did not make quite the splash that *Kinder- und Hausmärchen* (1812) did, but it did inspire the collection and publication of legend and folk belief across Europe. Nothing since has had an equivalent impact, but the Urban Legends Reference Pages, better known as Snopes.com, casts a long shadow. Snopes is the best-known and highest-traffic online repository of contemporary legend and rumor today. Barbara and David P. Mikkelson have maintained the site (in one web-based form or another) since 1995, making it as old as Hotmail.com and Yahoo![12] As of April 2010, it could boast of 7–8 million unique visitors per month (Stelter 2010). As of June 2012, Snopes's US traffic rank on Alexa is 626—its global traffic rank is 2,435—meaning that it is the 1,979th highest-traffic site on the web; 30,924 websites link to it (Alexa, Snopes. com). *Deutsche Sagen*, in contrast, though printed in multiple editions, was only translated into English in 1981 (Grimm and Grimm 1981).

Snopes's project is unmistakably one of curation rather than performance or participation in the legend conduit. The Mikkelsons present their material as artifacts—organizing it, indexing it, analyzing it, and making it consumable as edifying entertainment for those who know (or are about to know) truth from falsehood. That material is a mix of legends, rumors, anecdotes, folk etymologies, and e-mail warnings—secular belief genres lumped together under the rubric "Urban Legends."[13] These items are organized by subject matter into categories (Computers, Autos, Quotes, Food, Travel, History, Legal, Love, etc.) and subcategories (e.g., under Love: Betrayal, Dating Disasters, and Scorned Lovers Avenged), and then cross-indexed (as when Scorned Lovers destroy Autos). Overall, Snopes's material is more systematically arranged than the legends in *Deutsche Sagen*, which included a table of contents but no index. In fact, the Grimms' foreword detailed their struggle with how to organize their material (Grimm and Grimm 1816–1818, xv–xix). They might have appreciated hypertext.

---

not clear whether she would classify the contents of urban legend sites like Snopes as digital folklore (Heyd 2009, 254).

12　However, the domain name snopes.com was only registered in 1997. By way of comparison, David Emery has written about urban legends at About.com since 1997 (Emery n.d.). Rich Butler of TruthOrFiction.com has been active since 1999. The domain name urbanlegendsonline.com was registered in 2003.

13　Ghosts and ETs are absent, and there are only a few religiously themed items, many of the "signs from God" type, nearly all of which the Mikkelsons classify as "Glurge."

Snopes frames its material as quotations. Narratives are typically reproduced in one or more versions, directly quoted from whatever source they come from (rumors, folk etymologies, and the like are often paraphrased). Also indicated are the date of collection and nature of the source (print, e-mail, or the vaguer "Internet"). The Grimms also gave some account of their sources, including published ones (Grimm and Grimm 1816–1818, xx–xxiv), and they stressed the accuracy of their reproduction of genuinely anonymous folk creations; they wrote of *Treue und Wahrheit* (Grimm and Grimm 1816–1818, ix). For them, the truth of their legends was a philosophical, inner truth as well as the truth of reproduction faithful to an original.

As for factual truth, the Grimms published for an audience they assumed did not believe the content of the materials they documented, in contrast to the folk, who, childlike, "still believed their legends" (*das Volk hat noch nicht ganz aufgehört, an seine Sagen zu glauben*) (Grimm and Grimm 1816–1818, v). The Mikkelsons publish for an audience that wants to know whether or not they should believe—an audience that suspects that there is a division in the world between people who know no better and those who do. The site's design makes fact checking efficient: each item is labeled with a colored dot to indicate its degree of truth value: true, false, multiple truth values, undetermined truth value, and unclassifiable veracity. Analysis is often in the service of determining the origin of a given item, tracing it to, say, a misunderstood news report or an original and inaccurate e-mail, and thereby discovering its truth value.[14] Some entries include thoughts on the social and psychological function of specific stories.[15]

---

14   Searching for origins and truth value will likely strike today's professional folklorists, many of whom have been trained to equate analysis with interpretation, as an outdated approach. It is nonetheless an analytical approach. Certainly it is more than description, or even classification. I would also note that some seekers-after-origins conflate origin with meaning, which might further blur the line between the discovery of an item's origin and the work of interpretation.

15   For an example of interpretation, see the entry for "The Evangelical Prez," filed under "Glurge." After debunking the veracity of the tale of then-President-elect George W. Bush witnessing to a sixteen-year-old boy, Barbara Mikkelson unpacks it as a product of its historical moment: "Such tales also work to reassure folks, both those who voted for the newcomer and those who didn't, that this new man is a decent sort of guy and that he will do right by the country . . . Part of that transition is coming to see the President-Elect as someone the country can look up to, and part of that process is good, old-fashioned storytelling" (Snopes, Evangelical Prez).

Attempts to wipe out popular beliefs by publishing them in collected form with commentary predated the field of folklore as we know it. First published in 1646, Thomas Browne's wonderfully titled *Pseudodoxia Epidemica*, for example, essayed to "timely survey our knowledge; impartially singling out those encroachments, which junior compliance and popular credulity hath admitted" (Browne 1672, n.p.). Similar concerns were current in the nineteenth century. Andreas Faye's 1833 collection of legend, the first such published in Norway, addressed the question of whether putting tales of supernatural creatures in print would only further buttress continued erroneous belief. Not to worry, he wrote, for making such tales "objects of discussion among reasonable people" (*Gjenstand for fornuftige Folks Samtale*) and annotating them with information about their origins will act to correct that belief (Faye 1833, iv). For Faye, as for the Mikkelsens, discovering origins was the key to establishing truth value, and truth value is essential to the project.

Truth value is not all, however. Snopes's design also provides entertainment for the casual reader. A "randomizer" button appears at the top of each page. Useless for directed research, the button adds to an electronic resource a functionality familiar from print media: that of opening to a random page. Nineteenth-century legend collections might offer a similar experience, both in terms of pleasant diversion and the potential for intentionally haphazard access. Faye suggested his legends might provide children with adult-supervised entertainment (Faye 1833, vi). Jacob Grimm clarified in the third edition of *Deutsche Sagen* that the collection is not meant to be read cover-to-cover but rather dipped into; the reader who did so would find much to enjoy.[16] The same can be said of Snopes. Indeed, a columnist at *The Seattle Times* has remarked that "[y]ou could do worse than spending a rainy afternoon here" (Watanabe 1998). One might spend a similar day strolling among the cases in a museum. The pleasure of the two activities is the same—that of consuming a curated collection.

---

16 "Ein Lesebuch soll unsere Sammlung gar nicht weden, in dem Sinn, daß man alles, was, sie enthält, hinter einander auszulesen hätte. Jedwede Sage stehet vielmehr geschlossen für sich da, und hat mit her vorausgebenden und nachfolgenden eigenlich nichts zu thun; wer sich darunter aussucht, wird sich schon begnügen und vergnügen" (Grimm and Grimm 1977 [1891], xv).

FOLK SPEECH AND COLLABORATIVE CURATION

If Snopes is well known and respected, then its notorious counterpart in the cataloging of folk speech is Urban Dictionary (UD). While newer on the scene than Snopes, the Urban Dictionary website has significantly higher traffic.[17] UD's huge compilation of slang contains nearly 6 million definitions as of June 2011—though some percentage of them must be regarded as chaff.[18] The site organizes its items alphabetically, as one would expect in any dictionary, and each word appears on its own page with its definition or definitions and, frequently, examples of use.

Architecturally, the UD site is something between a group blog and a wiki. Users submit and define all items, and no registration is required to submit material. One may register oneself as an editor (at no cost) and vote with other editors on which submissions will be published. Editors also rate definitions, if more than one has been submitted for a single word; and the definitions deemed better by popular consensus appear higher up on the word's page. The UD platform does not support discussion of entries by either editors or nonregistered users (as do some other folklore curation sites and Wikipedia). But unlike Snopes, where the Mikkelsens exercise a firm editorial hand, the de facto editor and publisher of UD is not an individual but a collective.[19] In the language of web-based business, the task of building and maintaining this collection of folk speech is referred to

---

17   UD has been online since 1999 in one form or another (the domain name was regis-
      tered in 2001). As of June 2012, it has an Alexa global traffic rank of 872, US traffic
      rank of 418, and 44,371 links from other sites (Alexa, urbandictionary.com).

18   A *New York Times* columnist called Urban Dictionary an "exquisite and unorthodox
      resource" (Heffernan 2009). Use with care, however, as the site's stated policy against
      abusive commentary is not enforced and has not kept out some disturbingly racist
      definitions of certain ethnonyms. UD has also become a forum for posting purported
      definitions of personal names (e.g., "Chris, The most awesome person to ever live";
      "Maria, slut") and faux definitions of standard English words (e.g. "child, The mani-
      fest divine wrath of a vengefull [*sic*] God in punishment for screwing"). Ad hoc coin-
      ages also clutter the view; while not folk speech per se, they might be considered
      a form of artistic vernacular expression—one dependent on the dictionary context
      for its impact. The *Times* recognized the difficulties presented by UD: "Something
      interesting is being cataloged by Urban Dictionary; it's just not clear what" (Heffernan
      2009). Much of it, however, is clearly folk speech.

19   The founder (and CEO!) of Urban Dictionary, LLC, Aaron Peckham, does not project
      any sort of editorial authority into the virtual space of the project, and, in fact, his
      name appears nowhere on the site's pages. Peckham appears to reserve his editorial
      function for the print versions of the dictionary, published in 2005 and 2007. The
      issues raised by those publications are too many to be dealt with adequately here.

as "crowdsourcing." The coiner of the word defines *crowdsourcing* as "the act of taking a job traditionally performed by a designated agent (usually an employee) and outsourcing it to an undefined, generally large group of people in the form of an open call" (Howe 2006; see also Howe 2008). If we invert the focus of the concept, we see instead the act of contributing as one of an undefined, generally large group of people to a collaborative project traditionally performed by a designated agent—in other words, participation in a traditional practice.[20]

Ongoing solicitation of items is by no means unique to UD. The Mikkelsens of Snopes, though they appear to gather some of their items from their own spam filters and web wanderings, also actively solicit new material from their readers with a button marked "Submit a Rumor," visible on every page of the site. UD has an "add" button. Compare these to the preface of John Camden Hotten's 1859 dictionary of "Modern Cant, Slang and Vulgar Words . . . With Glossaries of Two Secret Languages Spoken by the Wandering Tribes of London," where he wrote that "[t]he compiler will be much obliged by the receipt . . . of any cant, slang, or vulgar words not mentioned in the dictionary" (Hotten 1859, iv). By 1872 Hotten had expanded the dictionary from about 3,000 words to almost 10,000 with the help of his correspondents, whom he thanks in the volume's preface (Hotten 1872, v, x).

Urban Dictionary takes greater advantage of the interactive possibilities of Web 2.0 than Snopes—possibilities to which Hotten did not have access. UD's model comes close to collapsing informants with publishers; although entries do not instantly appear online, any contributor may join a self-nominated (and seemingly uncritical group) that patrols the border between submission and publication. UD's slogan stresses contributors' role in editing and publishing: "Urban Dictionary is the dictionary you wrote. *Define your world.*" The call for submissions William Thoms wished the *Athenaeum* literary journal would issue (that would "gather in abundance" such tidbits as the Yorkshire children's rhyme he gives as a sample of his "folk-lore") is characteristically built into web-based collections of tradition in the form of a clickable button (Thoms 1999 [1846], 12). The technical

---

20   To be fair, the language of Web 2.0–based business models has increasingly focused on the agency of the collective. Talk of users and consumers has turned to editors, user-generated content, and prosumers (producer-consumers), and then to produsers (producer-users) and produsage. The vocabulary of folkloristics does not appear to have penetrated the discussion.

affordances of Web 2.0 permit these sites to automate collection and streamline it with editing and publication.

While Urban Dictionary is remarkable for its size and popularity, it is not at all unique. The online curation of slang, which is often user-submitted, is not limited to English slang or even to the Anglophone web.[21] The non-oral "folk speech" of SMS texting, instant messaging, e-mail, and other electronic and/or web-based channels of communication, sometimes called "netspeak," is also cataloged online in more than one place. Models vary from centralized editorship by an individual, as with the Internet Slang Dictionary & Translator (or NoSlang.com), which specializes in helping visitors crack the code of electronic communication among adolescents, to more collaborative efforts, as at NetLingo, where a volunteer editor pool helps maintain a large collection of user-submitted IT jargon, slang, and SMS abbreviations.

Particularly notable, if not particularly high-traffic, is the Online Slang Dictionary (OSD), an online dictionary of mostly offline slang.[22] The site contains a disproportionate amount of entries submitted by founder and administrator Walter Rader; it is not clear how much editorial power Rader chooses to exercise over the site, but its architecture resembles that of Urban Dictionary or NetLingo. Once again, visitors are invited to register (free) and submit words and definitions, but this particular site asks them to supply additional data. The site's interface allows for feedback on how often a visitor or others use a word, the word's level of vulgarity, and a visitor's location. A Google application uses this last piece of data to generate a map of a given word's geographical spread—a historic-geographic dream.

---

21   Cool Slang (www.coolslang.com) offers dictionaries of French, German, Hindi, Japanese, Korean, Norwegian, Serbian, and Turkish slang, as well as American and Irish English, some monolingual and others with English apparatus and translations. A quick dip into the northern end of the Internet turns up monolingual online dictionaries of nonstandard Icelandic (Slangurorðabókin, slangur.snara.is) and nonstandard Danish (Slangster, slangster.dk). They are both newer than UD and have, as yet, less chaff (it helps that Slangurorðabókin has a separate category for clever neologisms—*nýyrði*—which is a recognized genre of folk creativity in Iceland). All are compilations of words submitted by users. Slangurorðabókin (in English: "The Slang Dictionary") is the most collaborative of these. It invites not only the continuing submission of new words but discussion of those already cataloged; comment threads fill with discussions of individual entries.

22   As of June 2012, the Online Slang Dictionary's Alexa US traffic rank was 11,045; only 934 sites linked in (Alexa, onlineslangdictionary.com).

Examples of usage follow, supplied not by users but culled in real time from Twitter feeds by means of a search engine.[23]

The affordances of Web 2.0 make it possible for the Online Slang Dictionary to automate its collection of examples and replace the wandering researcher with pencils and notebooks with a search engine. Both editor-in-chief and collector-editors can contribute—if not while "seated on damask in [their] own drawing-room[s]," as nineteenth-century publisher John Camden Hotten (1872, xiii) imagined the ideally comfortable attitude in which to conduct a study of vulgar speech, then at least in a desk chair. Hotten contracted with his informants among the "chaunters and patterers" to check the contributions of their fellows for "deception and mistakes" (xiii); at OSD that ingenious but slow system is replaced by an editorial collective in ongoing communication. Code compiles and synthesizes the data into a list of statistics, making for an even richer curated collection that web surfers can consult as a reference work or sample for entertainment with a "random" button. Code also automates the ongoing updating of the site, speeding up the production of new editions.

Obviously, nineteenth-century editor-publishers did not have access to Internet technology, but it is interesting to view today's expressive modes of communication against the arduous efforts by Hotten to approximate the collaboration that is now so easily supported by Web 2.0. He not only solicited contributions for his next edition, but he made it easy for his readers to update their own copies. In the front matter of the third edition, he writes: "Copies of this work interleaved with finely ruled paper for the use of those who desire to collect such Slang and colloquial words as may start into existence from time to time can be obtained from the publisher price 9^8 6^d" (Hotten 1872, iv).

The interactive web speeds up everything by giving the reader the ability to make his revisions visible to himself and all other readers, but the collaborative principle is similar.[24] Technology, as Alan Dundes long since noted, can be "a vital factor in the transmission of folklore" (Dundes 1980, 17)—and this is as true now as it was then.

---

23 Twitter's register, like that of some e-mail and instant messaging, is notably oral in style. The Twitter search picks up many non-slang usages and so is imperfect in its application, but the idea is brilliant in principle.

24 For a comparative case, see Kennedy (2009) for an extended exploration of how the collaboration that creates Wikipedia may not be so fundamentally different from that behind an eighteenth-century example of the genre like Ephraim Chambers' 1728 *Cyclopædia*. Chambers incorporated much reader (user?)-submitted material into the work.

The Online Slang Dictionary and other such sites demonstrate how employing one-way technology is a vital tool in the transmission of artifactualized folklore—and not by academic or public folklorists but by semi-anonymous collectives without any kind of official status. Although we could say that the collection and curation of folklore is being crowdsourced, this is a passive construction that elides the agency of the members doing the actual work. More interesting to the folklorist is that large numbers of individuals are choosing to exercise their agency by collaboratively collecting and curating vernacular culture.

INTERNET MEMES AND A SCHOLARLY COMMUNITY

The Online Slang Dictionary provides no means for contributor-editors to communicate with each other, and so the site does not support a robust scholarly *community*, but other sites do. Notably, Know Your Meme (KYM) collects, archives, and researches Internet memes and discusses them in forums.[25] Those discussion forums are home to a community dedicated to the production of knowledge. First, however, the phrase "Internet meme" requires some explanation.[26]

On the Internet, *meme* has become a genre term, albeit a broad one. Meme may refer to nearly any creation or practice that has "gone viral," in which it is transmitted, transformed, and retransmitted quickly and widely enough across the Internet and other new media outlets to have attained status as a familiar cultural reference online. Examples may include catchphrases, edited photographs, image macros, and pranks.[27] This is the material Know Your Meme catalogues in a sizeable database.

---

25   KYM spun off from the *Rocketboom* blog, a site offering "daily Internet culture," tech news, and commentary. Other collections of memes can be found at whatport80.com and memedump.com.

26   The history of the term starts with Richard Dawkins's *The Selfish Gene* (1976), where it means a transmittable unit of culture. Folklorists and others already familiar with the idea later discovered that culture might be transmitted and used in discussions of folklore in general (Pimple 1996), fairy tales (Zipes 2008), urban legends (Heath, Bell, and Sternberg 2001), Anglo-Saxon literature and oral theory (Drout 2006, 2010), and image macros (Foote 2007). The viability of idea has also received criticism from Gregory Schrempp (2009).

27   *The New York Times* has recently noted these phenomena (Walker 2010). On social networking sites like Facebook and LiveJournal, "meme" can refer more narrowly to questionnaires passed from user to user to elicit trivial and, in an ideal world, interesting personal information (e.g., "Ten things you don't know about me"). On Facebook,

Know Your Meme began as a video webcast in which the creators affected a jokey scientifism, styling themselves as The Rocketboom Institute for Internet Studies. The short videos featured clipboard-toting men and women in lab coats discussing specific items of current Internet culture. While production of the video episodes has tapered off, the spinoff database and discussion boards are flourishing.[28] As at Snopes, entries in the database take the form of short articles explaining each meme and tracing its origin and development as far back as the researcher knows. Even more so than Snopes, KYM emphasizes the multiple existence and variation of each meme and always provides several examples of derivatives of the original image or phrase. "Spoofs, mashups, remixes, parodies, recontextualizations, and re-enactments" all qualify (Know Your Meme, FAQ).

Some entries include a graph generated by Google Analytics showing the fluctuation in interest in the meme over time based on the frequency of Google searches for related words or phrases. For example, the entry for Serious Cat—an image macro consisting of a picture of a dour white cat captioned with "I are serious cat. This is serious thread"—contains a graph showing that searches for the phrase "serious cat" began in October 2006, had a modest uptick in August 2008 (coinciding with a large upswing in searches for "LOLcat"), and have since leveled off.

Registered users research, write, and submit all KYM articles; this all-volunteer collective pools its expertise in an attached discussion forum labeled "Meme Research." The entries are then approved and expanded (or rejected and "Deadpooled") by a "professional editorial and research

---

a meme may be a request that one update one's status or profile picture in a particular way. There is relatively little overlap between these memes and those cataloged by KYM, though the site does offer an article on the sudden fad for posting the color of one's brassiere in January 2010 (KYM, Bra Status Updates).

28   Ownership of the KYM site has changed hands since I began my research. Rocket-boom sold KYM to the Cheezburger Network (cheezburger.com), a company that owns some of the web's highest-traffic image macro sites, in March 2011. While the "Rocketboom Institute for Internet Studies" banner no longer appears at the top of the site's pages, and four Rocketboom employees have become employees of Cheez-burger, forum members and researchers are still volunteers and the character of the site appears not to have changed. Said Cheezburger CEO Ben Huh, "People require context, history, and origins [that] helps them understand why [a meme or image macro on Cheezburger] is funny or why [it] isn't funny. And Know Your Meme was probably doing the best job of that out there" (Terdiman 2011). Given the size and commercial success of Cheezburger, KYM is now arguably a hybrid of folk and mass culture, "vernacular" in Robert Glenn Howard's sense of participatory media (Howard 2008). The distinction is not significant to the present argument.

staff" (Know Your Meme, About). KYM had 1,500 registered users on its discussion boards as of July 2009 and some 10,000–15,000 views per day (Menning 2009). As of June 2012, the Meme Research forum had 18,500 conversations in 2,467 threads in which members discuss memes, debate what qualifies as a meme, and share tips on research methods. Forum participants are not able to automatically add to or edit the database directly; they can request editorship of a particular entry from community managers or make specific suggestions for others to implement. Forum administrators have the authority to assign the writing of specific articles to members. Thus, KYM is collaborative, even if not as radically and democratically so as a wiki. It is still a case of collective curation. The explicit goal of the site, as articulated by one of the forum's community managers, is "to document and analyze memes from all over the web" and to study them as "cultural artifacts" (Menning 2010). The forum community imagines itself, in Andersonian terms (Anderson 1991 [1983]), as a group that produces and manages the knowledge necessary to that goal. The overall tone of forum posts makes clear that members take the project seriously, even as they joke around with each other.

It may amuse—or perhaps disconcert—professional folklorists to know that the typing, clicking, surfing masses understand the stuff KYM catalogs to be tradition by name. Proof of this arrives from within the material itself in the form of countless images with the caption "I am aware of all Internet traditions." The fertile catchphrase apparently made its first appearance in a comment thread on the blog *Lawyers Guns & Money*, where a reader, Vanderleun, accused the blogger of grossly misquoting Geraldine Ferraro. Others protested that the blogger had used the word "shorter" (in the phrase "shorter Geraldine Ferrero") to signal that what followed should be understood as a snarky paraphrase and not a direct quote. Vanderleun rejected this explanation: "I am aware of all Internet traditions and also of literary conventions in which placing something in quotes or in a blockquote means that your [*sic*] are quoting that person."[29] Vanderleun clearly was referring to punctuation and formatting conventions, not online traditions in the folkloric sense—namely, that the meaning of the word *traditions* changed once Vanderleun's phrase escaped its original discursive habitat.

---

29   The page on which this line originally appeared has since vanished. The exchange is
      quoted at length at KYM.

In KYM's terms, the phrase went viral, and the practice of reworking it became a meme; it has its own page in the database (Know Your Meme, "I am aware of all Internet traditions"). A now-dormant blog called *I am aware of all Internet traditions* preserves yet more examples of edited images captioned with versions of Vanderleun's famous phrase. In many of these images, created first to mock Vanderleun's perceived arrogance and then to perpetuate the growing joke, "tradition" refers to exactly the material and practices cataloged on sites like KYM: Serious Cat (noted above), the LOLrus (see Lynne McNeill's chapter in this volume), Badger Badger Badger, "I Hate Iceland," Rickrolling, and more.[30]

. *The Poor Man* blog (thepoorman.net) posted an excellent example of how Internet traditions have been used to construct memes. Styled like a motivational poster, the image features a white cat surrounded by visual quotations of various memes (Rick Astley of Rickrolling, the Dancing Baby, etc.) and captioned above with "I am aware of all Internet traditions" and below with "ALL INTERNET TRADITIONS: I am aware of them" (The Poor Man).[31] Says one commenter in the attached thread, "Internet tradition cat is traditional." And on the KYM page dedicated to tracing the history of the "I am aware of all Internet traditions" meme itself, commenter "Richie McNuggets" remarks, "this meme is traditional and been made aware of by all" (Know Your Meme, "I am aware of all Internet traditions"). The grammar is shaky, but the message is clear: memes are expressions of tradition. If we are keepers of the discipline of tradition, then so are the contributors to the KYM database.

CREATING KNOWLEDGE

We might understand the emergence of sites like KYM, and even those that do not support communities, as part of what William Westerman refers to as the "new knowledge industry [that] exploded across the World Wide Web in the late 1990s" (Westerman 2009, 150). Westerman is interested

---

30   For the uninitiated, these are, respectively: a cycle of visual jokes featuring a walrus or elephant seal bereft of his favorite bucket; a looped Flash animation featuring badgers doing knee bends; changes rung on a news clip of a Scottish traveler venting his frustration at being stranded by the April 2010 volcanic eruption of Iceland's Eyjafjallajökull, and the practice of redirecting unsuspecting web surfers to videos of Rick Astley singing "Never Gonna Give You Up." For more information, consult the Know Your Meme database.

31   This redundant sentence structure is itself a traditional formula indexed at KYM.

in Wikipedia, which definitely produces knowledge; and unlike KYM and Snopes, it also hosts original research. Nonetheless, Wikipedia and sites of folklore curation are part of this same larger picture. However, Wikipedia is also part of another, much longer history of the creation of encyclopedias that stretches back to the eighteenth century and beyond. The *Encyclopaedia Britannica* itself has been published since 1768; the *Chambers' Cyclopædia* is even older. In contrast, the production of collections and studies of folklore in the West boomed in the nineteenth century, when literacy expanded and printing technology became cheaper, and again now, as technical and economic barriers to online publication have been radically lowered.

Some curation of folklore occurred on Usenet, before mass access to the Internet and before the web and the graphical user interface that made the online world more practically accessible to people without an Information Technology background or university affiliation. The newsgroup alt.folklore.urban (AFU) supported a community "predicated on the production and transmission of information" (Tepper 1997, 47). AFU even maintained a long list of urban legends with information on their background and truth value (the FAQ)—exactly the information that Snopes now manages in website form. In fact, Snopes grew out of AFU, where "snopes" was merely the handle of a particularly prolific contributor whose real name was David P. Mikkelsen. He would go on to establish Snopes once the web took over from Usenet as the primary environment in which everyday people experienced the online world.[32] The shift from Usenet to the web has significantly affected user access. AFU resembled a club of amateur antiquarians holding semiprivate meetings at which they discussed their interest in certain items of lore. To become aware of their existence, one would have had to have been moving in certain computer-savvy circles; and it was difficult to stumble across them.

As closely as the AFU newsgroup's FAQ resembled Snopes's collection, the file was only available via FTP, and retrieving it required a level of technical proficiency that not everyone had. The FAQ was not comparable to a conventionally published collection of folklore. Snopes.com, on the other hand, publishes in a form easily accessible both technically and economically to a much-larger audience than AFU ever had. That audience is web-literate just as the emergent bourgeoisie of the nineteenth century

---

32   Something like the alt.folklore.urban community survives in the Snopes discussion
      forums at message.snopes.com. Participants have no editorial control over the main
      site, but they engage in wide-ranging discussion of urban legends.

was conventionally literate and able to consume the curated collections of its own day. Snopes is an example of how a small scholarly society could become a major curation project after moving to the web. The projects featured on other sites discussed here could only have emerged in the Web 2.0 environment. This boom is different from the one in the nineteenth century; instead of learned individuals going out among the supposedly tradition-bearing collective to collect material they will organize and publish for a newly expanded literate audience, the collective collects, organizes, and publishes the stuff for a newly expanded computer-literate audience. Technology and social factors have caught up with the metaphor Joseph Jacobs used when he wrote that "[t]he folk is a publishing syndicate" (Jacobs 1893, 230).[33]

ARTIFACTUALIZATION VS. PERFORMANCE

Snopes, Urban Dictionary, Know Your Meme, and the rest of the sites discussed here artifactualize vernacular expression by defining the borders of those expressions and moving them outside of the channel commonly conceived of as tradition. Snopes lies outside the legend conduit. The Mikkelsens do not *tell* legend and rumor or do the online equivalent (i.e., firing it unbidden at the inboxes of the unsuspecting). They do offer subscriptions to a weekly e-mail newsletter, but it is just that: news of updates to the site. Urban Dictionary and similar sites are not venues for using slang by employing it in sentences as part of a communicative act. Slang does appear in complete sentences in some entries, but these are only examples of potential usage or, in the case of the Online Slang Dictionary, real usage lifted out of its context.[34] Know Your Meme does not deploy image macros to add nuance to conversion, as when a chatboard participant tells his interlocutors to lighten up by posting a version of Serious Cat. To find such "authentic" usage, one must go to the KYM forums, where conversation is taking place. Just like collections of folklore, and just like

---

33   I am grateful to Kimberly Ball for this reference.

34   Showing a piece of slang in an invented example is analogous to exhibiting any other ethnographic object *in situ*, as the phrase is explained by Barbara Kirshenblatt-Gim-blett (Kirschenblatt-Gimblett 1998, 20). Where a genuine example of use is shown, the entirety of the quoted material is the ethnographic object. Once either example is accompanied by a definition, fitted into a classification, or explained in any way (as all words and phrases on the sites discussed here are), its presentation becomes an exhibit *in context*, also per Kirshenblatt-Gimblett.

scholarly articles that quote the data they analyze, these sites pull material out of the stream of "tradition" and insert it into the handing-on that is the practice of curation. As Andreas Faye did in 1833, they turn vernacular expressions into objects of discussion among reasonable people.

When we complain about the difficulty of finding traditional forms "in context" online, we may be demanding the privilege of artifactualizing the stuff ourselves. By failing to recognize the artifactualizing discourse of the individuals and collectives who maintain and contribute to sites like Snopes and KYM, we implicitly discredit and subordinate it relative to our own, professional discourse. However, doing so goes against the spirit of some of the most influential scholarship of recent decades. Charles L. Briggs has explored how the performance turn and the rise of ethnopoetics has brought with it calls for folklorists to handle their data lightly, resist asserting the power that comes with artifactualizing the expressions of others, and "allow the voices of actual native people to emerge, to speak out for themselves" (Sherzer 1990, 14; quoted in Briggs 1993, 419). If we follow through on this, and if "the intended shape of the text" (Hymes 1981, 7) that ethnopoetics seeks to reveal is itself a work of vernacular scholarship like Snopes or KYM, then the logic of ethnopoetic practice would seem to demand that we accord equal status to the discourse of which it forms a part.

Given all of the above, it could be argued that the word *curation* is a poor choice. Using it might import the hierarchies implicit in the history of the word and its close relatives.[35] To wit, a legal curator has the care of things belonging to children, the insane, the incompetent. A curate (the old title for vicar) is a clergyman who has the care of souls belonging to laymen. Even the self-styled curators of the new media offer us their selections from the informational flood because we are unable to find the quality news on our own. The implication throughout is that curators deal with things for people who, despite having a close relationship to those things, cannot be trusted with them. This is probably not how most contemporary folklorists would like to characterize themselves and their work. Nonetheless, I think

---

35   Properly, there are two words forming *curator*, both derived from the Latin *curare* but brought to English by different routes. Through Old French come the noun *curate* and related words having to do with religion, legal guardianship, and healing. Direct from Latin comes *curator*, from which the back-formed verb *curate* and *curation*—the vocabulary of art and museum curation. For more details, see entries for *curator*, *curation*, and *curate* in the *Oxford English Dictionary*.

the ghosts of hierarchy have a place here. Just as the curators of the British Museum face claims from Greece on the Elgin Marbles, the curators of KYM are charged by the protean masses of the Internet with "stealing [their] memes" and profiting from them.[36] For every curator of tradition that emerges, there spring up ten creators and users of that tradition who understand his caretaking as appropriation or theft. The seeming flaws in the word *curation* might serve to nod toward that fact.

In writing this essay, I am again privileging my own professional discourse and making an object of the discourse of others. As usual, there is no way out of the reflexive loop, and, as usual, we must carry on trying to say something meaningful anyway. In order to do so in the modern world, however, we ought to recognize that something analogous to the boom of collection and publication that signaled the foundation of our field in the nineteenth century is taking place once more, this time on the web instead of on paper. MacEdward Leach has written that the Grimms have been "referred to as the fathers of folklore because they themselves did systematic collecting and brought their finds to the desks and tried to analyze, classify, and explain them" (Leach 1968, 17). Whether or not you believe the Grimms in particular deserve the honor, taking the creation of the object of study out of context characterized folklore collections and allowed the establishment of the discipline.

The heirs to the Grimms' project are systematically collecting, analyzing, classifying, and explaining online. The medium matters, too; with the interactivity and collaboration supported by Web 2.0, the division between collector and informant is nowhere near as clear as it was when the Grimms published their books. Chatboards and comment threads permit near real-time discussions in virtual space instead of paper journals circulating in physical space. The number of people involved is significant. We see not merely the efforts of a handful of "amateur scholars" applying the methods of the professionals but a widespread folk practice. As we go forward in studying the nature of tradition in all its senses—process, expression, and construction—as it manifests itself on the web, we should be aware that not only are we not the only keepers of the discipline of tradition, but we may not even be the keepers of the only discipline of tradition.

---

36   See æ: Operation Stop Their Scheme for background on the vendetta. Be advised that the content is extremely offensive.

ACKNOWLEDGMENTS

I am grateful to Trevor J. Blank, Robert Glenn Howard, Kimberly Ball, Ray Cashman, and my anonymous reviewers for thoughtful comments at various stages of this essay's production. Thanks also go to Dorry Noyes for taking the time to compare ideas—and over a long weekend, no less. All ill-considered elements of the essay are, of course, my own.

REFERENCES

æ: Operation Stop Their Scheme. n.d. æ: Encyclopedia Dramatica. https://encyclopediadramatica.se/Operation:_Stop_Their_Scheme.

Alekseevsky, Mikhail. n.d. "The Anthropology of Internet/Studies on Internet Folklore." http://mdalekseevsky.narod.ru/biblio-Internet.html.

Alexa Internet, Inc. 2010. "onlineslangdictionary.com Site Info." Alexa: The Web Information Company. Accessed July 31. http://www.alexa.com/siteinfo/onlineslangdictionary.com#.

Alexa Internet, Inc. 2011. "snopes.com Site Info." Alexa: The Web Information Company. Accessed February. http://www.alexa.com/siteinfo/snopes.com.

Alexa Internet, Inc. 2011. "urbandictionary.com Site Info." Alexa: The Web Information Company. Accessed February. http://www.alexa.com/siteinfo/urbandictionary.com.

Anderson, Benedict. 1991 [1983]. *Imagined Communities: Reflections on the Origins and Spread of Nationalism*. New York: Verso Press.

Barry, Phillips, and Fannie Hardy Eckstorm. 1930. "What Is Tradition?" *Bulletin of the Folk-Song Society of the Northeast* 1: 2–3.

Bauman, Richard. 1975. "Verbal Art as Performance." *American Anthropologist* 77 (2): 290–311. http://dx.doi.org/10.1525/aa.1975.77.2.02a00030.

Blank, Trevor J., ed. 2009. *Folklore and the Internet: Vernacular Expression in a Digital World*. Logan: Utah State University Press.

Briggs, Charles L. 1993. "Metadiscursive Practices and Scholarly Authority in Folkloristics." *Journal of American Folklore* 106 (422): 387–434. http://dx.doi.org/10.2307/541905.

Bronner, Simon J. 2009. "Digitizing and Virtualizing Folklore." In *Folklore and the Internet: Vernacular Expression in a Digital World*, ed. Trevor J. Blank, 21–66. Logan: Utah State University Press.

Browne, Thomas. 1672. *Pseudodoxia Epidemica, or Enquiries into Very Many Received Tenents and Commonly Presumed Truths*. 6th ed. London. http://penelope.uchicago.edu/pseudodoxia/pseudo1.html.

Bruns, Axel. 2008. *Blogs, Wikipedia, Second Life, and Beyond: From Production to Produsage*. Digital Formations 45. New York: Peter Lang.

Cashman, Ray, Tom Mould, and Pravina Shukla, eds. 2011. *The Individual and Tradition: Folkloristic Perspectives*. Bloomington: Indiana University Press.

Crowston, Kevin, and Marie Williams. 2000. "Reproduced and Emergent Genres of Communication on the World Wide Web." *Information Society* 16 (3): 201–15. http://dx.doi.org/10.1080/01972240050133652.

Dawkins, Richard. 1976. *The Selfish Gene*. New York: Oxford University Press.

Dégh, Linda. 1999. "Collecting Legends Today: Welcome to the Bewildering Maze of the Internet." In *Europäische Ethnologie und Folklore im internationalen Kontext: Festschrift für Leander Petzoldt zum 65. Geburtstag*, ed. Ingo Schneider, 55–66. Berlin: Lang.

Drout, Michael D. C. 2006. "A Meme-Based Approach to Oral Traditional Theory." *Oral Tradition* 21 (2): 269–94. http://dx.doi.org/10.1353/ort.2007.0002.

Drout, Michael D. C. 2010. *How Tradition Works: A Meme-Based Cultural Poetics of the Anglo-Saxon Tenth Century.* Tempe: Arizona Center for Medieval and Renaissance Studies.

Dundes, Alan. 1980. *Interpreting Folklore.* Bloomington: Indiana University Press.

Emery, David. n.d. "David Emery: Urban Legends Guide." About.com: Urban Legends. http://urbanlegends.about.com/bio/David-Emery-1417.htm.

Faye, Andreas. 1833. *Norske Sagn.* Arendal: Gald.

Fialkova, Larisa, and Maria Yelenevskaya. 2001. "Ghosts in the Cyber World: An Analysis of Folklore Sites on the Internet." *Fabula* 42 (1/2): 64–89. http://dx.doi.org/10.1515/fabl.2001.011.

Foote, Monica. 2007. "Userpicks: Cyber Folk Art in the Early 21st Century." *Folklore Forum* 37 (1): 27–38.

Fox, William S. 2007 [1983]. "Computerized Creation and Diffusion of Folkloric Materials." *Folklore Forum* 37(1): 5–14. https://scholarworks.iu.edu/dspace/handle/2022/3235. Originally published in *Folklore Forum* 16(1): 5–20.

Frank, Russell. 2004. "When the Going Gets Tough, the Tough Go Photoshopping: September 11 and the Newslore of Vengeance and Victimization." *New Media & Society* 6 (5): 633–58. http://dx.doi.org/10.1177/146144804047084.

Frank, Russell. 2009. "The Forward as Folklore: Studying E-Mailed Humor." In *Folklore and the Internet: Vernacular Expression in a Digital World*, ed. Trevor J. Blank, 98–122. Logan: Utah State University Press.

Franklin, Adrian. 2001. "Performing Live: An Interview with Barbara Kirshenblatt-Gimblett." *Tourist Studies* 1 (3): 211–32. http://dx.doi.org/10.1177/146879760100100301.

Gehl, Robert. 2009. "YouTube as Archive: Who Will Curate This Digital Wunderkammer?" *International Journal of Cultural Studies* 12 (1): 43–60. http://dx.doi.org/10.1177/1367877908098854.

Grimm, Jacob, and Wilhelm Grimm. 1816–1818. *Deutsche Sagen.* 2 vols. Berlin.

Grimm, Jacob, and Wilhelm Grimm. 1977 [1891]. *Deutsche Sagen.* 3rd ed. Berlin. Reprinted in facsimile by Ayer.

Grimm, Jacob, and Wilhelm Grimm. 1981. *The German Legends of the Brothers Grimm.* Trans. Donald Ward. Philadelphia: Institute for the Study of Human Issues.

Grudin, Jonathan. 1994. "Computer-Supported Cooperative Work: History and Focus." *Computer* 27 (5): 19–26. http://dx.doi.org/10.1109/2.291294.

Handler, Richard, and Jocelyn Linnekin. 1984. "Tradition, Genuine or Spurious." *Journal of American Folklore* 97 (385): 273–90. http://dx.doi.org/10.2307/540610.

Heath, Chip, Chris Bell, and Emily Sternberg. Dec 2001. "Emotional Selection in Memes: The Case of Urban Legends." *Journal of Personality and Social Psychology* 81 (6): 1028–41. http://dx.doi.org/10.1037/0022-3514.81.6.1028. Medline:11761305

Heffernan, Virginia. 2009. "Street Smart: Urban Dictionary." *New York Times*, July 5. http://www.nytimes.com/2009/07/05/magazine/05FOB-medium-t.html?_r=1.

Heyd, Theresa. 2008. *Email Hoaxes: Form, Function, Genre Ecology.* Amsterdam: John Benjamins.

Heyd, Theresa. 2009. "A Model for Describing 'New' and 'Old' Properties of CMC Genres: The Case of Digital Folklore." In *Genres in the Internet: Issues in the Theory of Genre*, 239–62. Pragmatics & Beyond: New Series (P&B) 188. Amsterdam: Benjamins.

Hobsbawm, Eric, and Terence Ranger, eds. 1983. *The Invention of Tradition.* Cambridge, UK: Cambridge University Press.

Hotten, John Camden. 1859. *Modern Cant, Slang and Vulgar Words . . . With Glossaries of Two Secret Languages Spoken by the Wandering Tribes of London. . . .* London.

Hotten, John Camden. 1872. *The Slang Dictionary; Or, The Vulgar Words, Street Phrases, and "Fast" Expressions of High and Low Society. . . .* 3rd ed. London.

Howard, Robert Glenn. 2008. "The Vernacular Web of Participatory Media." *Critical Studies in Media Communication* 25 (5): 490–513. http://dx.doi. org/10.1080/15295030802468065.

Howe, Jeff. 2006. "The Rise of Crowdsourcing." *Wired* 14 (6). http://www.wired.com/ wired/archive/14.06/crowds.html.

Howe, Jeff. 2008. *Crowdsourcing: Why the Power of the Crowd Is Driving the Future of Business.* New York: Crown Business.

Hymes, Dell H. 1981. *"In Vain I Tried to Tell You": Essays in Native American Ethnopoetics.* Studies in Native American Literature 1. Philadelphia: University of Pennsylvania Press.

Jacobs, Joseph. 1893. "The Folk." *Folklore* 4 (2): 233–38. http://dx.doi.org/10.1080/00155 87X.1893.9720155.

Kennedy, Krista A. 2009. *Textual Curators and Writing Machines: Authorial Agency in Encyclopedias, Print to Digital.* PhD diss., University of Minnesota, Minneapolis.

Kibby, Marjorie. 2005. "Email Forwardables: Folklore in the Age of the Internet." *New Media & Society* 7: 770–90.

Kirshenblatt-Gimblett, Barbara. 1998. *Destination Culture Tourism, Museums, and Heritage.* Berkeley: University of California Press.

Know Your Meme. 2011. "About Know Your Meme." Know Your Meme. http://knowyourmeme.com/about#.TeKRRkcs2So.

Know Your Meme. 2010. "Frequently Asked Questions." Know Your Meme Forums: General. http://knowyourmeme.com/forums/general/topics/3937-frequently-asked-questions.

Know Your Meme. n.d. "Bra Status Updates." Know Your Meme Database. http://knowyourmeme.com/memes/bra-status-updates.

Know Your Meme. n.d. "I am aware of all Internet traditions." Know Your Meme Database. http://knowyourmeme.com/memes/i-am-aware-of-all-Internet-traditions.

Lawyers Guns & Money. n.d. *Lawyers Guns & Money* (blog). http://www.lawyersgunsmoney-blog.com/. Previously at http://lefarkins.blogspot.com.

Leach, MacEdward. 1968. "The Men Who Made Folklore a Scholarly Discipline." In *Our Living Traditions: An Introduction to American Folklore,* ed. Tristam Potter Coffin, 15–23. New York: Basic Books.

Menning, Chris. 2009. Discussion board post, March 26. Know Your Meme: Meme Research. http://knowyourmeme.com/forums/meme-research/topics/33-what-criteria-should-be-considered-when-submitting-a-meme-entry.

Menning, Chris. 2010. Discussion board post, July 27. Know Your Meme: Meme Research http://knowyourmeme.com/forums/site-related/topics/5743-the-database-is-no-place-to-get-self-referential.

Mould, Tom. 2005. "The Paradox of Traditionalization: Negotiating the Past in Choctaw Prophetic Discourse." *Journal of Folklore Research* 42(3): 255–94.

newcurator. 2010. You Are Not a Curator. *new curator.* March 9. http://newcurator. com/2010/03/you-are-not-a-curator.

Noyes, Dorothy. 2009. "Tradition: Three Traditions." *Journal of Folklore Research* 46 (3): 233–68. http://dx.doi.org/10.2979/JFR.2009.46.3.233.

Oring, Elliott. 2003. *Engaging Humor.* Urbana: University of Illinois Press.

Oring, Elliott. 2009. Untitled contribution to forum "Tradition in the 21st Century: Locating the Role of the Past in the Future." Presented at the American Folklore Society Annual Meeting, Boise, ID, October 21–24.

Peckham, Aaron. 2005. *Urban Dictionary: Fularious Street Slang Defined.* Kansas City, MO: Andrews McMeel.
Peckham, Aaron. 2007. *Mo' Urban Dictionary: Ridonkulous Street Slang Defined.* Kansas City, MO: Andrews McMeel.
Pimple, Kenneth D. 1996. "The Meme-ing of Folklore." *Journal of Folklore Research* 33 (3): 236–40.
Reno, Denis Porto. 2007. "YouTube, o mediador ciberespacial da folkcomunicação." *Revista Latina de Comunicación Social* 62: 190–6.
Revak, Kelly. 2010. "'You're Banned': Computer-Mediated Folk Games in Internet Forums." Paper presented at the Western States Folklore Society Annual Conference, Salem, Oregon, April 15–17.
Rosenbaum, Steve. 2009. "Can 'Curation' Save Media." *Business Insider*, April 3. http://www.businessinsider.com/can-curation-save-media-2009-4.
Rosenbaum, Steven. 2011. *Curation Nation: How to Win in a World Where Consumers Are Creators.* New York: McGraw-Hill.
Roth, Klaus. 2009. "Erzählen im Internet." In *Erzählkultur: Beiträge zur kulturwissenschaftlichen Erzählforschung; Hans-Jörg Uther zum 65 Geburtstag,* ed. Rolf Wilhelm Brednich, 101–20. Berlin: de Gruyter. http://dx.doi.org/10.1515/9783110214727.2.101
Sherzer, Joel. 1990. *Verbal Art in San Blas: Kuna Culture through Its Discourse.* Cambridge, UK: Cambridge University Press.
Schrempp, Gregory. 2009. "Taking the Dawkins Challenge, or the Dark Side of the Meme." *Journal of Folklore Research* 46 (1): 91–100. http://dx.doi.org/10.2979/JFR.2009.46.1.91.
Shifman, Limor. 2007. "Humor in the Age of Digital Reproduction: Continuity and Change in Internet-Based Comic Texts." *International Journal of Communication* 1: 187–209.
Snopes. 2007. "The Evangelical Prez." Urban Legend Reference Pages. Glurge Gallery. http://www.snopes.com/glurge/bushpray.asp.
Snopes. 1995–2011. "Snopes FAQ." Urban Legend Reference Pages. http://www.snopes.com/info/faq.asp.
Stelter, Brian. 2010. "Debunkers of Fiction Sift the Net." *New York Times*, April 4. http://www.nytimes.com/2010/04/05/technology/05snopes.html.
Tepper, Michele. 1997. "Usenet Communities and the Cultural Politics of Information." In *Internet Culture*, ed. David Porter, 39–54. New York: Routledge.
Terdiman, Daniel. 2011. "Cheezburger Network Buys Know Your Meme." CNET News. Geek Gestalt, March 28. http://news.cnet.com/8301-13772_3-20048067-52.html.
The Poor Man. 2008. "Make Every Day Internet Traditions Awareness Week." *The Poor Man* (blog). http://thepoorman.net/2008/06/18/make-every-day-Internet-traditions-awareness-week.
Thoms, William. 1999 [1846]. "Folk-Lore." In *International Folkloristics*, ed. Alan Dundes, 9–14. Lanham, MD: Rowman & Littlefield. (Originally published in *Athenaeum* 982: 862–63.)
Vander Wal, Thomas. 2007. Folksonomy Coinage and Definition. *vanderwal.net.* February 2. http://vanderwal.net/folksonomy.html.
Voß, Jakob. 2007. "Tagging, Folksonomy & Co—Renaissance of Manual Indexing?" arXiv preprint cs/0701072, 1–12. 10th International Symposium for Information Science. Cologne, January 10. http://arxiv.org/abs/cs/0701072.
Walker, Rob. 2010. "Taking Web Humor Seriously, Sort Of." *New York Times*, July 12. http://www.nytimes.com/2010/07/18/magazine/18ROFL-t.html?_r=1&ref=global-home.

Watanabe, Mark. 1998. "Site-Seeing—The Urban Legends Reference Pages." *Seattle Times.* May 3. http://community.seattletimes.nwsource.com/archive/?date=19980503&slug=2748530.

Westerman, William. 2009. "Epistemology, the Sociology of Knowledge, and the *Wikipedia* Userbox Controversy." In *Folklore and the Internet: Vernacular Expression in a Digital World*, ed. Trevor J. Blank, 123–58. Logan: Utah State University Press.

Zipes, Jack. 2008. "What Makes a Repulsive Frog So Appealing: Memetics and Fairy Tales." *Journal of Folklore Research* 45 (2): 109–43. http://dx.doi.org/10.2979/JFR.2008.45.2.109.

WEBSITES CITED

æ: Encylopedia Dramatica. http://encyclopediadramatica.ss.

Cheezburger, Inc. http://cheezburger.com.

Cool Slang. http://coolslang.com.

Crowdsourcing. http://crowdsourcing.typepad.com/cs/.

Internet Slang Dictionary & Translator. http://www.noslang.com.

KnowYour Meme. http://knowyourmeme.com/.

NetLingo: The Internet Dictionary. http://www.netlingo.com/index.php.

The Online Slang Dictionary. http://onlineslangdictionary.com.

Slangster. http://www.slangster.dk/.

Slanguroðabókin. http://slangur.snara.is.

Snopes. http://www.snopes.com.

6

Trajectories of Tradition
Following Tradition into a New Epoch of Human Culture

Tok Thompson

> *"To defy the laws of tradition is a crusade only of the brave!"*
>
> —Les Claypool

TRADITION IS A NEXUS OF THE PAST, THE present, and the prospective future, a place where human agency engages with some of the more substantive constructs of the past. As Henry Glassie once wrote, "(h)istory, culture, and the human actor meet in tradition" (Glassie 1995, 409). Today the world's societies are undergoing an unprecedented era of rapid change, in large part brought on by new communicative technologies. This opens up new ruptures and fissures in our relationships to the past and, alongside these, new possibilities for rearticulating the past for our present and future selves. The need for critical understanding of the concept of tradition may therefore increase in importance in our postmodern age as people create new linkages with the past.

Due to the shifting of traditions—in turn due to the rapid technological and social changes in the last two hundred years—and the current ongoing change brought on by the digital revolution, coming to understand the word *tradition* is both tricky and necessary. In this chapter, I examine tradition as a "living word"—a word that is constantly adapted and changing in a dynamic, productive language—a word that has been around before, during, and after modernity. With each epoch, tradition has been shaped in part by different communication technologies: from live performances, manuscripts, and printed literature to, most recently,

DOI: 10.7330/9780874218992.c06

digital traditions in the online realm. In following this line of reasoning, I propose a workable definition of tradition based on performative models, which, although borrowing heavily from folkloric theories, should apply to the concept in the most general sense, including literary traditions, cinematic traditions, and online traditions.

In searching for elemental meanings of multifaceted words, core definitions remain important as a sort of anchor for all the various meanings and reinterpretations; I think it is safe to say, as a most basic definition, that something absolutely, completely new cannot be considered traditional—a starting point, perhaps, but a limited one, since even most "new" things (a new prophecy, a new novel, a freshly coined word or joke) seem to have connections to other things (prophecies, novels, words or jokes) in the past. The measurement of "how original" a particular piece might be is often held in reverse correlation to its connections to the past.

When something *can* become traditional is a thornier question. Most of our actions have their counterparts in the past, but this does not mean that nearly everything is traditional. In a recent article, Jack Santino (2009) carefully delineates between etic and emic perspectives in tradition and ritual, arguing that what one person or group considers to be traditional might not be considered so by the next.[1] According to Santino, this implies that tradition (along with some other terms he explores, like *ritual*) must be viewed as at least slightly self-conscious: in calling something tradition, we are consciously evoking what happened in the past in our present activity, underlining the activity's rhetorical relevance and importance. As with much of folklore, traditions are self-conscious performances that frequently involve a good deal of questions about identity (such as whose performances are we referencing?). Hence, we have national traditions, religious traditions, family traditions, and even office traditions or online group traditions. When we celebrate traditions, we choose which traditions to celebrate and how to adapt them in the present, for the sake of the future.

Yet not all traditions are performed in the same way. One major differentiation has to do with the media of communication through which traditions are performed. Folklorists tend to focus on live events, yet we can certainly point to other traditions outside of this category, such

---

1   This continues a long line of anthropological inquiry into emic and etic categories, as chronicled and explained in Marvin Harris's (1976), "History and Significance of the Emic/Etic Distinction."

as literary, cinematic, or online traditions. This indicates the important role that communicative technologies play in the construction of the meaning of tradition, a role that will be investigated at length in this chapter. New communicative technologies thus necessitate a new, and more encompassing, view of tradition and perhaps hold out the possibility for transcending the long-dominant "tradition versus modern" binary.

Communicative technologies have changed greatly and helped usher in whole epochs of human history. The introduction of literacy heralded a new age of humanity where words, and thus time, could be inscribed into material objects. Even more important was the much later transposition of literary accounts into mechanical modes of reproduction, leading to widespread literacy, industrialization, and culture industries, generally.[2] More recently, the digital revolution has changed the rules of the game once again, allowing for a reemergence of participatory culture mediated through digital networks. The effects of this new technological revolution will likely be more profound than those of even the printing press—which is to say, if the printing press and the mechanical revolution gave us modernity, then the digital revolution has pushed us quickly into postmodernity. What will become of traditions and what will traditions become in this new age will be a central concern of our time.

This is not to say that traditions are doomed to die out—not at all. Today, a quick Internet search for "tradition" reveals all sorts of traditions being discussed, including national traditions, school traditions, regional traditions, sporting traditions, literary traditions, and political traditions. What sort of theory of tradition can be offered that can account for such a powerful word, in all its many manifestations? Given the complexities of such a task, in this chapter I strive to strip "tradition" down to its basics in order to better understand the outlines of the word. In doing so, I propose a basic definition based on a performative approach that works within folklore studies and beyond in order to continue an engagement in productive interdisciplinary dialogue on the important topic of tradition in the twenty-first century.

---

2   For Western societies, tradition after the printing press and the Industrial Revolution came to take on particular connotations, often relating to an imagined time before modernity and widespread literacy—namely, before the rupture of modernity. For an extensive theoretical account on the romanticization of tradition as "premodern," see Abrahams (1993) and Anttonen (2005).

WORDS AND DISCIPLINES

Few concepts are more central the discipline of folklore than that of tradition. Tradition, after all, is the backbone of everything that folklorists study—all folklore performances build on traditions and all folklore is traditional.[3] Yet the words are not equivalent; as a concept, tradition can relate to other disciplines: the literary, legal, and cinematic traditions and their like are not commonly considered folklore. Still, the discipline of folklore has a uniquely singular interest in traditions. Given this we may ask: What can the discipline of folklore offer in terms of a general theory of tradition? To better understand the many complexities, I find it necessary to engage in a careful and critical review of the word itself.

WORDS AND CHANGE

"Plant them, they will grow; watch them waver so
I'll always be a word man; better than a bird man."

James Douglas Morrison

Tradition is, in its most primary category, a word. While perhaps obvious, this dedication to remembering the linguistic constructs of our theoretical toolkit is necessary in order to set a basis for disentangling the rather complex package of "tradition." Such an approach utilizes the views of philosopher Ludwig Wittgenstein, who has been widely heralded as correcting a philosophical interpretive system with roots back to Plato's *eidos* and his postulated "ideal forms" that our words strive to describe. Following a lead introduced in linguistic anthropology, Wittgenstein (1958) was able to show that, rather, the reverse is true: words are used to create categories, boundaries, definitions. It is not that there is an ideal "tree" for which our words strive but rather that our word *tree* tries to accomplish a boxing-off of the world—a creation of a category called "tree"—in order to deal with multiple real-world

---

3   Literature on this subject is voluminous and informative, documenting the many ways in which the word has been employed, often nearly as a synonym for folklore. See, for example, Anttonen (2005), and Jones (2000). Folklorists study traditions: while it is true that individual performers often add new developments and insert their own agency within these traditionalist praxes (for a discussion, see Kirshenblatt-Gimblett 1989), the brunt of folkloristic study has not focused on these expressions of individual agency (and "authorship") but on aspects of the performance that are shared with others.

existences of somewhat related objects and actions. Confusion can set in when people fail to understand the power of the word in creating the category and confuse the symbol with that which it represents. Definitions, as always, are constitutively important, and perhaps nowhere more so than on a word like *tradition*, a word of great power and authority.

Tradition is a word that came into use at certain times and in certain languages; it is a word that has been consistently reinterpreted and changed in nuance and affiliation, depending on historical circumstances. Change, of course, is an essential aspect of any word in any living language, but the very nature of the word *tradition* invites a particularly close relationship to continued practice versus change. People pretend that words are stable, but they are not. Words have meaning only in usage; *tradition* is a word that refers to that very concept—the idea of a "real" past, yet one that is always changing and only existing in some enacted present moment.[4]

Tradition has been exported as a term to many parts of the world (including many Indo-European linguistic exportations), along with the spread of English, French, Italian, and other European languages. It translates somewhat easily into some other languages, and not so easily into others. It is a Romantic word, laden with manifold heartfelt connotations. As a word, its rhetorical power and Romantic bases make it a bit of a pied piper, leading countless starry-eyed followers down wayward paths. Many people wave the flag of "tradition" or try to assert traditionality in various situations, displaying the inherently social aspect of the word and its performative qualities. It is perhaps no surprise, then, that no other discipline has studied traditions to the degree and intensity as folklore studies; yet, it seems to be the case that folklore has not critically examined this category sufficiently, perhaps due to the sociopolitics of the discipline itself.

Folklore studies has played a large role in determining what people think of tradition, yet folklorists have not engaged extensively in boundary-making definitions of the term. Dan Ben-Amos complained that in American folklore studies, "tradition has been a term to think with, not to think about" (Ben-Amos 1984, 97). While some critical work on the term has appeared in recent years (Anttonen 2005; Ó Giolláin 2000), there is little agreement over its basic usable definitions. As Michael Owen Jones (2000) notes, folklorists have

---

4 Further, there are traditions of using the word *tradition*, which makes the inherently adaptable aspect of words and languages all the more complex. Such a line of inquiry forces the scholar to consider not only the word itself but the interplay between history writ large and the history of the word.

frequently employed the term to help define folklore but have left this key term itself largely undefined.

In spite of the word's importance, we can see that folklorists have not extensively problematized it. What *has* happened is that the view of tradition has slowly shifted, along with the discipline itself, toward being thought more in terms of its performances. From Carl von Sydow's (1948) tradition bearers, through the communication-centered approaches of Kenneth Goldstein (1971), Dell Hymes (1975), Dennis Tedlock (1983), Barre Toelken (1969), and others (see Bauman and Briggs 1990), folklorists and anthropologists have increasingly found tradition in the performances of people. As anthropologist Jocelyn Linnekin puts it, "Symbolically constructed traditions are therefore not inauthentic; rather, all traditions—Western and indigenous—are invented, in that they are symbolically constructed in the present and reflect contemporary concerns and purposes rather than a passively inherited legacy" (Linnekin 1991, 447).

The performative study of such symbolic constructions reveals the social contestations over the appropriate scope of the word and the claim that various social actors have to that social construction. Such contests may come to light especially in liminal areas—border zones—where definitions are often forged and where personal performative agents press their own cases as to words' definitions ("that's not how you're supposed to do it") or appropriate geographical scopes ("around here, hunting alligators is a time-honored tradition"). Such liminal zones are uncertain, contestive, and productive, forging the boundaries—the cleavages—between this and that.[5] This is how all words work, although in the case of tradition, such contestations frequently take on additional significance. Tradition, rather than being a word representing a thing, is clearer when viewed as representing a social process, enacted by individual agents.

PROPOSED DEFINITION

So what is the *this* and *that* of tradition? How can we productively define it? I propose a minimal, straightforward definition of "tradition" as

---

5   On this, see Pierre Bourdieu and the ideas of limits of meanings (Bourdieu 1973, 124–25), or Lévi-Strauss's (1968 [1962]) ideas on binary thought. Observing the process of determining what is traditional and what is not can reveal much of the social-cultural matrices at play, put into action via the interpretive and creative role of the social agent.

a mode of action that re-presents the past.[6] Tradition must be *performed*, and in its various performances, tradition refers to, re-collects, and re-articulates the past. This is not to say that tradition *is* the past but rather a recollection *from* the past, articulated by social agents and performed at some present moment. For example, a "very traditional" wedding in the United States does not mean that it is necessarily an accurate replication of a wedding from two hundred years ago but that the performance will invoke several key motifs and themes from yesteryear, such as the bride wearing white. *How* traditional a performance is may often indicate how many themes and motifs will likely be retained, perhaps including some generally considered anachronistic (following the US wedding example, a traditional wedding may or may not include the father "giving away" the bride, but a "very traditional" wedding would be much more likely to do so).

Such a minimal, straightforward definition should be applicable to the various sorts of traditions (national, family, literary, office, etc.) as well as the various genres (songs, proverbs, practical jokes, etc.). Also, it is not so broad as to include everything connected with the past. The emphasis on performance, for example, provides a stark contrast with other similar concepts such as heritage. Heritage, with its connotations of "inheritance," seems to presume some kind of inherited relationship to a particular culture (Klein 2001; Lowenthal 1996). One does not have to perform heritage, it just is—or at least is asserted to be. Meanwhile, traditions die out if not performed and ossify if not constantly changing with the times.[7] Similarly, while acknowledging the view that tradition incorporates all folklore, my definition allows for those elements that are not folklore but nonetheless clearly traditional.

To be sure, any usable definition must also consider the modes of communication through which words are expressed. Words are not only expressed in natural spoken language but through other realms of discourse such as mechanical reproduction or digital information. Some things get noticed, some do not; some things get repressed, celebrated, denigrated, and so on. For each performer, and for each group, "tradition" represents something slightly different—a reinterpretation that occurs with each performance, each changing generation, and each cultural milieu. This

---

6   Cf., anthropologist Pascal Boyer describes tradition as a "*type of interaction which results in the repetition of certain communicative events*" (Boyer 1990, 23; italics in the original).

7   I have previously contrasted heritage with tradition in these terms (see Thompson 2006).

intertextual approach toward studying "tradition" also reveals the word's strong ties to various ways of conceptualizing the past, ways that are themselves generated by historical and technological changes and developments and the modes through which language and culture are transmitted.

MODES OF COMMUNICATION: MEDIA AND MESSENGERS

Live Culture

The relationship between the producers of culture and the consumers of culture provides one way of thinking of these different modes. In the realm of folklore, traditions flow generally among all members of society. Although some may be more privileged to speak, relatively little social stratification difference exists between the producers of culture, and the consumers of culture. Everyone, to some degree, helps create the culture. Hence, my diagram would label this as a "horizontal mode" of producing culture. The idea represents the horizontal flow of culture, information, etc., in folklore; transmission is more or less evenly distributed throughout the population and people are both performers and consumers of shared traditions.

There are a few things to note about live, face-to-face interactions and the distribution of culture. One is that culture is always changing and always adapting yet often uses meanings derived from the past. This is how folklore works and this is why folklore is such an important part of nonliterary cultures. One can also note that this is the social and cultural situation into which homo sapiens evolved; newer modes pale in comparison to the time-depth of face-to-face culture. Furthermore, it may well be that in terms of our species we are "built" for face-to-face interactions and that later modes of establishing "tradition" may continue to be less psychologically satisfying than the more primary one of embodied, live social performances. This may be why live performances still rule the roost: from weddings to funerals, to festivals and family traditions, live performances are where tradition is perceived to be at its fullest. This is not to deny the impact of cinematic or literary or legal traditions but rather to suggest that these other, more literary, traditions are less "live" in the senses and, ultimately, in their affect, and perhaps therefore less important in terms of identity. To put it another way: people may be especially moved by the traditions in which they actively participate.

This horizontal mode of folklore still continues, of course, but its authority was gradually overtaken by the development of early literary models that very often imbued written accounts with a sacral (scriptic) quality, witnessed in languages such as Latin, Hebrew, Sanskrit, Ge'ez, Arabic, and others and associated with the super-national organizations of widespread religious institutions (see Anderson 1991). Such "sacred/scripted culture" allowed for a rise of widespread hierarchies and the introduction of a vast differential in social status between those who controlled the sacred/scripted culture and those who did not. Mandarin, although not a priestly language, played a similar institutional role. The archives became a repository for cultural power for those who had access (Lynch 1999).

Industrial Culture

The role of folklore was further supplanted by the technological revolution of the printing press, which heralded mass literacy, and new social rules and regulations more dependent on written records than on folkloric performances (see Emery et al. 1997). In short, with industrialization, and the industrialization of culture, began modernity.

Not surprisingly, perhaps, modernity has often been assumed to oppose tradition. Irish folklorist Diarmuid Ó Giolláin writes that "the modern age is inherently destructive of traditions" (Ó Giolláin 2000, 12). Meanwhile, Finnish folklorist Pertti Anttonen (2005) goes so far as to say that tradition is created as a sort of temporal foil for modernity, as a constructed Other, existing not so much on its own as in a constructed shadow of modernity. Modernity, in Anttonen's view, creates tradition.

Yet both views choose as their focus "traditional folklore"—namely, modernity's view of traditions, reflecting an imagined premodern way of life. At the same time, it remains clear that all sorts of traditions continued unabated in the modern world, with new ones constantly being created as well in the many associations and groups in the lives of everyday people (such as local high school traditions, etc.).

As has been investigated elsewhere, the move to the industrialized, modern world heralded the rise of nations (via such luminaries as Johann Gottfried Herder and the Grimm Brothers) through such media as the printing press and the development of national languages and national discourses.[8] Once culture was industrialized, national citizenship became an

8   See Anderson's (1991) seminal work on this.

increasingly important marker of identity. National languages and national discourses (newspapers, books, and, later, other media) helped create the notion of ethnicity as nationality, the modern ethnonationalism.

The mechanical world's creation of the new age of nations often did so with explicit reference to the premechanical days of yore, using traditions that predated the modernized, mechanized, literary world. In the increasingly literate world, the fascination with folklore reached a fever pitch, with the work of the Brothers Grimm being one of the most perennially popular and influential. Their work explicitly aimed to situate folklore performances as providing the necessary building blocks of national languages and national identities. Industrial, literate, and often cosmopolitan people looked to the preliterate past to help anchor notions of identity. In this way, industrial culture also increasingly consolidated ethnonationalism, frequently co-invoking the ideas of "blood and land" as a basis for political representation in the newly emerging nation-states—the "imagined communities," as Anderson (1991) called them.

Although much of modernity predicated itself on a split with the traditional, we can also see how actual political entities arising from modernity (the modern nation-state) relied on a fascination with ideas of premodern tribal "nations," leading to the birth of the nation-state, in what has been dubbed "ethnogenesis" (Geary 2002). In Europe, the literary elite undertook this project of nation-building after the Reformation and printing press revolution, re-imagining and re-creating stories of ancient tribes and ahistorical times ("once upon a time") from which to form new, "national" identities.

The formation of nations is a moment of inscription—in constitutions, official histories, and the like. This moment of the inscription (and freezing) of tradition is ironic in that the inscription is inherently at odds with living tradition. Still, this connotation cannot contain the core concept of tradition, as one also easily finds references to "modern traditions" and "traditions of progress" (Bronner 1998; Dundes 1969). With all the complexities linking modernity and traditionalism, it is clear that they are not as diametrically opposed as many have assumed.

Forces of modernity relied on appeals to "traditional society" in order to sustain and reinforce their authority, all the while undermining vernacular traditions and systems of authority. Premodern traditions became a favorite topic for much of the "original" and authored arts of painting, music, literature, and the like. Grand old traditions became best-selling bedtime stories for thoroughly modern children. The colonial, nationalist, and postcolonial uses of tradition have been well investigated; such uses often invoke references to the past and the re-articulation and re-creation of tradition.[9] This overlap of politics and folklore (studies and performances) has long been a problematic zone; conservative politicians frequently lay claims to "traditional values" in order to further various political agendas (as per Bronner 1998). In this way, tradition can take on a conservative or even reactionary flavor in common parlance. Folklorism *(folklorismus)* refers to the use of folklore themes taken out of place or context, often molded to advance a political agenda and presented on a national stage (see especially Bendix 1988).

Looking back, we can easily see that live traditions *did* result where traditions (or cultures) and geography overlapped—one found different traditions in different areas. The biological requirements of live performances gave rise to geographically variegated cultures, where endless variations played out in tandem with historical events such as wars, famine, and change in general. This led to the frequent misinterpretation of cultures as being biologically or genetically determined and rooted inseparably to the land. From the view at the time, people who looked different lived in different places and acted differently. Therefore, it was an easy (but false) step to assume some sort of causality between the two.

This widely held falsehood has become particularly problematic in recent racial and ethnonationalist discourses. "Heritage," as noted before, can also muddy these waters by implying some sort of innate link (note the problematic use of the term "genetic heritage"). In spite of anthropology's main lessons—that culture is not in the blood but the cradle—this notion of a causal link between genetics (or "blood") and traditions is often ongoing and has been brought into the age of mechanical reproduction by the development of the "national" (languages, cultures, and ruling governments), which often base notions of citizenship on "blood" (Bendix 2000; Geary 2002; Volkan 1997).

One should also not forget that the mechanical revolution included a media revolution that served to separate the producers of culture (such as

---

9   See, for example, the vast number works on cultural traditions and nationalism, including Hobsbawm and Ranger's (1984) famous *Invention of Tradition*, the concepts of fakelore and *folklorismus* (e.g., Bausinger 1990; Newall 1987), and the notion of "authenticity" (e.g., Bendix 1997).

the CEOs of major printing presses, record companies, and movie studios) from the consumers of culture, who were increasingly viewed as passive receivers of corporate-produced culture. I label this model the "vertical mode" of culture, due to the sudden differentiation between producers and consumers; only those who could afford expensive machines could exploit the media successfully. Authority became invested in printing press institutions and in the written word from the authorities, from the experts, from the "they" (as in the common phrase tag "that's what 'they' say"). The developing media industries replaced folklore performances for many people—instead of listening to various storytellers, people read the works of a few literary giants. Instead of hiring local musicians for a party, people could listen to glamorous star performers on the radio. Culture, through the corporate and institutional model, flowed asymmetrically from producers to consumers. In contrast to the idea of folklore and natural language discourse as "horizontal communication," the mechanical mode of replicating culture can be viewed as "vertical" in that power, authority, and money were lodged with the producers of culture (the "culture industry" of the Frankfurt School), and a vast gulf opened between the producers of culture and the consumers (now often viewed as "passive").

Alongside the rise of institutional and corporate culture came the consideration of folkloric culture as ignorant and backward, full of old wives' tales, "silly superstitions," and the like. The once-common proverb of modernity—"if it wasn't true, they wouldn't print it"—gives testament to the belief in print.[10] Real capital and cultural capital were invested in these culture-making institutions and seen as sources of authority. The historical rupture between these two modes of cultural reproduction profoundly shaped modernity's romantic gaze backward.

Many authors have critically gazed on one or another aspect of this topic, invoking tradition as a process (Gailey 1989), performance (Glassie 1995), personal relations (McDonald 1997), history (Vansina 1985), conservatism (Ó Giolláin 2000), public discourse (Bronner 2000), or self-identity (Jones 2000). All of these are necessary corrections to the as-yet-common positivist approaches that seek to detect "objective" traditions.[11] Although important, such approaches often fail to emphasize the central

---

10   It is interesting to note that the rise of the Internet surely provides an easy *terminus donec quem* for this proverb.

11   A case in point is sociologist Edward Shils's (1981) *Tradition*, which displays no awareness of such critical turns.

point that tradition itself is ongoing. It is what was, and what is and what will be, and it does not stop at any particular point of time. Over time, there can be change, stasis, repetition, and all sorts of agencies involved in various aspects of the performances that relate to the past (as per de Certeau 1984).

MODERN TIMES AND ITS EFFECTS

Charlie Chaplin, as the hapless everyman, wrestled with giant machines in the 1936 silent movie *Modern Times*, a classic of its era. The great comedian showed that modernity came with its share of discontents, particularly in relation to "the machine"; at this time of industrial culture and corporate performances, people followed the instructions of the machine or were torn up in their resistance. The Frankfurt School investigated how the late industrial age heralded the beginning of culture industries. The freezing of symbolic communications, gradually rising throughout the history of inscriptions and literacy, reached new and dizzying heights in the less-sacred-but-all-the-more-powerful frozen performances of modernity.

These frozen performances also created stars: individual "genius" authors creating "novels" and the like. It is surely no accident that the rise of the individual—perhaps one of the most important philosophical shifts in all of modernity—coincides with these modes of communicative technologies. Enlightenment philosophies extolled the individual's role as the proper locus for consciousness (René Descartes), political rights and representation (John Locke), and cultural advancement (Friedrich Nietzsche). Democracy, with its belief in "inalienable" individual liberties, likewise emerged from this epoch. With frozen performances, the focus turned to exceptional individuals rather than the masses and their traditional loci of power (chieftains, kings, bards).

Inscriptions (literally, *writings into*), and replications of inscriptions, shaped the very notions of art, identity, and authority in modernity. Our entire legal systems of copyright, for example, are based on such models. Yet such systems are coming under increasing strain as modernity retreats from view and we are ushered into a new epoch of human cultural communication—that of digitally (rather than mechanically) reproduced information spread via global (rather than regional or even national) networks. Modernity's gaze on tradition was predicated on tradition as the anti-definition of original authorship. This, in turn, was based explicitly on books, previously the repositories of the sacred, infused with a sacral authority. Just as the Bible was the "undeniable word of God," so the authored book was the undeniable word of the author. Our whole system of modern governance, philosophy, and society seems built on the mechanical reproduction of culture, with its fictions of temporal fixity, however much it may incorporate or base its claims on premodern traditions.

Even our views of the past (to which traditions are logically related) show the precedence of history—the study of the inscribed past—in determining the authority on the subject, even when discussing traditions themselves. For example, historians Eric Hobsbawm and Terence Ranger's (2002 [1984]) famous work *The Invention of Tradition*, focuses on the modern re-creations of tradition, which the authors see as being "invented" for a tradition-hungry public. While popular, the work shares a flaw with many other scholastic treatments of tradition in that the authors fail to recognize the power of the antecedents to modern works. Hobsbawm and Ranger relate their famed encounter with a clever English merchant who "created" Scottish kilts to sell to tradition-hungry (and gullible) Scots. For Hobsbawm and Ranger, this proves that "traditions" are inherently false indicators of historicity and that "historical" inscribed data tells the "real" tale. The authors mention only briefly that the English merchant in question derived his design from an earlier Scottish garment—the great kilt—in order to create his newer "small kilt" (*Fèileadh beag*), and they attach no particular significance to the precursor. They looked for that one original moment and found it for themselves in the heart of modernity—and in the English wool merchant's clever marketing. However, in doing so, they mistake a tree for the forest and a historical moment for vast passages of time.

This same privileging of inscription can be seen in what literary critics have long dubbed the "cult of the author," which focuses on a singular moment of origin deriving from the "eureka" moment of a literary genius. Such an approach seems to have blinded much of literary studies to the possibilities of studying traditions within literature—studying Shakespeare's *Hamlet* instead of the story of Hamlet, for example (an ancient and well-known story long before the birth of Shakespeare). Considering a book as a self-contained text, produced by a self-contained author, turns one away from the study of literature as a social and, yes, traditional performance—the moment, or moments, that Shakespeare "performed" Hamlet, through the recording medium of paper and ink. Although literary criticism has used dialogism and intertextuality (e.g., Bakhtin 1981) more recently to move away from this approach, it has not grappled—as folklorists have—with traditions, in spite of the many traditions that abound in that field. Likewise, although perhaps a bit less so than books, the study of films, music, and other "authored" works have also been influenced by the idea of the singular author—to the detriment of studying what the various works share in common.

In contrast to modernity's positivism, the élan of tradition remained and remains outside of the simple true or false, denigrated for its lack of modernity and venerated as repositories of some spiritual or identitarian value. Hence, traditions—especially those highly valued—are often scrutinized as to their *authenticity* (see Bendix 1997; Lindholm 2008). The question of authenticity seems to haunt the study of traditions due to the understandable desire for many people to have "true" representations of the past while at the same time acknowledging that traditions are an inherently changing process. Therefore, what is an "authentic" tradition? Unlike works by individual authors, which are more easily subjected toward quests of authenticity (as in an "authentic Robert Frost original poem"), traditions do not fit easily into the canonized realm of literature and inscriptions. Indeed, the very nature of tradition strains at the confines of modern discourse, entrancing and repelling, being subjected and overwhelming. Modernity and modern discourse, with its logos of inscribed fixity, ultimately prove ill-suited toward truly understanding traditions, a problem echoing loudly today in the realm of intellectual property (see Brown 1998, 2003; Hafstein 2004; Shand 2002).

MODERNITY IN HINDSIGHT

Many scholars would theorize that the modern world, arising out of industrialization, is being replaced quickly by a postmodern world, arising out of digitization of information; and I would agree. I further believe that this transition allows us new perspectives on modernity as well.

Modernity in particular has displayed an interest in premodern traditions—that very way of life that it was supposed to replace. There is a large amount of nostalgia and cultural romance in the interest of the premodern, agrarian times. In America, renaissance faires and "fairy tales" set in premodern Europe attest to this cultural interest while in Europe, whole towns dedicate themselves to performing "traditional" festivals, locked in the time just before the onset of modernity.[12]

---

12   See Mugnaini (2006).

This particular romance of modernity with premodernity has obscured the ongoing traditions within modernity itself and the vital role that all traditions perform in modern societies. The assumption that modernity is opposed to traditions is inherently at odds with the continuing importance of traditions throughout the history of modernity. It also obfuscates the very real roles that traditions continue to play in all walks of life. There are traditions for your first job interview, traditions for your child's birthday, and traditions for your interactions with your spouse. We interact with such traditions both in live performances and in recorded works such as newspapers, books, movies, television shows, and music videos.

The scholarly consideration of modern traditions—and traditions as modern—has been held back by the cultural emphasis on the original and the individual author as the genesis of the works (as in copyright law) as well as the nostalgia for premodern traditions that preoccupied the discourses of modernity.

Certainly, one of the core issues regarding copyright is the idea of "the original" work. This fiction is near and dear to our modern world. The individual is both a creator and a copier in every single act. Some actions are *more* derived from others, and others are *more* the results of individual agency and innovation. But all actions known to man are somewhere between these two ideal poles. This "continuum" view of authorship is clearly a break from the classic modern view of individually authored works and at clear variance from the legal fiction of copyright. Yet such a theoretical break is absolutely necessary in order to fully appreciate human culture. There is such a thing as a traditional detective show for television, for example, and many plots have been recycled from series to series. Even nominally authored work, on scrutiny, reveals varying degrees of a variety of traditional elements. As Icelandic folklorist Valdimar Tr. Hafstein (2004) argues, we must consider the notion of copying as a creative act to understand the social nature of creativity.

THE MEDIATED WORLD

The fall of the modern age happened as suddenly as its ascent. Within a decade, previous assumptions about the ways in which culture and information are shared were radically and forever altered. The digital age bypasses nations and national identities and at the same time allows for all sorts of new identities to come to the fore. Perhaps even more influentially, the digital age allows for the everyday person to once again become a producer, as well as a consumer, of culture. The elite grip on the solitary work of genius, provided via industries to the masses, was based on controlling the mechanical means of reproduction: printing presses, record labels, etc. *Time* magazine heralded its 2006 Person of the Year, featuring a mirror, as the everyday person. Why the change? This new focus on the everyday individual reflects the new technological revolution, the new ways of enabling anyone once again to produce culture, and to be *loci* of authority.

The new digital mode of communication may be thought of as "mediated horizontal": *horizontal* in its distribution of production and consumption across a wide demographic and *mediated* in that digital communication is mediated through computers. A wide demographic shares both the production and consumption of traditions, with nearly everyone both consuming and producing culture. This is where the digital medium is most similar to folklore, even to the point where some theorists label it *as* folklore (see Blank 2009). Yet the "mediated medium" of computers differs from the usual definitions of folklore. Folkloric traditions are performed live in a face-to-face setting. Even if one considers that some digital traditions are performed live, much of digital culture also includes archival, more inscripted aspects (Kirshenblatt-Gimblett 1995). Many digital traditions are recorded—recordings of "live" events, no matter how frequent, are recordings nonetheless. This aspect of online culture resembles the literary and mechanical modes with its archival and scriptal qualities, unlike the more ephemeral nature of non-digital, analog folklore.

Much in the way that Robert Glenn Howard (2008) has thought of online communications as a hybrid between vernacular voices and the institutional, so too are digital traditions a hybrid of the live and the recorded, a mishmash and conflation of several categories, previously easily separated.[13] While one may argue if user-generated digital culture is indeed "folklore" (I, myself, prefer the term "folklore 2.0"), it is undeniable that an explosion in online traditions has occurred within the brief few years of its existence. Such a view, focused on the performance of traditions throughout the different technological modes of communication, allows us to see the category of traditions in a view untethered from questions of folklore, literature, authority, or originality.

---

13   For example, see my work on the new art form of the "mashup," an expressive artistic form that celebrates such conflations (Thompson 2011).

For example, King Arthur, the legend of old, was inscripted into early manuscripts in what appears to be literary renditions of oral poems, some of which were copied into later manuscripts as well, stretching throughout the medieval period. King Arthur likely never really left the folkloric realm, and he remained popular in the countryside (as evidenced in various place names) as well as the medieval and renaissance courts. Early on, King Arthur entered the realm of authored literature and was among the first printings available in the new medium of the printing press. Tales of Arthur remain popular and include some of the finest works of English literature as well as comics (Prince Valiant, for example), film adaptations, and video games. King Arthur is all over the Internet; an online search on his name returns several million sites. The tradition of King Arthur stretches right from prehistory to the future. If tradition is indeed a mode of activity that represents the past, then which pasts are being invoked in, say, writing online fan fiction of King Arthur?

Similar, of course, are a plethora of other topics from folklore—from Christmas trees to the ancient art of the didgeridoo. More information dedicated to ancient traditions is available now than ever before, and more new re-creations and re-performances of such traditions occur online at any moment. Brand-new traditions, such as traditions of netiquette, are constantly being created, often varying from context to context and from group to group. Again, such a scheme is viewed as additive: folklore has never disappeared, and neither have the institutional, national, and corporate industries of culture—many of which have web presences—which both deny and venerate tradition. Yet the short story remains that the mechanical, industrial, vertical model of culture has, in its turn, been superseded by something much more communicative.

Technology has introduced new forms of cultural communications that incorporate both live performances and recordings, which reflect both the *vox populi* and elite institutions. As Robert Glenn Howard (2008) notes, a great deal of institutional and vernacular sources exist on the web. Traditions of stories, and traditional stories, are being produced and consumed via both vernacular and institutional sources. Communications scholar Henry Jenkins (2008 [2006]) points to "transmedia storytelling" as the entertainment industry grapples uneasily with user-generated culture in its myriad forms—for instance, in fandom.

The global proliferation of widespread, unlimited access to information that followed the introduction of user-based digital technology was, of course, an unprecedented achievement in world history. The postmodern builds on modernity, even as the modern built on premodernity. Yet, just as modernity reinterpreted the premodern for its own devices, so too will the postmodern reinterpret traditions and traditionality for its own meanings and trajectories.

Conceptions and performances of traditions in postmodernity will likely be far different from modern conceptions and performances, which, in turn, were far different than the premodern. Society itself will be rewritten, in large part by new performances of traditions. These new performances will take place in the live, the inscribed, and the mediated digital, and the concept of tradition itself must grapple with these epochal changes in the uses and connotations of the word.

POSTMODERN TRADITION

It is my contention that the forced reconsideration of tradition— including not only the live, performed, and folkloric but also the inscribed and institutional—opens up the study of tradition to something much broader than before. From the bedroom to the boardroom, traditions continue to play a formative and substantial part in what it is to be human.

For example, legal studies make it clear that law has many traditions, some of which can be reasonably described as folkloric (see Glenn 2007; Renteln 2004), and others that are not (traditions of habeas corpus, for example). Further, unlike folklore, a good deal of law is not comprised of tradition. Understanding traditions in general could presumably tell us a good deal about how traditions work in regards to law.

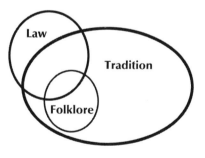

IDENTITY AND HUMANITY

Not only do traditions allow us to engage in our humanity, they also help us shape much more focused ideas of who we are. Which traditions are followed, celebrated, and venerated tell much about the culture and people involved. It may not be too much to say that identity itself is dependent on traditions; individual agency often appears as individual choices within a panoply of traditional options or at the very least, an assertion of agency either for or against, but nearly always determined by, the traditions in question. One can state that a joke is "not funny" or laugh along instead, but either way, one is performing in a field of traditionality.

Expressive culture is highly formative of individually held notions of group identity. What it is to be Mormon or Samoan (or Morman Somoan), a male hairdresser or a female prizefighter, a high school junior or a senior citizen, our self and group identities are made real by our performances of traditions—a point brought home eloquently many times in folklore scholarship. As traditions change, and the very concept of tradition changes in the newly emerging digital epoch of human culture, we can therefore be assured that group identities—indeed, the very concept of identity—will change with them.

The future of traditions in expressive cultures will be highly constitutive of the new humanity, with a reintroduction of the voice of the common man. Already we have seen many such new identities emerging. In many ways, the new builds on the old, as people reinterpret what it means to be Chinese or Sufi or Tuscan. In other ways, newer identities are also coming to the fore. In all of this, the discourse is global and mediated via the computer.

It is indeed a global village with businesses, artists, shopkeepers, entertainers, lovers, politicians—and a great deal of communication. The global village is vast beyond anything witnessed by humanity before, with millions of people participating in online discussions and the like. Its size means that a great deal of choice now exists in which traditions to perform online—more choices than ever before. Does one add their voice to an electronic school blog in planning a traditional graduation dance? Look through a webcam in hope of seeing a traditional ghost, via a ghost-hunting website? Play a swords-and-sorcery video game based on romantic ideas of premodern Europe?

Whatever online forum in which one expresses oneself, there are rules of the game, experienced performers, and newcomers ("newbs" or "n00bs," in common computer slang). Traditions are established and performed by all, with some members pushing the limits and some pushing the limits back. One can become a member of a community online, and one's identity can be entwined with one's online performances. There is individuality and agency in such performances, yes, but there are also many traditions that are informing the field within which the individual agent performs. Such wide-ranging, new ideas of community and identity are already evident in the first decade of the digital epoch. It remains to be seen where all this will lead, but there are at least two safe bets.

One is that with continued developments in the digital realm, not only will the individual agent continue to be involved in traditions but the individual may also be involved at one time with a number of different groups with different traditions. One may have many overlapping affiliations and groups, all of which may influence a person's identity to a lesser or greater extent and provide different traditions to carry forward (or not). Identity, therefore, looks likely to be increasingly fragmented, or segmented, rather than unitary. One performs identity through traditions, and these performances are increasingly taking place in multiple online social groups.

The second is that the largely despatialized medium of hyperspace will increasingly challenge older ideas of geographically homogenous tradition-sharing units, perhaps particularly the nation-state, a form that has long held ascendancy in world affairs. Although the nation-state is not going to suddenly disappear, I do think that we can already begin to speak of postnational identities (even beyond international, or transnational, identities), which will likely grow in importance over time.

THE FUTURE'S UNCERTAIN AND THE END IS ALWAYS NEAR

My outlook on the study of tradition attempts to connect performance studies to post-humanities by showing the way that new traditions question previously held notions of identity, allowing for new conceptions of identity through such things as post-racial or postnational identities, "cyborg" identities, or other new, emergent identities. Whatever the new forms of identity and community will be, they will be established through modes of activity that reproduce the past, performances of memories, and ways of making sense in an increasingly chaotic world.

Given the role that performances of traditions play in reproducing culture, I believe that studying the traditions that people engage in, both as performers and audience members, will be very instructive toward understanding the new emergent mode of communication—and indeed the future of humanity—and that the discipline of folklore, for so long the only discipline to study traditions, has a great deal to offer the understand of tradition writ large.

Here we can once more invoke the notion of tradition as a performance, and one of a particular type, as Glassie put it, where the past, present, and future meet. As Bauman (1984) and others note, public performances imply a certain heightened responsibility for one's actions, especially when speaking for the past. As always, tradition must be performed by a creative social agent engaging in both novelty and repetition. Although formulated by folklorists, such views on tradition have much wider applications, toward studies of tradition outside that of traditional folkloristics.

The ground is shifting underneath our feet. A new epoch in humanity will rewrite the way we conceive of ourselves. Enlightenment philosophies—for so long the guiding light in modern institutions and beliefs—may soon need to be discarded for newer models that can address the new humanity in which we find ourselves. Our grandchildren may have very different beliefs as to what it is to be human, much in the same way that the newly literate looked back on the premodern with amusement, nostalgia, and a fair amount of disdain.

Que sera, sera—"whatever will be, will be"—goes the old saying about the future. The modes of cultural communication have undergone a communication revolution likely larger than that of the printing press and the Industrial Revolution. With this, tradition will shift in meaning, nuance, and emphasis, as it has always done. The future is always hard to predict—never more so than in times of great upheaval—but one safe prognostication (besides death and taxes) is that there will very likely still be old sayings such as *que sera, sera*. Whatever the future will be, it will be a future of traditions.

REFERENCES

Abrahams, Roger D. 1993. "Phantoms of Romantic Nationalism in Folkloristics." *Journal of American Folklore* 106 (419): 3–37. http://dx.doi.org/10.2307/541344.

Anderson, Benedict. 1991 [1983]. *Imagined Communities: Reflections on the Origin and Spread of Nationalism*. London: Verso.

Anttonen, Pertti J. 2005. *Tradition through Modernity: Postmodernism and the Nation-State in Folklore Scholarship*. Helsinki: Finnish Literature Society.

Bakhtin, Mikhail M. 1981 [1930s]. *The Dialogic Imagination: Four Essays*. Trans. Caryl Emerson and ed. Michael Holquist. Austin: University of Texas Press.

Bauman, Richard. 1984 [1977]. *Verbal Art as Performance*. Prospect Heights, IL: Waveland.

Bauman, Richard, and Charles L. Briggs. 1990. "Poetics and Performance as Critical Perspectives on Language and Social Life." *Annual Review of Anthropology* 19 (1): 59–88. http://dx.doi.org/10.1146/annurev.an.19.100190.000423.

Bausinger, Hermann. 1990. *Folk Culture in a World of Technology*. Trans. Elke Dettmer. Bloomington: Indiana University Press.

Ben-Amos, Dan. 1984. "The Seven Strands of Tradition: Varieties and Its Meaning in American Folklore Studies." *Journal of Folklore Research* 21 (2/3): 97–131.

Bendix, Regina. 1988. "Folklorism: The Challenge of a Concept." *International Folklore Review* 6: 5–15.

Bendix, Regina. 1997. *In Search of Authenticity: The Formation of Folklore Studies*. Madison: University of Wisconsin Press.

Bendix, Regina. 2000. "Heredity, Hybridity, and Heritage from One *Fin de Siècle* to the Next." In *Folklore, Heritage Politics and Ethnic Diversity: A Festschrift for Barbro Klein*, ed. Pertti J. Anttonen, 37–56. Botkyrka: Multicultural Centre.

Blank, Trevor J. 2009. "Toward a Conceptual Framework for the Study of Folklore and the Internet." In *Folklore and the Internet: Vernacular Expression in a Digital World*, ed. Trevor J. Blank, 1–20. Logan: Utah State University Press.

Bourdieu, Pierre. 1973. "Cultural Reproduction and Social Reproduction." In *Knowledge, Education and Cultural Change*, ed. Richard Brown, 71–112. London: Tavistock.

Boyer, Pascal. 1990. *Tradition as Truth and Communication: A Cognitive Description of Traditional Discourse*. Cambridge, UK: Cambridge University Press. http://dx.doi.org/10.1017/CBO9780511521058

Bronner, Simon J. 1998. *Following Tradition: Folklore in the Discourse of American Culture*. Logan: Utah State University Press.

Bronner, Simon J. 2000. "The American Concept of Tradition: Folklore in the Discourse of Traditional Values." *Western Folklore* 59 (2): 143–70. http://dx.doi.org/10.2307/1500157.

Brown, Michael. 1998. "Can Culture Be Copyrighted?" *Current Anthropology* 39 (2): 193–222. http://dx.doi.org/10.1086/204721.

Brown, Michael F. 2003. *Who Owns Native Culture?* Cambridge, MA: Harvard University Press.

de Certeau, Michel. 1984. *The Practice of Everyday Life*. Berkeley: University of California Press.

Dundes, Alan. 1969. "Thinking Ahead: A Folkloristic Reflection on the Future Orientation in American Worldview." *Anthropological Quarterly* 42 (2): 53–72. http://dx.doi.org/10.2307/3316639.

Emery, Michael, Edwin Emery, and Nancy L. Roberts. 1997 [1972]. *The Press and America: An Interpretive History of the Mass Media*. 9th ed. Upper Saddle River, NJ: Prentice-Hall.

Gailey, Alan. 1989. "The Nature of Tradition." *Folklore* 100 (2): 143–61. http://dx.doi.org/10.1080/0015587X.1989.9715762.

Geary, Patrick. 2002. *The Myth of Nations: The Medieval Origins of Europe*. Princeton, NJ: Princeton University Press.

Glassie, Henry. 1995. "Tradition." *Journal of American Folklore* 108 (430): 395–412. http://dx.doi.org/10.2307/541653.

Glenn, H. Patrick. 2007. *Legal Traditions of the World: Sustainable Diversity in Law*. 3rd edition. Oxford, NY: Oxford University Press.

Goldstein, Kenneth S. 1971. "On the Application of the Concepts of Active and Inactive Traditions to the Study of Repertory." *Journal of American Folklore* 84 (331): 62–67. http://dx.doi.org/10.2307/539734.

Hafstein, Valdimar. 2004. "The Politics of Origins: Collective Creation Revisited." *Journal of American Folklore* 117 (465): 300–15. http://dx.doi.org/10.1353/jaf.2004.0073.

Harris, Marvin. 1976. "History and Significance of the Emic/Etic Distinction." *Annual Review of Anthropology* 5 (1): 329–50. http://dx.doi.org/10.1146/annurev.an.05.100176.001553.

Hobsbawm, Eric, and Terence Ranger. 2002 [1984]. *The Invention of Tradition*. Cambridge, UK: Cambridge University Press.

Howard, Robert Glenn. 2008. "Electronic Hybridity: The Persistent Processes of the Vernacular Web." *Journal of American Folklore* 121 (480): 192–218. http://dx.doi.org/10.1353/jaf.0.0012.

Hymes, Dell. 1975. "Breakthrough into Performance." In *Folklore: Performance and Communication*, ed. Dan Ben-Amos and Kenneth S. Goldstein. The Hague: Mouton.

Jenkins, Henry. 2008 [2006]. *Convergence Culture: Where Old and New Media Collide*. New York: New York University Press.

Jones, Michael Owen. 2000. "'Tradition' in Identity Discourses and an Individual's Symbolic Construction of Self." *Western Folklore* 59 (2): 115–41. http://dx.doi.org/10.2307/1500156.

Kirshenblatt-Gimblett, Barbara. 1989. "Authoring Lives." *Journal of Folklore Research* 26: 123–49.

Kirshenblatt-Gimblett, Barbara. 1995. "From the Paperwork Empire to the Paperless Office: Testing the Limits of the 'Science of Tradition.'" In *Folklore Interpreted: Essays in Honor of Alan Dundes*, ed. Regina Bendix and Rosemary Levy Zumwalt, 69–92. New York: Garland.

Klein, Barbro. 2001. "More Swedish than in Sweden, More Iranian than in Iran: Folk Culture and World Migrations." In *Upholders of Culture Past and Present*, ed. Bo Sundin, 67–80. Stockholm: The Royal Swedish Academy of Engineering Sciences.

Lévi-Strauss, Claude. 1968 [1962]. *The Savage Mind*. Chicago: University of Chicago Press.

Lindholm, Charles. 2008. *Culture and Authenticity*. Malden, MA: Blackwell Publishing.

Linnekin, Jocelyn. 1991. "Cultural Invention and the Dilemma of Authenticity." *American Anthropologist* 93 (2): 446–49. http://dx.doi.org/10.1525/aa.1991.93.2.02a00120.

Lowenthal, David. 1996. *Possessed by the Past: The Heritage Crusade and the Spoils of History*. New York: Free Press.

Lynch, Michael. 1999. "Archives in Formation: Privileged Spaces, Popular Archives and Paper Trails." *History of the Human Sciences* 12 (2): 65–87. http://dx.doi.org/10.1177/09526959922120252.

McDonald, Barry M. 1997. "Tradition as a Personal Relationship." *Journal of American Folklore* 110 (435): 47–67. http://dx.doi.org/10.2307/541585.

Mugnaini, Fabio. 2006. "Medieval Ever Since, Medieval Forever." In *The Presence of the Past: A Multidisciplinary Perspective*, ed. Fabio Mugnaini, Pádraig Ó Héalaí, and Tok Thompson. Catania, Italy: Edit Press.

Newall, Venetia. 1987. "The Adaptation of Folklore and Tradition (Folklorismus)." *Folklore* 98 (2): 131–51. http://dx.doi.org/10.1080/0015587X.1987.9716408.

Ó Giolláin, Diarmuid. 2000. *Locating Irish Folklore: Tradition, Modernity, Identity*. Cork, Ireland: Cork University Press.

Renteln, Alison Dundes. 2004. *The Cultural Defense*. New York: Oxford University Press.

Santino, Jack. 2009. "The Ritualesque: Festival, Politics, and Popular Culture." *Western Folklore* 68: 9–26.

Shand, Peter. 2002. "Scenes from the Colonial Catwalk." *Cultural Analysis* 3: 47–88.

Shils, Edward. 1981. *Tradition*. Chicago: University of Chicago Press.

Tedlock, Dennis. 1983. *The Spoken Word and the Work of Interpretation*. Philadelphia: University of Pennsylvania Press.

Thompson, Tok. 2006. "Heritage Versus the Past." In *The Presence of the Past: A Multidisciplinary Perspective*, ed. Fabio Mugnaini, Pádraig Ó Héalaí, and Tok Thompson. Catania, IT: Edit Press.

Thompson, Tok. 2011. "Beatboxing, Mashups, and More: Folk Music for the 21st Century." *Western Folklore* 70 (2): 171–93.

Toelken, Barre. 1969. "The Pretty 'Languages' of Yellowman: Genre, Mode, and Texture in Navajo Coyote Narratives." *Genre (Los Angeles, Calif.)* 2: 211–35.

Vansina, Jan. 1985. *Oral Tradition as History*. Madison: University of Wisconsin Press.

Volkan, Vamik. 1997. *Bloodlines: From Ethnic Pride to Ethnic Terrorism*. New York: Farrar, Straus, and Giroux.

von Sydow, Carl W. 1948. "On the Spread of Tradition." In *Selected Papers on Folklore*, ed. Laurits Bodker, 11–43. Copenhagen: Rosenkilde and Bagger.

Wittgenstein, Ludwig. 1958. *Philosophical Investigations*. 2nd ed. Oxford, UK: Blackwell.

7

And the Greatest of These Is Tradition
The Folklorist's Toolbox in the Twenty-First Century

Lynne S. McNeill

I CLEARLY RECALL THE MOMENT WHEN, IN AN ADVANCED Folkloristics graduate seminar, a classmate of mine gave in to her mounting frustration, slammed her book shut, and demanded to know how she *wasn't* an anthropologist. As a class, we were reading the works of several anthropologists, learning the techniques of ethnographic writing and research, and seeking to understand and explain the cultures of diverse groups of humans; what about our experience was setting us apart from anthropology students, other than the name of the department in which we studied? "Good question," I remember thinking.

Folkloristics and anthropology are close cousins, often treading the same academic ground despite the fact that folklore studies are just as commonly connected to the humanities as to the social sciences. Many of the qualities that once seemed to distinguish folklore studies from anthropology in the past—a focus on the researcher's own culture, a focus on smaller groups, a focus on the mundane or everyday aspects of lived experiences—now seem less unique to folklore as anthropologists increasingly turn to the same kinds of scholarship. Since that class, I have witnessed many a graduate student (and several perceptive undergraduates) note the perplexing similarities between the two fields, and I find myself exceedingly grateful to have taken that Advanced Folkloristics class from Diane Goldstein who, as it turned out, was more than ready to clear things up for us.

Almost twenty years ago, Goldstein presented a paper she later published that sought to illuminate this very relationship: distinguishing

DOI: 10.7330/9780874218992.c07

folklorists from anthropologists. She wryly notes that "saying that folklorists are smarter and nicer people only goes so far" (Goldstein 1993, 15) and proposes an examination of the unique skills and perspectives that a folklorist brings to the study of culture.[1] Through a consideration of the methods and approaches of folkloristics, Goldstein identifies three concepts that together form the "really significant components of the distinctiveness of [a folklorist's] skills and training": genre, transmission, and tradition (Goldstein 1993, 19). In her seminar, she described these three concepts as the "tools in the folklorist's toolbox," an explanation that has guided me through many trials of clarifying the field's distinguishing characteristics. And yet, twenty years after the article's original publication, the question remains. The work of folklorists continues to resemble the work of anthropologists and students of folklore continue to yearn for a clear-cut explanation of their own unique contribution to academia. It is time to reconsider the folklorist's toolbox. In the following section, I revisit Goldstein's analogy in an effort to reestablish her definitional efforts and demonstrate their continued applicability for our conceptualization of folkloristics (especially tradition) in the twenty-first century.

THE FOLKLORIST'S TOOLS

The first tool in the folklorist's toolbox is *genre*, which serves as a "framework for the production of and interpretation of communication" (Goldstein 1993, 19). The concept of precise or culturally objective generic classification has been called into question numerous times in the field of folkloristics (see Ben-Amos 1976; Bennett 1984; Harris 1995), but as far as distinguishing factors go, *genre* (especially the historical focus on the narrative genres of folktale, legend, myth, and even ballad) ties folkloristics as much to the humanities as it does to the social sciences; it provides folklorists with interdisciplinary methods of textual analysis and literary criticism that clearly separate their work from that of anthropologists. More than that however, even the nonnarrative genres of folklore clearly emphasize one of our main disciplinary boundaries: *lore*. While folklorists are certainly interested in folk culture in general, the discipline rests on a long history of studying specific enactments of expressive culture, which

---

1   Goldstein was originally addressing the specific comparison of medical folklorists to medical anthropologists. In the classroom setting, she extended this to folklorists and anthropologists in general.

always come to us in the frames of various genres, whether ethnically or analytically determined. Folklorists know that the communicative choice of one genre over another provides insights into a teller's or performer's motivation, identity, and worldview. The simple fact that folklorists seek to delineate such discrete expressive forms from within the wider cultural milieu—and acknowledge that those forms reveal much about what is being expressed—is another way in which they differ from anthropologists.

The second tool in the folklorist's toolbox is *transmission*, which deals with "how information moves through time and space" (Goldstein 1993, 20). Just as with genre, the mode of transmission of any given expressive form can affect our understanding of the message being passed on. Folklorists recognize that the process of folk transmission is typically person to person or small group to small group, reflecting the field's attention to the informal and the unofficial, the marginal and the common. The basic idea of transmission implies both a sender and a recipient—one to perform the folklore and one to observe, hear, or otherwise take in the folklore. Thus, the idea of person-to-person transmission is at the heart of the concept of "folk group"; lore that is kept within the bounds of a single mind or life experience is not *folk*lore. Of course, not all transmission is folk transmission either; simply being shared does not qualify a cultural expression as folklore. Cultural materials transmitted via mass broadcast or institutional networks—materials that are identical at every point of reception and are authoritative in their original form and content—are not folklore. The necessary folk transmission of information in order to identify it as folklore is at the root of the discipline's unique focus on performance, reception, and context.

The third tool in the folklorist's toolbox is *tradition*. Of all the tools that folklorists may use, tradition is "perhaps [the] most important of all" (Goldstein 1993, 23), given that the discipline's unique perspective on (and approach to) tradition is one of the main characteristics that distinguishes it from other disciplines working with culture. Drawing from Richard Bauman's contention of the existence of a "social need to give meaning to our present lives by linking ourselves to a meaningful past" (Bauman 1992, 32), Goldstein argues that there is a "universal need to recreate aspects of experience" (Goldstein 1993, 22) that also serves to reinforce the importance of continuity within groups. Thus, tradition is a social process more than an obviously temporal one. While the tool of transmission tells us that folklore must be passed on in order to qualify as folklore, tradition tells us that some sense of continuity must also be present; for as much as folklore is dynamic and variable, there must be a conservative element that remains to identify a new iteration as "the same thing" as a previous one. This emphasis on continuity over longevity leads to the important point that "traditional" does not mean "old"; without the concept of tradition, we would not be able to accurately assess how a group conceptualizes both their past and their present. Indeed, folklorists rely on understandings and perceptions of tradition to determine what is important to a given culture and relevant to a given current issue within that culture: "By recognizing traditional authority and the significance of cultural continuity, we recognize breaks with tradition, cognitive dissonance and incommensurability. But the reverse is also true—we recognize that which is commensurable and the resulting room for negotiation and mediation" (Goldstein 1993, 23). Taken together, these three tools—genre, transmission, and tradition—are the markers by which folklorists can identify their particular sphere of comprehension and significance. Tradition, as the most important of the three, is key to marking the boundaries of folkloric inquiry.

WHY THE TOOLBOX MATTERS

There is a very practical reason for taking the time to distinguish the expertise of a folklorist from the expertise of an anthropologist. Today, as was also the case twenty years ago, folklorists are vying with their colleagues in a number of related fields for the same jobs, the same grant money, the same external recognition of specialization over a given patch of the academic landscape. In order to compete successfully, it is not enough to simply trust that we hold a unique perspective; folklorists must be able to articulate that unique perspective to decision makers (be they hiring committees, granting agencies, publishers, or the consensus of the general public). Identifying the differences between folkloristics and other disciplines of cultural analysis— identifying what it is we do better than anyone else—is incredibly important to the ongoing viability of the field of folklore studies in the larger spheres of cultural studies and academia.

Folklorists have embraced the concept of tradition so readily and (at times) unreflectively likely because external elements are readily able to relate to the idea of folklore, not because they themselves haven't realized or considered the myriad complexities of such a concept. Tradition provides folklorists with an easily accepted realm of expertise in the eyes of non-folklorists, and that is an undeniably important consideration. This pragmatism does not, however, exempt folklorists from continually revisiting the utility of their tools, honing and refining them to suit the changing materials to which we apply them.

Folklorists may comprehend and construct the concept of tradition as elastic and malleable, but even a flexible understanding of tradition may quail under the pressure of new genres and new modes of transmission. A removal of the temporal qualities of tradition, for example, in favor of the social qualities seems prudent in the face of rapidly transmitted contemporary legends; but can the element of time truly be discounted from an understanding of tradition? And while the idea of tradition may no longer rely on intergenerational passage, can the idea of transmission truly dismiss the concept of space as well as time? The folklorist's toolbox needs to be tested in new contexts to ensure the ongoing utility of its contents.

NEW EXPRESSIVE FORMS AND NEW MODES OF TRANSMISSION

In contemporary folklore studies, communication via the Internet and other forms of technological mediation has—in spite of initial concerns to the contrary—provided a vast arena for the formation and proliferation of folklore; and throughout the many studies folklorists have conducted, the folklorist's toolbox has regularly been put to good use. Folklorists have considered the digital manifestations of genres both long-standing and newly identified, genres that easily traverse the boundary between analog and digital culture as well as genres that appear only in digital contexts. Elizabeth Tucker's (2009) study of online narratives of missing girls, Russell Frank's (2009, 2011) work with political jokes and rumors, and Robert Glenn Howard's (1997, 2009) considerations of apocalyptic and fundamentalist Christians' online networking practices take on the familiar genres of legend, joke, and folk belief in the newer context of electronic media. Strictly digital genres, reliant on the unique expressive capabilities of computers, have been a common point of focus as well. Barbara Kirshenblatt-Gimblett's (1996) early consideration of ASCII art; Monica Foote's (2007) work with Internet memes; Russell Frank's (2004, 2011) and Robert Glenn Howard's (2008) studies of Photoshopped images; Margaret Duffy, Janis Teruggi Page, and Rachel Young's work with conservative political e-mail images (Duffy, Page, and Young 2012); and my own work with Internet memes (McNeill 2009) and flash mobs (McNeill 2012) are evidence of the proliferation and expansion of the folkloric concept of genre to the study of vernacular digital culture.

The seminal concept of transmission hasn't been left out of the toolbox either; if anything, it has received more scrutiny than ever before. Given the striking similarities between computer-mediated communication (even at the vernacular level) and mass media, folklorists have been hard-pressed to stake out the territory of "folk" transmission within increasingly ambiguous boundaries. Over twenty years ago, John Dorst (1990) addressed the nature of folk transmission within a medium of instant and exact replication and Robert Glenn Howard (2008) addressed the blurred relationship between institutional and vernacular expressions on the Internet, where corporate sponsorship and advertising frames most personal expressions (be they e-mails, real-time chats, status posts, or blogs). Awareness of the diversity of social and cultural interaction on the web has also risen; folklorists have examined the form and function of a variety of digital folk groups such as early bulletin boards, more recent social networks, blogging circles, fan communities, and MMORPGs (Bronner 2009; Dobler 2009; King 2011; Howard 2011; Miller 2008; Westerman 2009), considering the ways that the unique characteristics of these communities impact the transmission of their folklore.

As an illustrative case study of the third tool in our kit—tradition—I have chosen one of the many new digital genres of folk expression: image "macros"—pictures, typically photographs, that are captioned with humorous, sometimes nonsensical text.[2] As with all forms of folklore, image macros evolve as they get passed around the Internet, exhibiting both consistent conservative elements and dynamic variable elements. Consideration of the genre of image macros as a framework for both the production and interpretation of communication leads to an immediate understanding that this form of folklore is both familiar and unfamiliar. Similar to faxlore (Dundes and Pagter 1978 [1975], 1987), computer-generated images allow for the representational abilities of image and text to be united and presented together; unlike faxlore, however, image macros can be disseminated (via e-mail, social networking sites, dedicated websites, and blogs) at a rate that fax technology has not made possible.

---

2   Macros are also discussed in chapter 5 of this volume, "Curation and Tradition on Web 2.0," by Merrill Kaplan.

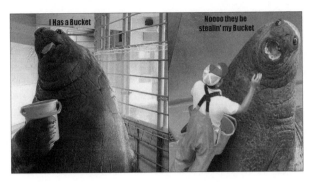

Figure 7.1. The lolrus in early form online.

A representative example of a popular image macro is the "lolrus" (Figure 7.1)—a portmanteau of the Internet slang term *lol* (laughing out loud) and the word *walrus*.[3] The original image showed two pictures side by side. The image on the left is a photo of a happy-looking large seal (not actually a walrus) holding a blue bucket and sticking out its tongue; the caption reads, "I Has a Bucket."[4] The image on the right shows the same seal with a horrified expression on its face as a person takes the bucket; the caption reads, "Noooo they be stealin' my bucket" (Cheezburger 2007).

This original image was posted to the popular lolcat and image macro site I Can Has Cheezburger? on January 14, 2007. Subsequent images that featured the same motifs began to be posted in March of that year. The first re-creation of the original shows a walrus holding a toy mobile phone with the caption "I has a cellular" paired with an image of the walrus hanging on to its toy in the presence of a person with the caption "They took mah bucket/You aint takin mah cellular" (Cheezburger 2007).

The adaptations spread from there fairly rapidly—within a month many more versions appeared: a shot of a sad-looking walrus captioned "miss mah bucket"; a picture of several walruses captioned "we has formed a team/to take back mah bucket"; an image of a walrus behind a cage door captioned "Day 76 without bucket. Was it red? Was it Blue? Sometimes I can't remember, and that scares me."[5] By the next month, there were pictures

---

3   The use of *lol* as a prefix is derived from the subset of image macros known as "lolcat" images: pictures of cats with funny captions.

4   The dialect known as "lolspeak," the language particular to lolcats and other image macros, involves regularly recurring mistakes with grammar and spelling.

5   This last example plays up the humor by explicitly shirking the rules of lolspeak grammar.

of buckets with captions from the bucket's perspective; one grainy black and white shot of a bucket is captioned "in soviet russia . . ./. . . bucket misses you." Other images brought in the element of relative lol-animal popularity by showing a cat in a blue bucket with captions like "stupid walrus" or "What you mean/'Unhappy Walrus is at the door'?"

While the presence of or reference to a walrus or large seal, the color blue, and references to buckets typically remained as conservative elements, details such as lol-spelling (bucket became bukkit or buhket), non-bucket objects, and additional animals began to evolve. Images of people (instead of animals) with captions that referenced the lolrus began to appear as well; one showed side-by-side images of former President George W. Bush— holding up a booklet with the caption "I Has a Budget" and with empty hands and the caption "Nooo they be stealing my budget!" (Lolpresidents 2007). The website LolPresidents.com features several images of Theodore Roosevelt—with his classic large, walrus-like mustache—and captions relating to buckets: "Do u has mah bukkit?" and "wen I findz you bukkit theef/I crush you."

Today the lolrus image macro has reached a point where, at least to those familiar with Internet culture, a picture of almost anyone or anything that references a lost bucket in the caption will automatically bring to mind walruses (and vice versa). The power of this otherwise random association is important because it illustrates the potential communicative power in many newly re-created image macros; this expressive form has made way for deeply coded communication among insiders to the tradition. We can clearly see Goldstein's concept of tradition at work here: an experience (the viewing of an image macro) is being re-created, and there is a clear effort made to link the present to the past.[6] But in the context of walruses and buckets, it seems fair to ask what the *point* of the tradition is.

Humor certainly comes to the forefront as an explanation for the prevalence of these forms. But much more than with textual jokes, image macros inspire people to contribute to the evolution of the image by altering the one they received rather than simply forwarding on the version given to them; there is an active creative engagement that isn't always present in other genres of folklore. In general, it can be assumed that folklore on the Internet has the ability to move faster and spread farther, reaching an exponentially larger audience in an exponentially shorter time than

---

6   Monica Foote (2007) has elaborated on this process of image macro evolution.

face-to-face transmission would typically require.[7] This is due, in part, to the blurring of folk and mass-mediated means of transmission (see Bronner 2009); while the network may still follow from one friend or acquaintance to another, it is possible for a single person to hit all their friends and acquaintances at the same time via posting to a social networking site or sending out a mass e-mail. Multiplying this process, it does not take long for a piece of Internet lore to reach a very wide audience indeed. So what is the significance here—will recognizing the concept of tradition in the lolrus canon provide the field of folkloristics with a much-needed foothold in the greater academic world?

SHARPENING THE TOOLS

While the simple enumeration of the folklorist's tools certainly helped me and my classmates comprehend the unique specialties of the folklorist, upon closer examination, it appears that these three tools are not equally configured within the toolbox. Rather, it seems that the interrelated yet significantly asymmetrical tripartite structure of these tools holds the key to many folkloristic endeavors. I would argue that genre and transmission are the generative components of the most important tool: tradition.[8] The concept of genre—even acknowledging all its inherent fluidity, its emic and etic forms and names, its overlapping and intersecting boundaries—basically addresses the "thing" of folklore: the song, the narrative, the custom, the object, and so on. Genre is the framework through which we apprehend the content or the "stuff" of the folklore. The concept of transmission, of passing that stuff along—whether face-to-face or technologically mediated, whether over the course of generations or in the span of hours—introduces the people, the group element that is necessary to consider the folklore shared. Adding these two elements together—expressive culture and informal process—creates tradition.[9]

Goldstein defines tradition most clearly as the "universal need to recreate aspects of experience" and traditions as "the various ways that we keep the

---

7   Whether or not this possibility is regularly borne out on the Internet is another question altogether.

8   Goldstein suggests this relationship—though does not develop it—when she notes, "Our knowledge of tradition permeates what I have already said about our training · and skills in genre and transmission" (Goldstein 1993, 21).

9   Both in the sense of *a* tradition and in the sense of the general concept of tradition.

past alive in the present" (Goldstein 1993, 22). It is vital to note the nouns used here: tradition is both a "need" and a "way." In other words, tradition is both a desire and the means to achieve that desire, an aspiration and the resources to obtain that to which we aspire. This concept of tradition requires both a *thing* (some cultural artifact, enactment, or concept) that expresses the *need* along with a *process* by which it is shared (some mode of transmission or passing on) that expresses the *way*. The presence of an expressive genre, plus the addition of some kind of informal process by which to share that genre, results in something traditional, or in a tradition. In shorthand: genre + transmission = tradition. In a way, this is similar to what folklorists have been getting at for some time now with summative phrases like "artistic communication" (genre) "in small groups" (shared group transmission), or even the more basic equation of "folk" (shared group transmission) plus "lore" (genre). In this sense, it could be argued that folklore simply *is* tradition, the stuff that gets passed or transmitted informally among a group of people.[10]

CONCLUSION

The concept of tradition, growing as it does out of the necessary elements of genre and transmission, remains seminal to the field of folklore studies. Taken in the context of a contemporary example of both genre and transmission—image macros shared via the Internet—the abstract value of tradition stands out. The "thing" in this case—repeated humorous references to an animal and/or a bucket—seems disproportionately minor as a "need" when compared to the efforts being made to effect its "way" or its continued expression. Bauman said that tradition gives "meaning to our present lives by linking ourselves to a meaningful past" (Bauman 1992, 32), but what if it doesn't really matter if that past is especially *meaningful*? What if there is simply a universal need to continually link ourselves to *any* past, even a relatively recent or silly one? Barbara Kirschenblatt-Gimblett has noted that in the electronic vernacular, "playful uses of the medium may be even more revealing than strictly practical applications" (Kirschenblatt-Gimblett 1996, 22). One reason for this may be that the more playful the message, the more the use of the medium is highlighted as the source of meaning. Thus, we find continuity for the sake of continuity rather than for the sake

---

10   Although I am not necessarily arguing it here.

of expressing a particular idea—a sense of connection to the culture we see before us without necessarily needing a preexisting or significant *meaning* to the form.

Many people are familiar with the experience of joining in with a group's traditions simply (or at least initially) for the sake of enacting group membership more than for the expression of any genuine cultural significances that the traditions embody. I propose that sometimes the entire meaning of a tradition is, in fact, initially formed and subsequently maintained simply through the process of communal recreation. The history of folklore studies contains many examples of how people make meaningful things traditional, keeping them present in their lives by recreating them with others; but we should also consider that we sometimes bestow meaning on things in the first place through the act of making them traditional. Simply by choosing to adapt and transmit an image macro to others, we spark a chain of shared experience that is meaningful simply because it forms a chain. The abstract enactment of continuity is the goal. In this sense, tradition remains a seminal tool for folkloristics regardless of the nuances of spatial or temporal significance. As long as expressive forms are being informally transmitted, we will have tradition. And we will have folklore.

REFERENCES

Bauman, Richard, ed. 1992. *Folklore, Cultural Performances, and Popular Entertainments: A Communications-Centered Handbook.* New York: Oxford University Press.

Ben-Amos, Dan. 1976. "Analytical Categories and Ethnic Genres." In *Folklore Genres*, ed. Dan Ben-Amos. Austin: University of Texas Press.

Bennett, Gillian. 1984. "The Phantom Hitchhiker: Neither Modern, Urban, nor Legend?" In *Perspectives on Contemporary Legend*, vol. 1, ed. Paul Smith and Gillan Bennett, 45–63. Sheffield, UK: Center for English Cultural Tradition and Language.

Bronner, Simon J. 2009. "Digitizing and Virtualizing Folklore." In *Folklore and the Internet: Vernacular Expression in a Digital World*, ed. Trevor J. Blank, 21–66. Logan: Utah State University Press.

Cheezburger. 2007. *I Can Has Cheezburger.* www.icanhascheezburger.com. Cheezburger, Inc. Accessed 13 June 2011.

Dobler, Robert. 2009. "Ghosts in the Machine: Mourning the MySpace Dead." In *Folklore and the Internet: Vernacular Expression in a Digital World*, ed. Trevor J. Blank, 175–93. Logan: Utah State University Press.

Dorst, John. 1990. "Tags and Burners, Cycles and Networks: Folklore in the Telectronic Age." *Journal of Folklore Research* 27 (3): 179–90.

Duffy, Margaret, Janis Teruggi Page, and Rachel Young. 2012. "Obama as Anti-American: Visual Folklore in Right-Wing Forwarded E-mails and Construction of Conservative Social Identity." *Journal of American Folklore* 125 (496): 177–203. http://dx.doi.org/10.5406/jamerfolk.125.496.0177.

Dundes, Alan, and Carl R. Pagter. 1978 [1975]. *Work Hard and You Shall Be Rewarded: Urban Folklore from the Paperwork Empire.* Bloomington: Indiana University Press.

Dundes, Alan, and Carl R. Pagter. 1987. *When You're Up to Your Ass in Alligators: More Urban Folklore from the Paperwork Empire.* Detroit: Wayne State University Press.

Foote, Monica. 2007. "Userpicks: Cyber Folk Art in the Early 21st Century." *Folklore Forum* 37 (1): 27–38.

Frank, Russell. 2004. "When the Going Gets Tough, the Tough Go Photoshopping: September 11 and the Newslore of Vengeance and Victimization." *New Media & Society* 6(5): 633–58.

Frank, Russell. 2009. "The *Forward* as Folklore: Studying E-Mailed Humor." In *Folklore and the Internet: Vernacular Expression in a Digital World*, ed. Trevor J. Blank, 98–122. Logan: Utah State University Press.

Frank, Russell. 2011. *Newslore: Contemporary Folklore on the Internet.* Jackson: University Press of Mississippi.

Goldstein, Diane E. 1993. "Not Just a 'Glorified Anthropologist': Medical Problem Solving through Verbal and Material Art." *Folklore in Use* 1(1): 15–24.

Harris, Trudier. 1995. "Genre." *Journal of American Folklore* 108(430): 509.

Howard, Robert Glenn. 1997. "Apocalypse in Your In-box: End Times Communication on the Internet." *Western Folklore* 56 (3/4): 295–315. http://dx.doi.org/10.2307/1500281.

Howard, Robert Glenn. 2008. "Electronic Hybridity: The Persistent Processes of the Vernacular Web." *Journal of American Folklore* 121 (480): 192–218. http://dx.doi.org/10.1353/jaf.0.0012.

Howard, Robert Glenn. 2009. "Crusading on the Vernacular Web: The Folk Beliefs and Practices of Online Spiritual Warfare." In *Folklore and the Internet: Vernacular Expression in a Digital World,* ed. Trevor J. Blank, 159–74. Logan: Utah State University Press.

Howard, Robert Glenn. 2011. *Digital Jesus: The Making of a New Christian Fundamentalist Community on the Internet.* New York: New York University Press.

King, Whitney. 2011. "Mormon Mommy Blogs: 'There's Gotta Be Some Women out There Who Feel the Same Way.'" MA thesis, Utah State University, Logan.

Kirshenblatt-Gimblett, Barbara. 1996. "The Electronic Vernacular." In *Connected: Engagements with Media*, ed. George E. Marcus, 21–64. Chicago: University of Chicago Press.

LolPresidents. 2007. LolPresidents.com. http://lolpresident.com/category/bukkit/. Accessed June 13, 2011.

McNeill, Lynne S. 2009. "The End of the Internet: A Folk Response to the Provision of Infinite Choice." In *Folklore and the Internet: Vernacular Expression in a Digital World*, ed. Trevor J. Blank, 80–97. Logan: Utah State University Press.

McNeill, Lynne S. 2012. "Real Virtuality: Enhancing Locality by Enacting the Small World Theory." In *Folk Culture in the Digital Age*, ed. Trevor J. Blank, 85–97. Logan: Utah State University Press.

Miller, Kiri. 2008. "Grove Street Grimm: *Grand Theft Auto* and Digital Folklore." *Journal of American Folklore* 121 (481): 255–85. http://dx.doi.org/10.1353/jaf.0.0017.

Tucker, Elizabeth. 2009. "Guardians of the Living: Characterization of Missing Women on the Internet." In *Folklore and the Internet: Vernacular Expression in a Digital World*, ed. Trevor J. Blank, 67–79. Logan: Utah State University Press.

Westerman, William. 2009. "Epistemology, the Sociology of Knowledge, and the *Wikipedia* Userbox Controversy." In *Folklore and the Internet: Vernacular Expression in a Digital World*, ed. Trevor J. Blank, 123–58. Logan: Utah State University Press.

8

The "Handiness" of Tradition

Simon J. Bronner

I ARGUE IN THIS ESSAY THAT GRASPING THE "HANDINESS" of tradition is the key to the analytical strategy of folklore studies; the way people *perceive* the hand (active, immediate, instrumental, gestural, and visible), particularly in relation to the mind (passive, remote, nonproductive, individualized, and unseen), dictates the way scholars *conceive* folklore as pervasive, relevant, contemporary, functional, expressive, and ultimately meaningful. Being a cultural resource *at hand*, tradition represents everyday processes of social control and expression, and these processes are often set in contrast to modernization associated with standardization, commercialization, discontinuity, and artificiality. The idea of tradition is "handy" or effective in the sense that people regularly invoke it to refer to a purposeful, creative process of sustaining social connections through cultural expression, whether literally, in greeting traditions of shaking hands and celebratory customs of clapping hands for applause, or figuratively, in handing down stories and songs—and values—between generations. That is not to say that the influence of tradition on present-day life is easily averred, particularly by an intellectual elite. Because of a modernist concern that tradition restricts individualism, progressivism, and free will, the force of tradition has been denied or even protested (Adorno 1993; Giddens 1994, 66–74; Nussbaum 2010, 2, 25; Williams 1983, 318–20).

The handiness of tradition is not the only consideration in how people think with tradition, but it is arguably the central one. In other publications, I have traced the rhetorical use of tradition in scholarly discourse to the idea of social authority evident in references to the "following" of tradition,

DOI: 10.7330/9780874218992.c08

both as an analytical strategy of tracking activity perceived to be traditional and an assumption about tradition serving as a guide to action (Bronner 1992, 1998, 2000; see also Bronner 2009a, 2009b, 2011). Another concern I have addressed is the variability of tradition as a result of creative and elaborative processes (rather than creation, which suggests the fabrication of something totally new) in the conceptualization of folklore. I have pointed out that despite the humanistic construction of tradition and creativity as polar opposites, they are intertwined in the process of transmission and reproduction of cultural practices (Bronner 1992; see also Bronner 2012).

In this essay, I ask why the hand is rhetorically emphasized to express the character of tradition and how folklore embodies this metaphorical meaning. My answer hinges on the historical and linguistic roots of the term *tradition* in Roman law and language and culturally on the cognitive categories created between brain and brawn. Bringing the use of tradition up to the present, I examine the way that the handiness of tradition both embraces and resists modernity. Against this historical and cultural background, I draw on practice theory and the philosophy of language to interpret the handiness of tradition as a *phemic* quality that drives an analytical agenda for folklore study into the future (Bronner 2011, 2012). As I maintain that this agenda challenges modernist conceptualizations of twenty-first-century Western society as being "post-traditional," and hence postmodern, in the end, I discuss a theoretical reorientation to account for the hand that tradition has in modern life.

DEFINING FOLKLORE WITH THE HAND OF TRADITION

The hand figures prominently in definitions of folklore that invoke tradition. Such definitions imply *handing* involves social learning. This kind of knowledge acquisition leads to expressive practice and involves repetition and variation characteristic of folklore. References to the hand as a learning process imply a contrast to cerebral, elite, or academic learning that appears removed from everyday life and often practical, social engagement with lived experience. For example, a popular set of pamphlets on various traditions compiled and re-titled *Handy Folklore* (Cooperative Recreation Service 1955) emphasizes folklore's characteristics of facilitating social expression, participation, and activity. Under the opening heading of "Do You Like People?," the anonymous writer declares that "folklore is a means of communication everywhere. It is a sharing of mutually enjoyable skills, of our common humanity." Tradition enters the picture because "these arts must be learned anew by each generation, nurtured by parents, and schools" (Cooperative Recreation Service 1955, 1). Rhetorically, the material in this popularized presentation is "handy" because it is easily accessible, involves social as well as expressive exchange, and is handed down—that is, socially learned or "passed" and practiced through generations.

Stith Thompson's classic academic statement of folklore being socially "handed down," and therefore equated with tradition, in *Funk & Wagnalls Standard Dictionary of Folklore, Mythology, and Legend*, echoes through most introductions to folklore during the mid-twentieth century: "The common idea present in all folklore is that of tradition, something handed down from one person to another and preserved either by memory or practice rather than written record" (Thompson 1949, 403). His contemporary Archer Taylor revised the handing process to be more historical when he defined folklore as "materials that are handed on from generation to generation" (Leach 1949, 402–3). But answering the question "What Is Tradition?," Phillips Barry and Fannie Hardy Eckstorm (1930, 2) considered "handing over" as important as "handing down" to the designation of folk material. As a synchronic process of being "passed on," Barry and Eckstorm construed tradition to be widely distributed over space, as well as persistent over time, and face-to-face interaction involved in its diffusion resulted in variation of the material called *folkloric*.

Scholars of later generations continued to invoke the hand to describe the communicative process of tradition in folklore. Probably the most used folkloristic textbook of the twentieth century, *The Study of American Folklore: An Introduction*, by Jan Harold Brunvand (with four different editions between 1968 and 1998), referred to folklore as "unrecorded traditions" characterized as "communication from person to person" (Brunvand 1998, 3). In a kind of motific substitution, Brunvand abstracts Thompson's emphasis on the hand in "handed down from one person to another" in the use of "communication," presumably to draw attention to transmission of traditions by recording, telephone, photocopy, facsimile machine, television, and computer (Brunvand 1998, 3). Remaining in the concept of passing is the generation of repeatable, varied expressions arising out of social interaction. According to Brunvand, folklore is "passed on" figuratively, if not literally hand to hand or person to person, and from elders to their juniors: "Folklore is oral or custom-related in that it *passes* by word of mouth and informal demonstration or imitation from one person to another and from one generation to the next" (Brunvand 1998, 12; italics added).

Elsewhere in Brunvand's textbook, one reads of folklore as an action or performance guided by tradition. He states that "folklore is traditional in two senses in that it is passed on repeatedly in a relatively fixed or standard form, and it circulates among members of a particular group" (Brunvand 1998, 12); folklore is "transmission [that] creates different versions" (15); and it is "expressed partly in commonplace terms or patterns" (16). Circulating traditionally, that is, with the idea of being handed down or over, folklore constitutes, in Brunvand's words, "processes of traditional performance and communication" (15). In the twenty-first century, Martha Sims and Martine Stephens (2005), in their textbook *Living Folklore*, characterize folklore as "knowledge . . . *handed on* orally from person to person" (131; italics added) and "expressive communication within a particular group" (6), thus suggesting the semantic equation of "handing" with "communication," "circulation," "transmission," "expression," and "sharing" as essential generative processes resulting in traditional material usually summarized as folklore.

The trouble is, as Åke Hultkrantz (1960, 229) notes in his definition of *tradition* in *General Ethnological Concepts*, equating folklore with tradition presents a "very general and vague definition, since tradition appears in at least three different senses": a body of material, a process of transmission or generation, and a mode of thinking (Bronner 1998, 9–12). All the senses of tradition, though, refer in some regard metaphorically to the action of hands. As a body of material, tradition is literally and figuratively associated with being hand-wrought—that is, personally rendered, manipulated, or conveyed, whether a basket or a well-delivered story. As a process of transmission and generation, folklore may be referred to as being handed (passed) down, handed over, and, more recently with digital culture, handed up (Bronner 2009b, 32) to draw attention to the social interaction, even with electronic mediation, out of which framed expressions or practices emerge. As a mode of thinking and social source of authority, tradition may represent conventional wisdom often expressed as a "rule of thumb" or a "guiding hand." Although handing may be replaced in modern rhetoric often related to digital culture, because scholars perceive the term to narrow folkloric production to face-to-face encounters, it nonetheless provides the basis for the social interaction and variable repetition given as hallmarks of tradition.

TRADITION IN FOLKLORISTIC ANALYSIS

Tradition informs folkloristic analysis because if folklorists are concerned with the handing over, as Thompson stated, of "memory or practice" from one person to another, they tend to objectify knowledge in the form of expression that draws attention to itself to render it observable or recordable (Ketner 1973, 1976). Unlike a record that renders a memory or practice in officious, finalized form such as a contract, engaging the hand means the expression is socially affective because the transaction between people needs to be reenacted and presumably raises emotions and personal connections. Metaphorically moving from hand to hand, folklore involves an exchange and suggests a simultaneous pattern of continuity and change. The label of "folk" for the observable expression implies a previous transaction that informed the continual, if variable, production of culture. If the individuals and events represented by the central folkloristic question "where and how did you learn that?" are not always apparent, they are nonetheless allusive in the idea of presently observable practices that owe inspiration to previously enacted transactions.

One can detect this allusion in the emphasis on the agency of tradition bearers performing and "passing on" folklore in the textbook *The Dynamics of Folklore* by Barre Toelken (1996 [1979], 32): "Its primary characteristic is that its ingredients seem to come directly from dynamic interactions among human beings in vernacular performance contexts rather than through the more rigid channels and fossilized structures of technical instruction or bureaucratized education, or through the relatively stable channels of the formally taught classical traditions." "Tradition," he writes, "is a compendium of those pre-existing culture-specific materials, assumptions, and options that bear upon the performer more heavily than do his or her own personal tastes and talents." The use of tradition, according to Toelken, means that "matters of content and style have been, for the most part, *passed on* by the culture, but not invented by the performer" (Toelken 1996, 37; italics added). Elsewhere he refers to "exchange" as dynamic because creativity is exercised *within* a tradition: "Generally speaking, the performers of traditional expressions do so because they want to or must, and usually their audience is made up of participating members of the same group in which the dynamic exchange of traditions through the years has formed the matrix out of which the performer operates" (37). The rhetoric of dynamism in this text reminds readers that the repeatable transactions of tradition, such as a goodbye wave or bow, are structured but not fixed. Individuals can strategically alter them in different contexts or with other persons and thereby in their agency give them situated symbolic meanings.

No wonder, then, that folklore studies emphasize "fieldwork." This scholarly labor outside the formal environments of institutions and archives implies that observation of the action of handing, the thing being handed, and the hands (that is, participants) involved reveals the active, naturalized character of the memory or practice labeled "folk" and framed as expressive, repeated, and connotative relative to various contexts (Bronner 2006a, 419–20; 2009b, 21–22; Georges and Jones 1980). Emblematic of this intellectually constructed division between formal institutions and informal tradition is Richard Dorson's oft-cited initiatory narrative of transversal into a naturalized realm of activity in need of ordering and deciphering: "The folklorist is crossing the square, or scaling the walls, that divide the book-learned from the tradition-oriented sectors of society, and in my foray into the Upper Peninsula of Michigan in 1946 [from Michigan State University in East Lansing] I crossed the Straits of Mackinac by ferry to enter an uncharted world of folk societies. As I now realize, I could have found the folk anywhere, but at the time I needed a symbolic crossing in my voyage of discovery" (Dorson 2008 [1952], xxvi). The moral of his story is that the field is a frame of social activity, or myriad expressive transactions, in need of exposure, and appreciation, through documentation (Bronner 2010).

Fieldwork presumes that folklore embodies tradition by revealing people in cultural production or metaphorically in "handwork." Folklore as a kind of expressive gesture therefore carries meaning that is discerned from recordable, repeatable practices. Folklore's traditionality presumably distinguishes it from other kinds of practices that are restricted to fixed forms of a solitary creator or are deemed culturally inert (as in "routines" of brushing teeth or putting on socks). Folklore, as with stylized hand motions of which the person is not aware, might become significant to record even if it is ordinary or routine if it signifies a form of cultural inheritance and body of traditional knowledge. If the framed expressive activity of tradition is to stick around, or have purpose, then it needs to be reproduced through transmission; and the work in the field to comprehend this learning and expressive process is typically central to a folkloristic analysis.

The reproduction of folklore can be selective, as in the idea of social groups gaining identity by the formation of informational conduits and shared traditions among their members (Blumenreich and Polansky 1975;

Dégh and Vázsonyi 1975; Dundes 1980, 1–19). Although approaches to fieldwork certainly vary, fieldwork essentially differs as an analysis from "doing a reading" or executing a "proof." Trained to discern manifestations of tradition, the analyst tends to frame events into repeatable, variable actions (such as singing, telling, and making), extrapolate knowledge gained and symbols communicated through the action, detect the exchange or direction of the transmission, and infer the character of people and settings in the exchange. The analysis frequently rationalizes activity that may appear out of the ordinary and aestheticizes material that might be construed as usual or routine. Folklorists apply fieldwork strategies to the study of the past, typically through archivable documents, by tracing social transactions resulting in an expressible product or practice and finding relationships of a present practice to other times and places.

   Another analytical ramification is the distinctive folkloristic emphasis on annotating lore to discern relationships of material to tradition bearers, groups, expressive precedents, and contexts (Bronner 2006b; Dorson 1972, 15–17; Oring 1989). The annotation locates cognates of a practice and determines if their contexts are comparable in time and space to establish its "traditionality." In other words, the annotation provides evidence of social transactions resulting in the practice or memory becoming culturally embedded. The annotation raises questions in its paucity or abundance about the agency, persistence, change, structure, and function of lore that by definition involves "passed," or traditionally gained, knowledge. Tradition therefore implies an element of time, in the sense of folklore representing precedence of knowledge and presence of an expressible product or reproducible practice. Tradition also involves space because the transaction is located or situated in a place, and the folklorist infers social connections that make it possible for the expressions to diffuse as a result of cultural transactions and exchanges. A relational factor sought in the annotation is the cultural association of tradition to folklore by determining where the knowledge passed from and where (and by whom) it became planted (another reference to the hand).

   From a structural viewpoint, the characteristic of folklore arising from the transmittive process of tradition allows for comparison of material that otherwise would be separated by genre. In the historiography of folklore studies, scholars used the characteristic of handed-down tradition to counter popular assertions that "lore" was restricted to the singular form of stories. William Thoms in 1846 suggested that customs, superstitions, proverbs, and ballads appear as "minute facts" were it not for their connection with a traditional "system" that he characterized as "links in a great chain" (Thoms 1965 [1846], 4–6). Picking up on Thoms's call, Charlotte Burne, in *The Handbook of Folklore*, generalized folklore as "the learning of the people" and labeled its parts as all being "traditional": "traditional Beliefs, Customs, Stories, Songs, and Sayings" (Burne 1913, 1). Later in the century, Alan Dundes noted that "if, then, there are non-verbal analogues (e.g., games) for verbal folklore forms (e.g., folktales), then folklore as a discipline cannot possibly be limited to the study of just verbal art, oral literature, or folk literature, or whatever similar term is employed" (Dundes 1964, 286). Tradition is the analytical basis of relating and comparing a range of cultural practices with the goal of deriving meaning out the usage, milieu, and content of these practices.

ON *TRADERE*: HISTORICAL AND LINGUISTIC ROOTS OF TRADITION IN ROMAN LAW

Most linguistic and philosophical considerations of tradition begin with a singular source citing the Latin root *tradere*, "to hand over or deliver," and adapting it to the popular idea that tradition is "handed down" from generation to generation, especially by oral means. This gap between the linguistic root and popular discourse raises the question of how speakers moved from the Roman conception of a social act involving contemporaneous transfer of material goods to the dominant narrative of receiving knowledge from a predecessor.

The answer lies in the changing perception of the distinction of knowledge gained by tradition. The source of the term *tradition* is typically traced to Roman jurisprudence, suggesting a literal meaning of tradition as a material transaction (Gross 1992, 9). Roman laws of inheritance dealt with goods considered valuable, and meanings arose from the root *tradere*, including *traditio* for the process by which transmission occurs and *traditum* for the thing transmitted. Historian David Gross points out that *traditio* implies that "(a) something precious or valuable is (b) given to someone in trust after which (c) the person who receives the 'gift' is expected to keep it intact and unharmed out of a *sense of obligation* to the giver" (Gross 1992, 9; italics in the original). As an inheritance, the gift, or *traditum*, often comes from a predecessor or ancestor, and with it is the expectation that the thing would be cherished and preserved and considered valuable enough to be passed on to someone else (Gross 1992, 9). The obligation to keep and honor the item is driven presumably out of respect for the memory (and wishes) of the predecessor, whose name may be obscured over time as the *traditum* is passed on generations later. This sense of obligation shows up in an alternative meaning of *traditio*—"surrender"—and suggests an association with authority because the recipient submits to the sway of the elder.

Getting to the abstraction of tradition from Roman law, a metaphorical shift occurred from thing to knowledge, which was probably based on the symbolic connotations of transmitting the *traditum*. Rituals accompanying the transmittal provide a major clue. To mark the transfer of a piece of land, an agent physically handed over a clod of dirt from the property to the recipient; to legally recognize the acquisition of a house or a shop, keys would ritually pass from one person to another (Congar 2004, 9). The earth and keys not only act as a synecdoche for something larger; they also inspire memory and narrative of the possession and the figures associated with it. Enacting *traditio* drew attention to itself by the use of a repeatable symbolic practice that relied on a shared knowledge between agent and recipient about the consequences of the act. The tradition became noticeable in the flow of life because it was ritualized and framed as time out of time. In that special occasion, differences between present and past collapsed. One was aware in the tradition that the action had precedent, but especially important was a transcendent concern about what it stood for. Other actions, including telling a story or singing a song that evoked the transference of something expressive or valuable, could be attached to the process of *traditio*. In this way, both tangible and intangible "gifts" recognized by their expressive and connotative characteristics became equated. Recalling what these things represented constituted a narrated knowledge that was not so much institutionally taught or read as it was socially engaged in practice. It connoted socialized or localized knowledge popularly designated as lore. As medieval English scholars began to gloss Latin texts, they indeed used *folclic lār* ("folklike lore") to designate sayings coming out of vernacular or noninstitutional settings drawing attention to themselves for being expressive or representative of a locality or group, particularly in contrast to the kind of fixed, widely distributed forms represented by the use of printing, which was then modern (Mazo 1996).

Setting the process of *traditio* apart is its consecutiveness. In a business deal, an agreement is concluded; it does not have to be reenacted to be valid. The business deal is a matter of record. In tradition, transmittal needs to occur repeatedly, often by word of mouth and practice, which further sets it apart from modernization characterized by the rule of official law and record. The socially communicative characteristic of a transaction in tradition is crucial to the perpetuation of lore. Every action in *traditio* involves a giver as well as a recipient, and the participants are aware that something like it has occurred before and will happen after they are gone. They understand that the action of *traditio* is consecutive from one person and one moment to the next. A commonly used metaphor is that they are links in a chain, each separate but connected to one another in a consecutive pattern. The liturgical introduction to the mourner's prayer (Kaddish) in Judaism for example, states that it is "testimony to that unbroken faith which links the generations one to another." Commenting on the ritual, famed philanthropist Henrietta Szold observed, "The Kaddish means to me that the survivor publicly and markedly manifests his wish and intention to assume the relation to the Jewish community which his parent had, and that *the chain of tradition* remains unbroken from generation to generation" (Lowenthal 1942, 92–93; italics added). Tradition requires agency to continue, and part of the obligation to keep the *traditum* intact is to reenact the process. Traditions can disappear and be revived after lapsing, but psychologically, a fear exists that the chain—the order—of tradition will be broken if it is not enacted consecutively (see Dundes 2007, 424–25).

Referring to tradition suggests not only that cultural reproduction occurs but also that a meaning may be changed through variable repetition of a precedent that creates a situational or local version. This broadening of the social implication of tradition is a semantic development beyond the one-to-one relationship implied in Roman law. As lore, traditions can be transmitted to a crowd and move in different directions with the travels of the recipients. When individuals engage in the process of *traditio*, traditions vary as they are adapted to different settings or are recalled with changes in content and meaning, even if they are structured similarly to the lore that went before them. As populations move and social needs change, traditions inevitably evolve, increasing or altering by fusion with other traditions or declining in practice and memory. Cognitively, there may be an inclination to believe that traditions by their nature as valued social artifacts grow from simpler to more complex forms in an evolutionary pattern, but this may be countered by a devolutionary belief that modernization and the passage of time renders traditions fractions of what they once were (Dundes 1969).

The former belief supports the folk idea that "Mighty oaks from little acorns grow," with the corollary view that tradition is a living faith and force. The latter belief often reveals the attitude that modernity and industrialization displace ways of life centered on the primary transmission of wisdom from elders to children.

The reverence for the flowering of tradition in the past commonly supports perceptions of a former golden age or the "good old days" in which traditions are rooted, whereas the devolutionary outlook frequently supports the conceptualizations of traditions as relic manifestations of an unenlightened past (Bronner 1998, 73–140). Participants may be unaware of the origins or original meanings of traditions as they take the form of practices and become integrated into everyday life, such as the unself-conscious cultural practices of shaking hands, bowing, and waving. Consequently, the consecutiveness of *traditio* can be expressed structurally as a circle rather than as a linear progression typical of the arts, from creation to imitation, because of the view that persons are joined together as participants in the dual roles of givers and recipients instead of as originators. Theologian Yves Congar (2004, 9–10) understood this structural basis when he offered the circular relay race as a metaphor for tradition, where runners standing at intervals both take and pass batons and in the process are bonded as a team. A ritual action is embedded in the transfer of the *traditum* to represent continuity; and as expressed in the idiom "passing the torch," a responsibility is implied in the handling of the *traditum*.

Recognizing that *tradita* can be preserved as relics without the enactment of *traditio*, Congar makes a distinction between active and passive traditions (Congar 2004, 45). In active traditions capable of accretion, agents, often called "tradition bearers," pass an expression. Edward Shils (1981, 13) refers to them as "custodians" or "exemplars." Passive traditions contain preserved content, often in the form of recorded or remembered texts, but they are not relayed ritually. In this theologically oriented rhetoric, traditions in the plural refer to expressions or practices, whereas the singular tradition, often capitalized, signifies the totality of belief. For Congar (2004, 10), tradition "encloses and dominates" existence by representing a mode of thought held by believers. In contrast to particularized, plural traditions, a capitalized Tradition broadly thematizes everything a group does (Congar used it to universalize Catholicism) and often carries a sacred connotation. One can view this usage of a capitalized Tradition as a theme in references to "Judeo-Christian Tradition," "Great Tradition," and "Western Tradition." They may not be culturally constituted by participation, but they are identified, organized, and mapped by institutions. Broadly imagined, the capitalized Tradition points to a shared transcendent faith in the understanding of belief as a truth and value.

Rather than categorizing the capitalized Tradition as *traditum*, philosopher Josef Pieper refers to *tradendum* as "what is supposed to be handed down." It is a useful addition to the lexicon of tradition because it differentiates localized cultural expressions from institutional canons, scriptures, or doctrines (Berkhof 2002, 105; Pieper 2008). *Tradenda* are not practices engaged in socially or things passed on; they are the ideals or values connected organizationally. They have a connection to the sense of tradition as a "mode of thinking," which is often the least conspicuous to observers but most pervasive in everyday life. This sense is expressed when someone explains that "tradition holds" (another hand metaphor) that something is done a certain way or tradition is equated with an outlook characteristic of a place or people.

Much of the semantics of tradition, whether as *traditio, traditum,* or *tradendum,* revolves around the process of "handing," which implies that the thing being handed over metaphorically has tangible value. For many people unaware of Roman law, what is relevant about tradition is the symbolism of social and emotional attachment in the hand. The hand is important to tradition because of its capacity to grasp objects physically and intellectually and attach meanings to them. Being "in hand" suggests the tradition's value of being possessed for human purposes. "Handing it over" as the basis of tradition implies a social connection, made with deliberateness, much like the transporting of a valued possession. Giver and recipient come together at that moment and become familiar as a consequence. The image of the hand gives the transaction a "personal touch," the ability to "reach out and touch someone" rather than being thought about in solitude. Being "handed down" brings elders or predecessors into the scene but in a way that implies a familial tie from one generation to another. In other words, a social bond or identity goes "hand in hand" with tradition. Whereas intellectual pursuits are associated with reading, memorization, and individualized study, knowledge to navigate through one's culture is seen as experiential—that is, gained through "hands-on" experience. "Hands-on" or "hand-me-down" shows social continuity with either a mentor in a workplace or an elder in a family, whereas observers attached to vision imply detachment and perhaps apartness from social norms.

HANDWORK AS CULTURAL WORK

The "common knowledge" of handed-down lore takes on a vernacular cast because of the association of handwork and domesticity with tradition, especially the perceptions that handmade, hand-hewn, or homespun materials are naturally traditional by virtue of their being rooted in a locality and its environment (see Bronner 1986; Jones 1975). The mechanical-sounding action of handing down may not be deemed intellectual, or more accurately "scholastic," but it suggests active participation and hence authenticity in culture by the passing of something socially significant involving memory and narrative (Bourdieu 1990, 127–40). It is often "practical" in the sense of being applied to lived experience and variable in social situations (Bourdieu 1990, 80–97).

Unlike intellectualized sight that allows for looking broadly out on the horizon, or reading alone, the sense of touch represented by the hand is immediate, involves bodily action, and implies certitude. Vision associated with a future orientation and the mechanical reproduction of images in photography became emblematic of modernity while handwork raises preindustrial images that persist into the present. Suggesting handiness as materialized and localized, the practical statement of "business at hand" refers to a matter in front of us that demands action. In conversation, "wanting to see something," with its reference to distance, is weaker than the possessive gripping imagery of "wanting to get my hands on something." "Seeing is believing," the English proverb states, but it admonishes in the second part that "feeling's the truth" (Bronner 1982; Dundes 1980, 86–92). "The hand is quicker than the eye," another proverb reminds people, also suggesting that the power of the hand is often overlooked. One might understand the hold of tradition by noting the "tangible proof" provided by touching with the hand. No doubt, one wants to have the certainty of knowing "hands down" or else behold the mistrust of "virtual images." One therefore longs to be "in touch with reality."

In references to being "handy," someone using handwork is often associated with pragmatic concerns about the conduct of everyday life. Handwork accomplishes tasks and orders or changes one's environment. The hand is directly or personally experienced, so one might be assured "you're in good hands" and might also be reminded that "one in the hand is worth two in the bush," meaning that the thing in the hand is definite, whereas those things one yearns for in the distance are uncertain. The root of tradition as an inheritance or gift being handed over is relevant because of the idea that practical wisdom is passed along with the touched thing rather than with the artifice of words. From these associations, tradition brings to mind a type of learning and teaching outside of institutional control. In popular usage, this vernacular knowledge or lore is related to everyday experience grounded in place. Tradition as a concept to describe the acquisition of this knowledge through repeated, enculturated practice implies a social, often localized predisposition that informs one's conduct in life (Bronner 2012).

The handed-over knowledge is more than the delivery of information. By referring to the hand's ability to gesture and touch, tradition is referential—even symbolic—in the actions produced. More than any other part of the body, the hands are images of symbolic actions and feelings: formed into a fist, folded in (prayer), or giving an affectionate pat or caress. As a sign of humanity, hands are valued for their special ability to hold tools—as an extension of the body—and thus work as well as play. Humans view the hand as a tool that requires skills to be productive. Overall, hands are perceived as instruments of purposeful activity: they make things happen.

According to psychologist Susan Goldin-Meadow, the hands are distinctive in being gestural, and, behaviorally, the gesture is the minimal unit of expressing meaning. This view follows from pragmatic philosopher George Herbert Mead's concept of the gesture as a social act, because whether in the form of language or bodily action, it elicits a response and is formed out of a communicative need or purpose (Mead 1962, 13–17, 68–81). In the form of folklore, gesture takes on the attribute of the "significant symbol" because meaning is attached by virtue of giver and recipient in a transaction similarly anticipating responses to connotative actions. Goldin-Meadow (2005, 25) elaborates on this crucial implication of the hand's ability to gesture when she writes, "Gesture conveys meaning globally, relying on visual and mimetic imagery. Speech conveys meaning discretely, relying on codified words and grammatical devices." People link handiness with objects rather than words because of the hand's ability to grasp and form objects that are supposed to stand the test of time more so than words uttered in a moment. I contend that "mimetic imagery" includes not just imitation but also the enactment of intentional representations, which is especially important for the production of culture (see Cantwell 1993). Neuroscientist Merlin Donald (1991, 168), for example, notes that mimetic skills or mimesis basic to tool making, child rearing, and custom rest on the ability to produce "conscious, self-initiated, representational acts that are intentional, but not linguistic" and these constitute the foundation of human culture. This "results in the sharing of knowledge without every member of the group having to reinvent that knowledge," or what we think of as tradition (Donald 1991, 173; see also Wilson 1999, 48–49).

Although people are often unaware of the hand gestures they make to express emotions or provide information, they understand such movements as a basic form of communication, especially when trying to make themselves understood to someone who does not share the same words or when emphasizing a point. In this way, the handy knowledge of tradition is a fundamental communicative behavior that both underlies speech and is independent of it. These associations affect the perceptions of tradition because of the cognitive categories of thought expressed as reasoned ideas in words by an individual, whereas tradition is construed as emotional action or gesture that is shared socially.

The source of time in handy knowledge is usually less certain than for institutional work because of tradition's imagery of collectivity and continuity. Saying that something is old implies that it can be dated, whereas labeling an artifact or story as "traditional" means that it has been transmitted *through* time. Tradition's time can refer to the last millennium or last week, but in popular usage it suggests "time immemorial" because tradition's nonlinear associations result in uncertainty of how traditions get started. This reference to time is apparent when tradition is used as a synonym for culture in the sense of representing the totality of arts, customs, lore, and institutions for a group. Thus, when one reads of "Dutch tradition" or "aboriginal tradition," the compound term emphasizes the culture's long, steady existence, which may not be clear from the use of *culture* with its connotation of a bounded social group in place (Ben-Amos 1984, 119–21; Hultkrantz 1960, 229–31). Individuals are probably conscious of plural traditions that are repeatable activities, but they consider a singular tradition to be an internalized mode of thinking or worldview.

People might be said to be born into tradition, as well as participating in traditions, but with the singular mode of thinking places an added emphasis on the lifelong effect of which people are probably unaware because it is all around them. Artist Mamie Harmon, for instance, refers to tradition as "comprising that information, those skills, concepts, products, etc., which one acquires almost inevitably *by virtue of the circumstances to which he is born*. It is not so much deliberately sought (like learning) as absorbed. It is not deliberately invented; rather, it develops. It is present in the environment, is accepted, used, transformed, transmitted, or forgotten, without arbitrary impetus from individual minds" (Harmon 1949, 400; italics in the original). Tradition so conceived can be said to be superorganic in the sense that it is constant and even controlling beyond one's consciousness. Modern sensibilities, however, usually dictate that individuals select and adapt traditions organically, allowing them to participate in various cultural scenes and take on various identities.

Linked to the life cycle, tradition revolves around generational time. The length of time qualifying to categorically constitute a tradition is often in dispute. Gross declared a minimal stretch of time for a tradition to be authentic to be three generations (i.e., two transmissions), although folklorists conceive of lore as being traditional or "handed over" spatially by virtue of the fact that someone passes it along to someone else (such as telling a joke one has just heard). What appears to be important is that a precedent for action exists. It is traditional because it resembles something that went before and was known in a social unit. Gross distinguishes tradition's "temporal duration" from history's occurrence in time and summarizes this aspect of tradition's meaning as "continuity between the past and the present" (Gross 1992, 10). Upon receiving tradition according to this perspective, people have a feeling of consecutiveness, the sense that they are part of a sequential chain stretching back in time and from one person or group to another. Tradition is therefore prescriptive by virtue of being repeated because it was done before in contrast to history which records what occurred previously (Gross 1992, 8).

Habit and custom also rely on precedent, but they are distinguished from tradition by their relative lack of emphasis on intergenerational connection and symbolic connotation. A habit is an action, often a mannerism, that is regularly repeated until it becomes involuntary (see Aboujaoude 2008). Rather than constituting a connotative message, habit is often considered "routine" by being unvarying, an addiction, or a rote procedure for an individual. Its manifestation in individual behavior is often differentiated from custom, which is a repeated social occasion. Although *traditional* and *customary* are often used interchangeably to refer to the prescriptive repetition of activities based on precedent, customary activities do not have the degree of consecutiveness and connotation expected of tradition. One does not hear of the *chain* or *authority* of custom in the way these terms are applied to tradition. Indeed, an event might be intentionally referred to as a custom to imply that it does not have as strong a consecutive hold on its participants as tradition or that it is irregularly enacted.

Both traditions and customs can be symbolic, but the implication of tradition having a hold from the rhetoric of the hand is that it draws attention to itself by its ritualistic connotation of idea and faith. Social psychologist Edward Alsworth Ross includes the criterion of involvement in the distinction he insightfully draws between custom and tradition: "By custom is meant the transmission of a way of *doing*; by tradition is meant the transmission of a way of *thinking* or *believing*" (Ross 1909, 196; emphases in original; see also Clark 2005, 4). The commonality of tradition and custom is their involvement of action in the form of practice, but tradition often brings into play a mode of thought or social learning associated with lore. Tradition—more than custom—brings out the handing down and over of values.

.

A PHEMIC PERSPECTIVE ON TRADITION

Separating brushing one's teeth in the morning as a daily routine or custom from the tradition of the tooth fairy is a quality that has been labeled "phemic" by philosophers, particularly those incorporating theories of language developed by J. L. Austin (1961, 1968; see also Warnock 1989). For some observers, the imaginative content of the tooth fairy, along with other beliefs, rituals, games, and narratives, sets it apart as a tradition; however, many utilitarian practices that are socially or geographically situated, such as craft, medicine, and agriculture, would not be perceived as fantasy or play and yet are viewed as noticeable traditions. Phemic material denotes an implicative message that is impelled to be transmitted, and the material becomes associated with the process of its transmission. Austin approaches the analysis of these messages similarly to Mead's gestures to account for the way they are *ordinarily used*—that is, transacted with others—to produce symbols and elucidate meaning.

Austin's contribution to a theory of tradition based upon practice is to rubricate forms of transmission that result in actions (he called them "illocutionary acts") we might recognize as traditional. Austin calls the production of sound a *phone*, whereas a *pheme* is a performative utterance with a definite sense of meaning (a subset of a pheme in his system is a *rheme* to refer to a sign that represents its object). Colloquially, the pheme may be said to "say something" that might be used on different occasions of utterance with a different sense (Warnock 1989, 120). The nuance to tradition as "regularities" Austin introduces is that the illocutionary act is one performed *in* saying something; the locutionary act is one in the act *of* saying something while the perlocutionary act occurs *by* saying something. Indeed, the example in everyday life that Austinian philosopher John Searle uses to exemplify this distinction among the acts invokes the role of the hand as the response that signals a transaction and the occurrence of a tradition. The locution might be a query of whether salt is on the table and the illocution is of requesting it. The perlocution is causing someone to hand the container of salt over or "pass it" (Searle 1969, 53). The rules or traditions governing the transaction are often unstated and learned by participation in cultural scenes or regular responses to what Searle calls "the presence of certain stimuli" or "intentional behavior" (Searle 1969, 53).

The term *pheme* comes from Pheme of Greek mythology, who personified renown and was characterized by rumor spreading (Austin was trained in the classics as well as linguistics). Symbolically important to the conceptualization of tradition as consecutive transmission *in vulgus populo* is her status as a daughter of the earth and one of the mightiest, if not the most elegant or beautiful, of the goddesses (Burr 1994, 231; Chisholm 1910, 158). She had a proclivity to repeat what she learned for better or worse (in art, she is often depicted with multiple tongues, eyes, and ears), to the point that it became common knowledge. Along the way, though, the information had varied greatly and was often made larger in proportion to the original bit of news. Pheme did not fabricate knowledge; her skill was in framing material in such a way that it would be passed around. She was a relay station of sorts, serving as both recipient and transmitter of earthy material that drew attention to itself by being shared from person to person. The knowledge transmitted was known as much for the process it went through as for its content. Because it was subjected to this verbal and nonverbal transmittal process associated with earthy rumor, the content invited evaluation of its truth and value. In its "larger" form, the material raised questions about its sources and its combinations and reconfigurations, forming a whole with multiple connotative layers created along the path of transmission.

In Plato's dialogues, pheme shows up as a circulating rumor or report, but, in repetition, it has religious and political values embedded into speech used by a collective of people. In a dialogue about what constitutes an ideal city, Socrates relates a Phoenician story but points out that the narrative is more than news of an event; it represents the involvement of a whole generation of parents transmitting the material to children with a moralistic message about proper behavior (Grube 1992, 92). He declares, "let us leave the matter to later tradition (*h ph me agag i*)" (Ophir 1991, 95). Pheme, in the long term, emphasizes the persistence of the material and the process by which it is preserved. In classicist Luc Brisson's reading, "*Ph m* in the long term designates collective speech what today we call 'tradition,' whether this tradition refers to a religious sphere—gods, daimons, heros, and even the world of Hades—or to a secular sphere—institutions, heroic military deeds, etc. From this perspective *ph m* designates collective speech which is destined to be preserved" (Brisson 2000, 31; italics in the original). This Platonic idea of tradition bridging religious and secular worlds and containing multiple messages inherent in the process of transmission within a collective group informs the semiotic notion of a pheme as a sign layered with meaning and "intended to have some sort of compulsive effect on the interpreter of it," or what Austin and Searle might term a perlocutionary act (Ochs 1998, 209).

Phemic transmission can be distinguished from phatic communication in what anthropologist Bronislaw Malinowski characterized as a "type of speech in which ties of union are created by a mere exchange of words," such as the greeting formula "How are you?" followed by "Fine, thank you" (Laver 1975, 215; see also Warnock 1989, 120–22). As action, phatic speech corresponds to the routine or custom of practice intended, according to linguist John Lyons, "to establish and maintain a feeling of social solidarity and well being" (Lyons 1968, 417). Tradition often serves this social function as well, but it is distinguished as purposeful activity with a repeatable, multilayered message that can be called phemic because it compels "handing down" and variation in the long term by means of social, especially face-to-face, interaction.

A modern-day example of repeatable or phemic behavior that is observable every academic semester is classroom seating. In most college classrooms, students choose where they sit. Once students settle on a seat, they tend to return to the same location. Their choice is often cognitively derived from a number of beliefs and structures: sitting in the front increases chances of academic success and attracts the professor's notice of the student as an individual; sitting in the back gets one away from the authority of the instructor and shows to others that the back-wall hugger is more social or rebellious; and seats are traditionally arranged linearly in rows. Some students believe that being near the door allows for an early exit or that being by the window is healthier by being closer to the natural outdoors. Students might sit near people they know for social connection, and many choose a similar location in all their classrooms. This common practice repeated throughout academe might seem like habit, except that students tie their location to student identity (i.e., "where I am dictates who I am" and gender considerations are often at work when women tend to cluster in the front) and relate action to outcomes. Students, for instance, insist on sitting in the same seat during finals when classrooms may change. They may indeed feel discomfort when forced to relocate. They believe that having the same seat imparts luck and insures success. As a proctor, I have often heard them explain beliefs to others about why certain seats are important to claim. Or they assert that being in a certain area and taking the examination in a certain way (suggesting a traditional response to anxiety) is a tradition to them.

Associated with precedent, continuity, and convention, tradition in all the senses discussed is commonly put forward to direct future action. Whether one wants the future to break with or continue a customary pattern dictates judgments of tradition as negative or positive. Especially common in the modernist literature of culture are statements emphasizing tradition as a guide or a choice. Folklorists frequently have the attitude that "living" folklore located within a mass society suggests that in the modern push toward novelty, choosing tradition—a social connection hearkening back to the past—is a threatened human freedom. Barry McDonald offers an example in a study of the Archibald family of musicians: "I see tradition as founded upon personal choice. In the Archibalds' case, this translates as the conscious decision to engage in a certain sort of historical relationship, involving a network of people and a shared musical activity and repertoire" (McDonald 1997, 58). Hence, folk musicians, folk artists, and folk tradition bearers may appear to be touted as exemplars of free will in a mass society that applies pressure to conform.

There is a noticeable irony in the invocation of tradition—a social connection to the past—as a sign of individualism. Reacting to the modern ability, or pressure, to create a personal identity to differentiate oneself from the mass of society, Jay Mechling and Michael Owen Jones posit that tradition can indeed be formed for oneself rather than for a collective. Mechling (2006), for instance, regards "talking to oneself" as a folkloric practice because it involves a cultural frame in which an exchange occurs. Jones describes artists who create apparently unique objects intended to express their personalities, and yet they self-consciously draw from different traditions (Jones 1995, 266–68; 2000). Although the social component of handing may not be as apparent in this conceptualization of tradition as transactions, the folklorization of the self nonetheless brings to the fore the handiness of constructing (or hybridizing) an identity out of the materials of tradition.

Handy knowledge conceived as "natural" or "earthy" may be devalued by academicians positioning themselves outside of tradition as fantastical old wives' tales, bawdy (or dirty) ditties or irrational superstition because in modern terms, such knowledge stands outside the rule of law and the reign of (clean or sacred) gentility. Yet by relating directly to experience and being perceived as accompanied by down-to-earth wisdom, it may be popularly viewed as a perlocutionary or phemic force because, in Gross's words, it carries "a certain amount of spiritual or moral prestige" (Gross 1992, 10). An emotional or even spiritual connotation to tradition exists that belies objective chronologies or social inventories. To claim tradition, after all, is to bring into play the presence (and guilt) of countless generations of ancestors—and perhaps the gaze of present-day neighbors. In political usage, it allows for a natural state; it refers to the givens of public practice and suggests, problematically, that the long-standing character of a practice is justification for its continuation.

For religion, following tradition may be construed as keeping the faith and therefore defying rationality. To break with tradition is to risk apostasy. Hence, there is a vibrant legacy of writing on tradition from the view of how religion draws its meaning from continuities of shared ritual and belief and how individual expressions of art and literature respond to socially inherited aesthetics, symbols, gestures, and themes. This is not to say that attempts to clinically objectify tradition have not been made, particularly in folkloristics, a discipline that, above all other disciplines, claims tradition for its sense of being. Tradition can be calculatedly viewed as a biological specimen and given the look of a genealogical chart. It can be stolidly computed as a series of motions and minutely analyzed bit by bit or frame by frame. Traditions can be "collected" as empirical evidence of everyday practice or tradition in the singular can be described as some conceptual, almost mystical whole, often outside the awareness of individuals. In both directions, scientific and humanistic, the problem of tradition questions the sources on which people base their actions and attitudes.

CONCLUSION: THE ANALYTICS OF TRADITION

The perception of tradition as handy, vernacular, colloquial, social, or earthy is conveyed by an attachment in most senses of the term with "folk." This folkness can represent the "we-ness" of a small group; peoplehood by region, nation, language, age, gender, or ethnicity; or refer back to the "folk process" of transmission through generations or among peers. The rationality of tradition is consistently expressed as a "folk logic," generated out of social interaction. Small groups associated with folkness constitute the logic of "folk tradition" structured as belief and handy knowledge. Headlines in the popular press and scholarly discourse manifest a tension in modern societies over whether this logic is anachronistic, senseless, pragmatic, or wise (Bronner 1998, 48–55). The stakes of resolving the anxiety is nothing short of directing the course of everyday life and the faith and metaphors by which people live.

The beginning of the twenty-first century marked for many thinkers a time to reassess tradition in modern life (Bronner 2002). With rhetorical use of the new century to represent a radically different millennium and observation of revolutionary changes in communicative technology, the new calendrical era to many pundits represented a new age in which tradition was no longer necessary or desirable (Giddens 1994, 66–82). By this thinking, personal computers and mobile devices displaced face-to-face social connection and gestural cultural production that was provided formally by rituals, stories, songs, and customs that we recognize as traditions. Tradition in a cyber age is supposedly rendered as meaningless repetition or even compulsive neurosis (Giddens 1994, 66–74). Although a collaboration between modernity and tradition was viewed as crucial in earlier phases of modern social development, in postmodernity represented by the cyber age, "modernity destroys tradition," according to social theorist Anthony Giddens (1994, 91). Globalization forces the evacuation of the local and community levels of society associated with tradition. Tradition in a "post-traditional society," Giddens asserts, becomes memory rather than action. The handiness of tradition has been turned into nostalgia or relic form, in other words. Giddens predicts that a few guardians of tradition take responsibility for reminding the populace about practices that should be repeated for "old-time's sake" (Giddens 1994, 63). His presumption is that technology and mobility cause individuals narcissistically to lose interest in one another, and they have no need to form and express community or ritualize occasions through tradition. Following this line of argument for a post-traditional society, tradition loses authority as a place to begin or a guide to action. To Giddens, "tradition lapses into custom or habit," which is to say it loses meaning (defined by Giddens as "ritual and formulaic truth") as it descends into personal routinization, and it can no longer function to engender social trust (Giddens 1994, 79). If such a futuristic scenario carries the promise of globalism, progress, freedom, and free will often associated with late modernity, it also has a risk of limiting the mechanisms that tradition provided for "settling clashes between different values and ways of life," according to Giddens (1994, 104); he warns that post-traditional society impels violence and social fragmentation. With its extremes of individualism and alienation, is Giddens's version of modernity an example of society gone terribly *out of hand*?

The tradition in danger of disappearance in Giddens's influential social theory is not one based on the handiness and phemic quality of folk process or *traditio*; as an artifact or *traditum* of a homogeneous, isolated society, tradition is imagined to be eradicable and phatic. This kind of tradition takes its cue from a hegemonic modernity that makes it possible to forego a sense of community or identity as a human need. Expressiveness in Giddens's scenario is taken care of by technology and individualized as well as globalized. While technology appears to enhance human agency, the recipients of connotative messages or the contextual frames in which they operate are ambiguous, Giddens observes. Tradition in this modernist theory operates as the authority of a society, and usually one that is homogeneous, rooted in place, ancient, rural, and small in scale, much as sociologist Robert Redfield (1947) described a "folk society." As supposedly premodern, tradition-centered groups studied as folk societies, the Amish or Hasidic Jews, for example, have been regularly viewed as doomed in modern society, even though they have expanded in size and distribution (Kraybill 2001; Mintz 1992).

There is no denying that digital technology has dominated communication in twenty-first-century globalism, and this could lead to presumptions that the kind of tradition based on localized face-to-face transactions in handing down and handing over expressive material will vanish. The assumption in such a "folk society" zero-sum game is that tradition cannot work with modernity because the *traditum* is a static relic of the past. It does not function as a gesture. Ethnographic observation, however, has revealed tradition as a process that is necessary to human interaction, even that which is mass mediated, to first provide a behavioral frame or foundation and then connect people socially, often providing a sense, if not reality, of gesturing "we-ness" for identity and size. Folklorist Paul Smith, in an early observation of joking on the computer, for example, noted that "little difference exists between the transmission of a tradition and any other type of communicable information, in that a tradition-bearer will not only use word of mouth but *any relevant and available medium*, including, nowadays, computers" (Smith 1991, 258; italics in the original; see also Bronner 2011, 398–449). Rhetorically, the process of transmission stated by Smith is key to convey gestures that carry the connotation of tradition, usually repeatable, variable, and playfully, artistically, or ritually framed. Tradition in this conceptualization is dynamic—that is, constantly reconstituted to achieve instrumental purposes. Some of those purposes may indeed be outside the awareness of users, such as gaining a human hand over the corporate, official World Wide Web in defiance of globalism or ritualizing, and therefore controlling, technological dominance over human expression. Others are intentionally applied to simulate or replace celebratory and memorial practices in analog culture. These actions are not post-traditional as much as they are adaptive and strategic in the context of modernization to effect the *praxis* of tradition (see Bronner 2012). Tradition as cultural practice goes hand in hand with modernity because it shapes the frames by which people know how to act in a novel world. The cognition of tradition has undoubtedly changed in this process to be more future oriented, and what I have identified as phemic, conceived often as socially negotiated or individually conceived frames of action in the immediate hereafter rather than the distantly heretofore.

Despite politicized attempts to silence or dematerialize tradition as part of modernist discourse, tradition keeps coming back into public-square negotiations of culture because it is still noticeable in life worked by, and on, people at the grassroots level and in national halls of power. It may come up in discourse of lost heritage or in efforts to revive and invent tradition; it is wrapped up in talk of technological and social change and searches for solutions to various problems facing communities and nations cognizant of the force of tradition. Rather than being relegated to the dumpster, tradition shows up in multiple guises and creeps into major headlines of the day. Suffice it to say here that tradition must still be thought to be persuasive, or why else mold it for public consumption? "We fall for 'tradition,'" an advertising adviser declares, noting that marketers emphasize tradition at times of crisis because "we unconsciously adhere to familiar, comforting rituals" (Lindstrom 2009). In the reference to ritual is an aspect of tradition that communicates behavioral repetition and social bonding—and a lasting symbolism. Yet in lived experience, adults may think of tradition as child's play—mere kids' stuff—if not a survival of long ago, thus evading its impact on markers throughout one's life course. Children are usually oblivious to the rhetoric of tradition, despite being brought up in it at home and in the playground. They may be aware of it in a negative way because they resent parental invocations of authority in handed-down proverbs and parables but unmindful of the way they hand up trends and technological skills (see Mechling 2004).

The image of modernity as the new order sweeping out the old traditions conveys a linear, evolutionary narrative in place of a layered picture of cultural dynamics in a variety of social settings. An assumption underlying this linear narrative is that in the past, folks unswervingly followed tradition and were therefore stuck in place and mind; now people are supposedly liberated and in control of their destinies. In the backwoods domains of tradition, popular belief holds, people lack choices, and having options is a hallmark of modern individualism. Or else tradition is condemned for distorting cold, hard facts joined to scientism; in yet another binary, tradition is soft or ineffable while science is solidly certain. A set of associations arises along with these rhetorical strategies: tradition is backward, old, irrational, illiterate, unimaginative, simple, frivolous, ephemeral, irrelevant, limiting, reactionary, and fogeyish while modernity is forward, scientific, cosmopolitan, creative, innovative, young, and vibrant. The impression might be given that there is a natural inclination toward modernity, or at least a pronounced social favor for it.

Where does that leave tradition? Does it bite the dust or is it reintegrated into modern life? In the hierarchy of culture implicit in educators' binary of traditional and modern, tradition is intellectually conceptualized as belonging to the lowly folk and modernity accords to the elite. Raymond Williams points out that within modernization theory, *tradition* and especially *traditional* are "now often used dismissively, with a similar lack of specificity" (Williams 1983, 319). In Williams's vocabulary, as a result of its controversial nature in intellectual circles and public practice, *tradition* constitutes a significant *keyword* of culture and society. He is not alone in his estimation that the modern appears to be known or empirical when intellectuals place tradition in the realm of the troubling, bizarre, unknown, unseen, and especially, the inexplicable. Compared to modernity, he editorializes, *tradition* is the more difficult word to fathom; or maybe scholars have oversimplified it to validate the complexity of modernization.

Instead of setting tradition in opposition to rationality, modernity, and popular culture, I advocate for tradition as a factor, rather than a foil, of modernity. We should highlight the elaboration and variation of tradition rather than presume its limitation and uniformity. We should uncover the human agency in tradition and its importance for containing and conveying symbols, deep-seated values, and political and psychological implications in modern culture, often in response to social anxieties and conflicts. The analysis of tradition is needed to comprehend the frames by which the force of perlocutionary acts become apparent, the formation of guiding rules and structures to life, and the phemic practices in which symbols, meanings, values, and truth are conveyed.

The fact is that every day, people are involved in events they recognize as traditional and at the same time look to establish precedents for traditions of the future (Georges and Jones 1995, 1). They do so because tradition fuels their culture; it provides the precedents by which they make their cultural choices and locate themselves in place and time. It signifies in countless gestures of speech, play, and rituals scripts embedded with values, symbols, and anxieties in their lives—and the heritage from which they come. In short, tradition's "handiness" informs people where to begin and guides them on how to proceed. But they may be troubled to engage in practices about which they do not have background. That is why so often I hear questions about common rituals and customs such as "how did this start?," "why did it last?," "why do we do it now?," and "what does it mean?" These questions are evidence that tradition is so pervasive that it is hard for people to separate from it so as to recognize it, no less analyze it. And apparently getting answers to these questions does more than satisfy curiosity; they relate to one's sense of belonging in a mobile, individualistic society. They speak to the fit of what people do "naturally" with the world that has been artificially built.

People have a need to get answers not just to hear about the old days but to assess their behavior—as well as their cultural identity and life passage—today. They are well aware of tradition as a keyword in public discourse but most likely are unsure of its meaning in their personal experience or of tradition as a mode of thought and learning. Tradition has multiple meanings and applications as a type of communicated expression, mode of thought, and representation of precedent; but that multiplicity is not necessarily a drawback to its handiness. In the face of uncertainty about tradition in a modern, supposedly progressive society, people may relate metafolklore—a narrative explanation based on oral tradition—to redirect the assumption of the questioner that tradition in whatever form holds meaning for the present. Here is an example I collected from a student of metafolklore found in many variations about an Easter tradition:

On Easter Sunday, a young mother prepared a ham for her family. As she pulled the thawed ham from the refrigerator, she placed it on the counter and took to removing the top and the four sides of the ham with a knife in order to form a perfect square. The husband was a little curious as to why she did this and inquired about the removal of what he saw as perfectly good meat. "That's just the way my mother has always done it," replied the young woman. Her curiosity piqued, the woman decided to call her mother to find out the reason behind cutting the ham into a perfect square, thus losing all that meat. "That's the way my mother always did it," she replied to her daughter's phone inquiry. The young woman then called her grandmother. "That's the way your great-grandmother always did it," her grandmother replied over the phone. The young woman, now completely fascinated by her interest in the matter, decided to call her great-grandmother, who was still alive and living in a retirement community in Florida. "Oh, that," the great-grandmother replied to the question, "we had to cut the ham, otherwise it wouldn't fit in the oven!" (Fansler 2008, 8; cf. Dundes 1994, 85).

The defensive fallback position represented by the narrative is to deny reason in tradition by underscoring a social inertia of "we've always done it" (Pieper 2008, 15). Yet analysts might incisively ask why some traditions are chosen to be continued and others are not. They could also question why the context of the holiday dinner framed by the presence of family evokes tradition and the realization that participants enact it for themselves. Is there something special or symbolic about the ham (or in the motific slot, the turkey) as a ceremonial dish? The family's appreciation and symbolization of a custom that distinguishes their social unit from others owes to the concept of tradition and serves functions in the present even if family members are not aware of the origin of the pragmatic behavior that later become ritualistic. Analysts might even ask why a story is necessary to relate a tradition about a tradition. The migratory, variable story contains a cultural assumption, as told in a modernist context, that whereas behavioral continuity is exhibited in the formation of the nonnormative square drawing attention to itself, a social discontinuity exists between generations. The story can be seen as a folk rationalization that avoids confronting social conflict and even admonishes listeners not to dig deeper. But dredge and discover we should to get to the bottom of tradition and reveal these cultural undersides that explain the need for folk production.

To be sure, folkloristic definitions have been proposed that take tradition out of the equation. Most notably, Dan Ben-Amos, in suggesting the definition of folklore as "artistic communication in small groups," sought to dispose of time as a criterion for folklore so as to allow an expansion of the material covered. He wrote, "The artistic forms that are part of the communicative processes of small groups are significant, without regard to the time they have been circulation" (Ben-Amos 1971, 14). Yet the "communicative processes" still entails the social exchange, or "handing over," of tradition. Writing later, Ben-Amos reflected, "*Tradition* has survived criticism and remained a symbol of and for folklore. It has been one of the principal metaphors to guide us in the choate world of experiences and ideas" (Ben-Amos 1984, 124; italics in the original). The experiment to deny or mask tradition in the conceptualization of folklore reflects an effort to emphasize the contemporary practice of folklore so as to remove the popular association of folk material with a relic, irrational past and its bearers with a backward or primitive reputation.

Elliott Oring finds that emphasis on the artistic element of folklore, evident in "verbal art" as a modernist (and, he adds, characteristically American) definition for folklore in lieu of "oral tradition," "reflects the current anthropological preoccupation with the cultural present as well as the effort to explain social and cultural forms in terms of the larger social and cultural systems in which these forms play some part" (Oring 1986, 14; for examples of verbal art conceptualizations, see Bascom 1955; Bauman 1975, 1984 [1977]). Although designed to expand the categories of folklore to include intermingling with modern popular culture, the terminology of "verbal art" removes the sense of cultural practices not involving speech. An alternative view is that those practices are tied by a process of transmittal that can be called traditional; tradition is the structure that connects different genres under the category of folklore (Bayard 1953; Bronner 2000; Dundes 1964). Without the burden of annotation to trace transactions back in time and over space, however, the analyst can assume a unique or emergent meaning within a particular context or situation. This often leads to a problem of disabling comparison or generalization. It precludes an explanation of locating a precedent in a series of transactions or a cognitive response and social agency in the construction of symbols (see Bronner 2009a; Dundes 2005; Oring 2009). It frequently replaces the analytical implication of tradition constituting meaning outside the awareness of participants with an empiricist stance that the participants' views represent the only reality. The goal of analysis should be to assess and explain the hand of tradition in thought and action.

REFERENCES

Aboujaoude, Elias. 2008. *Compulsive Acts: A Psychiatrist's Tales of Ritual and Obsession.* Berkeley: University of California Press.

Adorno, Theodor W. 1993. "On Tradition." *Telos* 94: 75–82.

Austin, J. L. 1961. *Philosophical Papers.* Oxford: Clarendon Press.

Austin, J. L. 1968. *How to Do Things with Words.* New York: Oxford University Press.

Barry, Phillips, and Fannie Hardy Eckstorm. 1930. "What Is Tradition?" *Bulletin of the Folk-Song Society of the Northeast* 1: 2–3.

Bascom, William R. 1955. "Verbal Art." *Journal of American Folklore* 68 (269): 245–52. http://dx.doi.org/10.2307/536902.

Bauman, Richard. 1975. "Verbal Art as Performance." *American Anthropologist* 77 (2): 290–311. http://dx.doi.org/10.1525/aa.1975.77.2.02a00030.

Bauman, Richard. 1984 [1977]. *Verbal Art as Performance.* Prospect Heights, IL: Waveland Press.

Bayard, Samuel. 1953. "The Materials of Folklore." *Journal of American Folklore* 66 (259): 1–17. http://dx.doi.org/10.2307/536742.

Ben-Amos, Dan. 1971. "Toward a Definition of Folklore in Context." *Journal of American Folklore* 84 (331): 3–15. http://dx.doi.org/10.2307/539729.

Ben-Amos, Dan. 1984. "The Seven Strands of Tradition: Varieties and Its Meaning in American Folklore Studies." *Journal of Folklore Research* 21 (2/3): 97–131.

Berkhof, Hendrikus. 2002. *Christian Faith: An Introduction to the Study of the Faith.* Rev. ed. Trans. Sierd Woudstra. Grand Rapids, MI: Wm. B. Eerdmans.

Blumenreich, Beth, and Bari Lynn Polansky. 1975. "Re-evaluating the Concept of Group: ICEN as an Alternative." In *Conceptual Problems in Contemporary Folklore Study,* ed. Gerald Cashion, 12–17. Folklore Forum Bibliographic and Special Series, no. 12. Bloomington: Indiana University.

Bourdieu, Pierre. 1990. *The Logic of Practice.* Trans. Richard Nice. Palo Alto, CA: Stanford University Press.

Brisson, Luc. 2000. *Plato the Myth Maker.* Trans. Gerard Naddaf. Chicago: University of Chicago Press.

Bronner, Simon J. 1982. "Feeling's the Truth." *Tennessee Folklore Society Bulletin* 48: 117–24.

Bronner, Simon J. 1986. *Grasping Things: Folk Material Culture and Mass Society in America.* Lexington: University Press of Kentucky.

Bronner, Simon J. 1992. "Introduction." In *Creativity and Tradition in Folklore: New Directions,* ed. Simon J. Bronner, 1–40. Logan: Utah State University Press.

Bronner, Simon J. 1998. *Following Tradition: Folklore in the Discourse of American Culture.* Logan: Utah State University Press.

Bronner, Simon J. 2000. "The Meaning of Tradition: An Introduction." *Western Folklore* 59 (2): 87–104. http://dx.doi.org/10.2307/1500154.

Bronner, Simon J. 2002. "Questioning the Future: Polling Americans at the Turn of the New Millennium." In *Prospects: An Annual of American Cultural Studies*, vol. 27, ed. Jack Salzman, 665–85. New York: Cambridge University Press. http://dx.doi.org/10.1017/S036123330000137X

Bronner, Simon J. 2006a. "Folk Logic: Interpretation and Explanation in Folkloristics." *Western Folklore* 65: 401–33.

Bronner, Simon J. 2006b. "Folklorist." In *Encyclopedia of American Folklife*, ed. Simon J. Bronner, 422–26. Armonk, NY: M. E. Sharpe.

Bronner, Simon J. 2009a. "Digitizing and Visualizing Folklore." In *Folklore and the Internet: Vernacular Expression in a Digital World*, ed. Trevor J. Blank, 21–66. Logan: Utah State University Press.

Bronner, Simon J. 2009b. "The Problem and Promise of Tradition." *Levend Erfgoed: Vakblad voor Public Folklore and Public History* 6: 4–11.

Bronner, Simon J. 2010. "Framing Folklore: An Introduction." *Western Folklore* 69: 275–97.

Bronner, Simon J. 2011. *Explaining Traditions: Folk Behavior in Modern Culture.* Lexington: University Press of Kentucky.

Bronner, Simon J. 2012. "Practice Theory in Folklore and Folklife Studies." *Folklore* 123 (1): 23–47. http://dx.doi.org/10.1080/0015587X.2012.642985.

Brunvand, Jan Harold. 1998 [1968]. *The Study of American Folklore: An Introduction.* 4th ed. New York: W. W. Norton.

Burne, Charlotte Sophia. 1913. *The Handbook of Folklore.* London: Sidgwick & Jackson.

Burr, Elizabeth. 1994. *The Chiron Dictionary of Greek and Roman Mythology: Gods and Goddesses, Heroes, Places, and Events of Antiquity.* Wilmette, IL: Chiron.

Cantwell, Robert S. 1993. *Ethnomimesis: Folklife and the Representation of Culture.* Chapel Hill: University of North Carolina Press.

Chisholm, Hugh, ed. 1910. *Encyclopaedia Britannica: A Dictionary of Arts, Sciences, Literature and General Information.* Cambridge: Cambridge University Press.

Clark, D. Anthony Tyeeme. 2005. "Indigenous Voice and Vision as Commodity in a Mass-Consumption Society: The Colonial Politics of Public Opinion Polling." *American Indian Quarterly* 29 (1): 228–38. http://dx.doi.org/10.1353/aiq.2005.0039.

Cooperative Recreation Service. 1955. *Handy Folklore: Fun with Folklore.* Delaware, OH: Cooperative Recreation Service.

Congar, Yves. 2004 [1964]. *The Meaning of Tradition.* Trans. A. N. Woodrow. San Francisco: Ignatius Press.

Dégh, Linda, and Andrew Vázsonyi. 1975. "The Hypothesis of Multi-Conduit Transmission in Folklore." In *Folklore: Performance and Communication*, ed. Dan Ben-Amos and Kenneth S. Goldstein, 207–54. The Hague: Mouton.

Donald, Merlin. 1991. *Origins of the Modern Mind: Three Stages in the Evolution of Culture and Cognition.* Cambridge, MA: Harvard University Press.

Dorson, Richard M. 1972. "Techniques of the Folklorist." In *Folklore: Selected Essays*, by Richard Dorson, 11–31. Bloomington: Indiana University Press.

Dorson, Richard M. 2008 [1952]. *Bloodstoppers and Bearwalkers: Folk Traditions of Michigan's Upper Peninsula.* 3rd ed. Ed. James P. Leary. Madison: University of Wisconsin Press.

Dundes, Alan. 1964. "On Game Morphology: A Study of the Structure of Non-Verbal Folklore." *New York Folklore Quarterly* 20: 276–88.

Dundes, Alan. 1969. "The Devolutionary Premise in Folklore Theory." *Journal of the Folklore Institute* 6 (1): 5–19. http://dx.doi.org/10.2307/3814118.

Dundes, Alan. 1980. *Interpreting Folklore*. Bloomington: Indiana University Press.

Dundes, Alan. 1994. "Towards a Metaphorical Reading of 'Break a Leg': A Note on the Folklore of the Stage." *Western Folklore* 53 (1): 85–89. http://dx.doi.org/10.2307/1499654.

Dundes, Alan. 2005. "Folkloristics in the Twenty-First Century (AFS Invited Presidential Plenary Address, 2004)." *Journal of American Folklore* 118 (470): 385–408. http://dx.doi.org/10.1353/jaf.2005.0044.

Dundes, Alan. 2007. "Chain Letter: A Folk Geometric Progression." In *The Meaning of Folklore*, ed. Simon J. Bronner, 422–25. Logan: Utah State University Press.

Fansler, Joshua. 2008. "Flag Retirement Ceremony." Student Paper in American Folklore. Archives of Pennsylvania Folklore and Ethnography, Pennsylvania State University, Harrisburg.

Georges, Robert A., and Michael Owen Jones. 1980. *People Studying People: The Human Element in Fieldwork*. Berkeley: University of California Press.

Georges, Robert A., and Michael Owen Jones. 1995. *Folkloristics: An Introduction*. Bloomington: Indiana University Press.

Giddens, Anthony. 1994. "Living in a Post-Traditional Society." In *Reflexive Modernization: Politics, Tradition and Aesthetics in the Modern Social Order*, by Ulrich Beck, Anthony Giddens, and Scott Lash, 56–109. Palo Alto, CA: Stanford University Press.

Goldin-Meadow, Susan. 2005. *Hearing Gesture: How Our Hands Help Us Think*. Cambridge, MA: Belknap Press.

Gross, David. 1992. *The Past in Ruins: Tradition and the Critique of Modernity*. Amherst: University of Massachusetts Press.

Grube, G. M. A., trans. 1992. *The Republic/Plato*, revised by C. D. C. Reeve. Indianapolis: Hackett Publishing.

Harmon, Mamie. 1949. "Folklore." In *Funk & Wagnalls Standard Dictionary of Folklore, Mythology, and Legend*, 2 vols., ed. Maria Leach, 399–400. New York: Funk & Wagnalls.

Hultkrantz, Åke. 1960. *General Ethnological Concepts*. Copenhagen: Rosenkilde and Bagger.

Jones, Michael Owen. 1975. *The Hand Made Object and Its Maker*. Berkeley: University of California Press.

Jones, Michael Owen. 1995. "The 1995 Archer Taylor Memorial Lecture: Why Make (Folk) Art?" *Western Folklore* 54 (4): 253–76. http://dx.doi.org/10.2307/1500307.

Jones, Michael Owen. 2000. "'Tradition' in Identity Discourses and an Individual's Symbolic Construction of Self." *Western Folklore* 59 (2): 115–41. http://dx.doi.org/10.2307/1500156.

Ketner, Kenneth. 1973. "The Role of Hypotheses in Folkloristics." *Journal of American Folklore* 86 (340): 114–30. http://dx.doi.org/10.2307/539745.

Ketner, Kenneth. 1976. "Identity and Existence in the Study of Human Traditions." *Folklore* 87 (2): 192–200. http://dx.doi.org/10.1080/0015587X.1976.9716034.

Kraybill, Donald B. 2001. *The Riddle of Amish Culture*. Rev. ed. Baltimore: Johns Hopkins University Press.

Laver, John. 1975. "Communicative Functions of Phatic Communion." In *Organization of Behavior in Face-to-Face Interaction*, ed. Adam Kendon, Richard M. Harris, and Mary Ritchie Key, 215–40. The Hague: Mouton. http://dx.doi.org/10.1515/9783110907643.215

Leach, Maria, ed. 1949. *Funk and Wagnalls Standard Dictionary of Folklore, Mythology, and Legend*. Vol. 1. New York: Funk and Wagnalls.

Lindstrom, Martin. 2009. "How Subliminal Advertising Works." *Parade* (January 4): 12–13.

Lowenthal, Marvin. 1942. *Henrietta Szold: Life and Letters*. New York: Viking Press.

Lyons, John. 1968. *Introduction to Theoretical Linguistics.* Cambridge: Cambridge University Press. http://dx.doi.org/10.1017/CBO9781139165570

Mazo, Jeffrey Alan. 1996. "A Good Saxon Compound." *Folklore* 107 (1/2): 107–8. http://dx.doi.org/10.1080/0015587X.1996.9715925.

McDonald, Barry M. 1997. "Tradition as a Personal Relationship." *Journal of American Folklore* 110 (435): 47–67. http://dx.doi.org/10.2307/541585.

Mead, George Herbert. 1962. *Mind, Self, and Society: From the Standpoint of a Social Behaviorist.* Ed. Charles W. Morris. Chicago: University of Chicago Press.

Mechling, Jay. 2004. "'Cheaters Never Prosper' and Other Lies Adults Tell Kids: Proverbs and the Culture Wars over Character." In *What Goes Around Comes Around: The Circulation of Proverbs in Contemporary Life*, ed. Kimberly J. Lau, Peter Tokofsky, and Stephen D. Winmick, 107–26. Logan: Utah State University Press.

Mechling, Jay. 2006. "Solo Folklore." *Western Folklore* 65: 435–53.

Mintz, Jerome R. 1992. *Hasidic People: A Place in the New World.* Cambridge, MA: Harvard University Press.

Nussbaum, Martha C. 2010. *Not for Profit: Why Democracy Needs the Humanities.* Princeton, NJ: Princeton University Press.

Ochs, Peter. 1998. *Peirce, Pragmatism, and the Logic of Scripture.* Cambridge: Cambridge University Press. http://dx.doi.org/10.1017/CBO9780511582851

Ophir, Adi. 1991. *Plato's Invisible Cities: Discourse and Power in the Republic.* Savage, MD: Barnes & Noble.

Oring, Elliott. 1986. "On the Concepts of Folklore." In *Folk Groups and Folklore Genres: An Introduction*, ed. Elliott Oring, 1–22. Logan: Utah State University Press.

Oring, Elliott. 1989. "Documenting Folklore: The Annotation." In *Folk Groups and Folklore Genres: A Reader*, ed. Elliott Oring, 358–74. Logan: Utah State University Press.

Oring, Elliott. 2009. "The Problem of Tradition." Paper presented in the panel "Tradition in the 21st Century: Locating the Role of the Past in the Future" at the American Folklore Society Annual Meeting, Boise, ID, October 21–24.

Pieper, Josef. 2008. *Tradition: Concept and Claim.* Trans by E. Christian Kopff. Wilmington, DE: ISI Books.

Redfield, Robert. 1947. "The Folk Society." *American Journal of Sociology* 52 (4): 293–308. http://dx.doi.org/10.1086/220015.

Ross, Edward Alsworth. 1909. *Social Psychology: An Outline and Source Book.* New York: Macmillan.

Searle, John R. 1969. *Speech Acts: An Essay in the Philosophy of Language.* Cambridge: Cambridge University Press. http://dx.doi.org/10.1017/CBO9781139173438

Shils, Edward. 1981. *Tradition.* Chicago: University of Chicago Press.

Sims, Martha C., and Martine Stephens. 2005. *Living Folklore: An Introduction to the Study of People and Their Traditions. Logan.* Utah State University Press.

Smith, Paul. 1991. "The Joke Machine: Communicating Traditional Humour Using Computers." In *Spoken in Jest*, ed. Gillian Bennett, 257–78. Sheffield, UK: Sheffield Academic Press.

Thompson, Stith. 1949. "Folklore." In *Funk & Wagnalls Standard Dictionary of Folklore, Mythology, and Legend*, 2 vols., ed. Maria Leach, 403. New York: Funk & Wagnalls.

Thoms, William. 1965 [1846]. "Folklore." In *The Study of Folklore*, ed. Alan Dundes, 4–6. Englewood Cliffs, NJ: Prentice-Hall.

Toelken, Barre. 1996 [1979]. *The Dynamics of Folklore.* Rev. ed. Logan: Utah State University Press.

Warnock, G. J. 1989. *J. L. Austin: The Arguments of the Philosophers.* London: Routledge.

Williams, Raymond. 1983. *Keywords: A Vocabulary of Culture and Society.* Rev. ed. New York: Oxford University Press.

Wilson, Frank R. 1999. *The Hand: How Its Use Shapes the Brain, Language, and Human Culture.* New York: Vintage.

About the Contributors

TREVOR J. BLANK is assistant professor of communication at the State University of New York at Potsdam. He earned his PhD in American studies from the Pennsylvania State University, Harrisburg and an MA at Indiana University's Folklore Institute. He is the editor of *Folklore and the Internet: Vernacular Expression in a Digital World* (2009) and *Folk Culture in the Digital Age: The Emergent Dynamics of Human Interaction* (2012) and author of *The Last Laugh: Folk Humor, Celebrity Culture, and Mass-Mediated Disasters in the Digital Age* (2013). Currently, Blank serves as editor to the open access journal *New Directions in Folklore* (http://newfolk.net). Follow him on *Twitter* @trevorjblank.

SIMON J. BRONNER is the Distinguished University Professor of American Studies and Folklore at the Pennsylvania State University, Harrisburg, where he chairs the doctoral program in American studies. He has also taught at Harvard University, Osaka University (Japan), and the University of California at Davis and held the Walt Whitman Distinguished Chair of American Cultural Studies at Leiden University in the Netherlands. He is author or editor of over thirty books, including most recently *Campus Traditions: Folklore from the Old-Time College to the Modern Mega-University* (2012), *Explaining Traditions: Folk Behavior in Modern Culture* (2011), and the *Encyclopedia of American Folklife* (2006). He also serves as editor of the *Encyclopedia of American Studies* online, the Material Worlds book series for the University Press of Kentucky, and the Jewish Cultural Studies book series for the Littman Library of Jewish Civilization. He is president of the Western States Folklore Society and the Fellows of the American Folklore Society.

STEPHEN OLBRYS GENCARELLA is associate professor in the Department of Communication at the University of Massachusetts, Amherst, where he offers courses in folklore studies and rhetorical studies. He was twice elected to the board of directors for the Massachusetts Teachers Association, one of the largest unions and democratic organizations in the commonwealth. He holds a joint PhD from the Folklore Institute and the Department of Communication and Culture at Indiana University and is the coeditor of the textbook *Readings on Rhetoric and Performance* (2010).

ROBERT GLENN HOWARD is professor in the Department of Communication Arts at the University of Wisconsin–Madison. His teaching and publications span several fields, including communication, folklore studies, journalism, and religious studies.

Focusing on everyday expression in network communication technologies, his 2011 book *Digital Jesus: The Making of a New Christian Fundamentalist Community on the Internet* documents a grassroots religious movement using the Internet to prepare for the "End Times." His other work expands his exploration of the possibilities and limits of empowerment through everyday expression on the Internet by focusing on the intersection of individual agency and participatory performance. In 2012 Howard cofounded the Digital Studies Program at UW–Madison and currently serves as its director. He is also the director of the Folklore Program at UW–Madison and editor of the journal *Western Folklore*. If you would like to contact Rob, e-mail him at rgh@rghoward.com or check out his most current research and teaching at http://rghoward.com.

MERRILL KAPLAIN is associate professor of folklore and Scandinavian studies at the Ohio State University. She holds an AB in folklore and mythology from Harvard College and a PhD in Scandinavian from the University of California, Berkeley. Her work focuses on Old Norse-Icelandic literature and mythology, legend and folk belief, and folklore on and off the Internet. She is the author of *Thou Fearful Guest: Addressing the past in four tales in Flateyjarbók* (2011) and coeditor, with Timothy R. Tangherlini, of *News from Other Worlds: Studies in Nordic Folklore, Mythology and Culture in Honor of John F. Lindow* (2011).

LYNNE S. MCNEILL holds a PhD in folklore from Memorial University of Newfoundland and currently teaches in the folklore program at Utah State University. Her main research interests include legend and belief, the supernatural, and digital culture, and she has published on diverse subjects including Canadian inuksuit, Internet memes, cats in folklore, and contemporary ghost hunting. She is currently the reviews editor for the journal *Contemporary Legend* and has appeared on the *Food Network* and *Animal Planet*.

ELLIOTT ORING is professor emeritus of anthropology at California State University, Los Angeles. He has written extensively about folklore, humor, and cultural symbolism. His books include *Israeli Humor: The Content and Structure of the Chizbat of the Palmah* (1981), *The Jokes of Sigmund Freud: A Study in Humor and Jewish Identity* (1984), *Jokes and Their Relations* (1992), and *Engaging Humor* (2003). Oring was editor of *Western Folklore* and currently serves on the editorial boards of *Humor: International Journal of Humor Research* and the *Journal of Folklore Research*. He was president of the International Society of Humor Research and has served on the executive board of the American Folklore Society. He is a Fellow of the American Folklore Society, a Folklore Fellow of the Finnish Academy of Arts and Sciences, and was a Fulbright Scholar at the University of Iceland in Reykjavík.

CASEY R. SCHMITT is a lecturer and doctoral student in communication arts at the University of Wisconsin–Madison, with a focus on rhetoric, politics, and culture. He holds an MA in folklore from the University of Oregon and an MA in communication arts from UW–Madison. His current research examines both rhetorical use of narrative and narrative construction of ethos and space through representations of so-called "rugged individual" character types. His work has appeared in *Cultural Analysis*, the *Journal of American Folklore*, and *Folklore*, and he has served on the editorial staffs of *Western Folklore* and the *Oral History Review*.

TOK THOMPSON was born and raised in rural Alaska. At the age of seventeen, he began attending Harvard College, where he received his bachelor's degree in anthropology. In 1999 he received a master's degree in folklore from the University of California, Berkeley and three years later received a PhD in anthropology from the same institution, all the while studying under the late Alan Dundes. He has researched and taught at Trinity College (Dublin, Ireland), the University of Ulster (Northern Ireland), the University of Iceland, and the University of Addis Ababa (Ethiopia) and is presently an associate professor of teaching in the Department of Anthropology at the University of Southern California. His research spans the time frame of human expressive culture, from evolutionary questions regarding hominid narrative development to the future of communication and its implications for humanity.

Index